William Wycherley: A Biography

B. EUGENE MCCARTHY

William Wycherley:
A Biography

Ⓓ Ohio University Press: Athens, Ohio

Library of Congress Cataloging in Publication Data

McCarthy, B. Eugene, 1934-
   William Wycherley: a biography.

   Includes bibliographical references.
      1.   Wycherley, William, 1641-1715.   2.   Dramatists,
English—Early modern, 1500-1700—Biography.
PR 3776.M3   822′.4 [B]   79-9210
ISBN 0-8214-0410-5

to Barbara
for and because of whom

CONTENTS

PREFACE

The research for this biography began some years ago in criticism and ended in record offices and libraries. In his essay on Milton's "Lycidas" Northrop Frye remarks that some critics can find things in the Public Records Office, and others like himself cannot find the place. I found it well enough, not to test Frye's remarks, for certainly the dust drifting from the parchment of old law cases has little beneficial effect on one's critical sensibilities. But this study ended at the Public Records Office necessarily and inevitably. I suppose then I am one of those who find things there, but I hope not to have fallen into the trap of pseudo-criticism Frye warns against. Scholarship and criticism are both in this book, but I hope I have kept the two disciplines separate.

What brought me to the Chancery Lane Public Record Office and, in a sense, initiated the formal research for this biography was the pathfinding work of previous scholars who discovered important documents there and thus illuminated new aspects of Wycherley's life, such as H. P. Vincent on the death of Wycherley, or Eleanore Boswell on his suit with his servant Barnaby. Without them and others, I would not likely have begun there. The search there was fascinating and tedious, and some of what I found may be of more importance to social historians than literary scholars. Sam Johnson said, I believe, that one may turn over a whole library to write one book and one sometimes has the feeling that is so; but the work of scholars provided both the direction and the motivation, and it is to them, and such as Montague Summers and Willard Connely, that this book is initially indebted; for even when I do not accept their word, I respect the value of their achievements.

It seemed apparent some time ago that a new biography of Wycherley was due. My design to make Wycherley a little more visible, a little more knowable and enjoyable thus determined what I tried to do in this biography, for it seemed that what was most needed at this time in his biographical history was a factually accurate chronology of his life. Since Connely's *Brawny Wycherley* in 1930, a good deal has been published in articles which had to be fitted into a coherent unity, and whatever additional I discovered filled in even more spaces. Thus because of the primary intention to rely on documented information as a basis for my views and comments on Wycherley, I did not attempt to speculate on his life beyond what the information warranted.

Admittedly the current interest in psychological criticism and even psychobiography would suggest that my directions were retrogressive; nevertheless, I felt that Wycherley could be best served by revealing as much factual material as possible and not by probing into areas where I felt least comfortable. One other very tempting direction for the book that came to mind, and was then reinforced by a "life" that Gerald Weales published in the *Michigan Quarterly Review* (Winter 1973), would be to exploit the richly anecdotal aspects of his life and proceed in a novelistic manner. But that may come later.

In spite of the information gathered here much of Wycherley's life remains very shadowy. There is still almost nothing available about his habits of writing, why he wrote, his thoughts on his contemporaries or his own later life. Contradictory stories, false stories, dubious stories do not help us clarify his life. At times we have to aim at a midpoint between stories for a generalized truth and abandon any desire for the literal truth. For example, after John Dennis reported how the Duchess of Cleveland hailed Wycherley in his carriage by saying, "You, Wycherley, are the son of a whore," Alexander Pope's version, "Sir, you're a rogue," sounds like a different translation for a rather prim audience. But apparently she said something significantly arresting to make him stop, turn around, and follow her to her bed. Problems of authenticity of sources are not unique to Restoration biography but certainly are annoying difficulties which we can only attempt to surmount.

Concerning the plays, though by right they should only be read—or seen—for their marvelous fun and pleasure, another decision had to be made: whether to treat them as biographical events only—when performed, where, by whom and so forth—or venture into criticism of them at the risk of violating the announced factual approach. But it seemed finally that we could attain a glimpse into the mind of the playwright by examining some of the issues that appear in them, and so I wrote about the plays for the purpose of exploring what Wycherley was thinking, what he believed, to some extent what his sources of belief were, and thus related the plays to an intellectual biography. The essays on the plays are not designed to be polemical, but as possible new ways of seeing the plays, as challenges to critical opinion.

As I said, many scholars before me have actually made this book realizable. But there are others who have made this effort come to completion and who have contributed in no less important ways. The dedication of this book to my wife, Barbara, marks the primacy of my debt to her. In a special sort of way, our children, Dan, Caroline, Maura, Stephen, and Alison have made such a venture worthwhile; I hope they will understand this better in later years. A man of high scholarly ideals and achievements, Fr. Frank Larkin (editor of the Tudor and Stuart Royal Proclamations), has always made the accomplishment of this book seem beyond question; his help has been spiritual and professional and personal; he is a dear friend to our family. A former student, Randall Caudill, and his wife Eileen, offered marvelous hospitality in Oxford, and guided me into the resources of the Duke Humphrey at the Bodleian. My friend and former colleague Frank Devlin, of Salem State College, read with his usual meticulous care the first chapters and showed me how to reshape them into something a good deal better. Others have helped in other ways, my colleague Joan Winslow, my former teacher at the University of Kansas, Ed Ruhe, and others whom I mention in the text. And there are the anonymous generous people who work in Record Offices in London, Shrewsbury, Winchester, Dublin, who always amazed me with their learning and assistance; and librarians there and in this country from Harvard to the Newberry have made the tasks much easier.

Holy Cross College has been generous in providing me the time and support to research this book on sabbatical in England and in grants to continue research to complete this book and to assist in its publication. The cooperation of Holy Cross librarians Jim Mahoney and Selina Martin has made work much easier through their kindness and interest. And my excellent typist, Mrs. Jane Iannini, has seen humor in typing endless footnotes: who could ask for more?

In order to abbreviate footnote entries for works often cited, I have made full entry only the first time each appears and thereafter only by author or editor: the former in the cases of Willard Connely, *Brawny Wycherley* (New York, 1930); Samuel Garbet, *The History of Wem* (1818); Richard Gough, *Antiquities and Memoirs of Myddle* (1875); and the latter in such cases as E. N. Hooker, ed., *The Critical Works of John Dennis*, 2 Vols., (Baltimore, 1939); George Sherburn, ed., *The Correspondence of Alexander Pope*, 5 Vols., (Oxford, 1956); Montague Summers, ed., *The Works of William Wycherley*, 4 Vols., (New York, 1964); George Watson, ed., *John Dryden, Of Dramatic Poesy and Other Critical Essays*, 2 Vols., (New York, 1962); and the following, James M. Osborn, ed., *Joseph Spence, Observations, Anecdotes, and Characters*, 2 Vols., (Oxford, 1966), by short title, *Spence, Anecdotes*.

The selection in Chapter V from Charles Dickens' *Bleak House*, ed. Morton Dawen Zabel (1956) is printed by permission of Houghton Mifflin Company.

William Wycherley: A Biography

Chapter I

Ancestry and Parentage

The Wycherley family had been in existence for several hundred years when Daniel Wycherley, father of the playwright William, was born in the early seventeenth century. Most genealogies have succeeded in tracing the family line back to the tenth year of the reign of Henry IV, in 1410,[1] but we can go back yet farther to the apparent origins of this long and manifestly gentlemanly line out of which Daniel emerged, a proud, intelligent and acquisitive man. A modern descendant of a branch of the Wycherley family—there are no descendants from Daniel's line—Mr. Frank Wycherley of Grinshill, Shropshire, has traced the line back two generations further to Wycherley of Wycherley but has been unable to fix a date earlier than 1409.[2] In Daniel's own day a search was made on his claim to the rank of gentleman at the insistence of a number of Shropshire gentry who apparently disbelieved his ostensible rank and thought it worth challenging, and this search, made during the years 1676 to 1679, settled the status of the Wycherley family and their arms, as well as the locale and state of their residence. The Earl Marshall of England received the challenge and sent his several deputies to search appropriate records and visitation books to determine whether the complaint against "one Daniell Wicharley" who "by a false and erroneous Pedegree with arms and quarterings"[3] did assume arms, was indeed justified. Their report is a precise and valuable record of the place called Wycherley and the persons who lived there.

Wee fynd, that there is a place now, & auntiently called ye Hamlett, or village of Wycherley, now in ye parishes of

[3]

Baschurch & Ellesmere in ye County of Salop, of all which ye family of Wycherley were Owners, & had aunciently their residence thereat; at which place (as we are credibly informd) there is yet remayning an auncient Mannour House, called Wycherley Hall, for ye most part moated about, & a Dovecote, or Pigeon House aunciently there . . .

As to ye possessours thereof we fynd, that one Richard de Wycherley 8⁰ R.2. which falls in ye yeare of our Lord 1385 by a Fyne then leavyed, acquired certaine Lands in Eyton neare Baschurch aforesayd, & that this Richard de Wycherley had yssue (as wee conceive) two sonns, Richard & Roger; from which Richard junior (after five Descents) descended Margarett ye sole Daughter, & Heyre of one other Richard (which Descents are entred in ye most auncient Visitation of that County in ye Heralds Office) who marryed Richard Onslow of Onslow in ye sayd County of Salop Esq. which Richard Onslow by reason thereof became possessed of Wycherley aforesayd, from which Family of Onslow ye worshipfull Family, now residing in ye County of Surrey is lineally descended.

The principall Braunch of this Family being thus gone out by ye sayd Heyre female, we come to Roger de Wycherley, ye younger sonn to Richard de Wycherley first abovenamed, & doe fynd that 10 H. 4. viz 1409 he obteyned a Graunt & confirmation of all those Lands & tenements in Clyve, & Sansaw in ye County of Salop aforesayd to himselfe, & his heyres, . . . & that ye lineall heyre Male Descendants of this Roger have had their residents att Clyve above mencioned to this day. . . .[4]

The year 1385, the eighth year of Richard II's reign, thus seems to be the earliest traceable date of origin of the family line. The arms to which Daniel claimed right, i.e., "partie per pale Argent & Sable, three eagles displayed & counterchanged of the field two, & one," were also verified by the report.

The Wycherley family was obviously of long and estimable standing, firmly rooted in the soil of Shropshire, a few miles north of Shrewsbury, scarcely ever moving except for the branch that married into the Onslows and moved to Surrey. They were landowners those many years, and gentry, not extraordinarily notable but successful and steady enough that Daniel's contemporaries insisted they were mere yeomen, not gentry at all.

It would be presumptuous to assume that Daniel continued the family traditions in every respect. Although he was a landowner in large fashion, a steadfast loyalist in politics, and a father concerned for the welfare of his descendants in property and learning, he in other ways marked a divergence. For though rooted to his properties in Shropshire, he ranged widely across the country to the center of English life, and once the sensation of property ownership, as well as business and social standing came within his reach, he stretched as far as he could, perhaps finally too far, to claim them for himself and for his children, who did not, it will become evident, follow his lead in all things nor continue that long-lived name of Wycherley beyond one generation, scarcely beyond the death of Daniel at the vigorous old age of eighty-one.

Biographer Montague Summers sketched a reliable picture of Daniel for us:

> a man of imposing physique, great strength of character, polished and urbane manners, iron resolve, and indomitable will. A thorough and exact classical scholar, a critic of no mean judgment with the particular gift of being able to impart information . . . , he was also well read in modern polite literature, especially philosophy and the poets.[5]

It was this strength of character and devotion to learning that Daniel passed on to his children; other of his characteristics are less admirable in themselves and less a benefit to their inheritors, and at the same time less easy to verify. He is, for instance, excessively charged with a passion for legalism;[6] his selfish and tyrannical treatment of his sons is certainly exaggerated, and his supposed love for the country and aversion for the city[7] is rendered implausible by his years of training and service in London, his associations with kings and other nobility, and his contact with persons throughout England, besides being contradictory to the cultured image Summers has given of him. It becomes, in short, imperative

[5]

to reexamine the life and character of Daniel, partly for his own sake but mainly to bring into clearer focus his very important and lifelong relation to his son William.

Daniel was born in 1617, the first son of Daniel Wycherley (who died in 1655) and Margaret nee Wolph; following Daniel there were four other children: John, who was closely associated with Daniel's later business affairs, Elizabeth, Alice and Mary.[8] His education was chiefly under the tuition of one Mr. William Sugar who had been brought by Daniel senior to be "Clarke Curate & Minister of Clive" and tutor to young Daniel about 1630; Sugar continued as curate at Clive for some 46 years and resided in the Wycherley home[9] gaining a reputation as a fine teacher. Shropshire historian and contemporary of Daniel, Richard Gough, asserted that Daniel "was well educated with all sorts of learning the country would aford, and haveing the advantage of a good naturall witt and a strong memory."[10] It is possible that he attended the Shrewsbury school, founded in 1552 by Edward VI,[11] judging from his benefaction to that school's library in 1681.[12] Following his education, no doubt hoping to surpass the limitations of his father's debt-ridden and dour life,[13] Daniel was eager to get on with a career and travelled to London.

By 1640, Daniel was apparently involved in some sort of work for the Marquis of Winchester, at Basing House in Hampshire, then called Southhampton or Southton, for it was there he met the twenty-two year old Bethia Shrimpton, daughter of William Shrimpton and attendant to Lady Honora de Burgh, second wife of John Paulet, fifth Marquis of Winchester. From what we discover later about Bethia's abilities in running Daniel's business affairs and her concern for her children, she was probably a very bright and accomplished woman and a good match to Daniel's energies. They were married in St. Martin's in the Fields parish, London, on 20 February 1640,[14] and about fifteen months later their son William was born.

The connection with the estates of the Marquis of

Winchester was at first only partial, for Daniel had a variety of other employments, free lancing as we might call it, in legal and financial matters, for instance, as solicitor for one John Thimebly of St. Giles.[15] These employments he had to relinquish almost entirely when he assumed high stewardship of the Marquis' estates and began to "wholly employ himself in and about these affairs."[16] The position of high steward or land steward was not precisely one that would seem appropriate to a member of the gentry for it was of the servant class, albeit the topmost rank. This may have been one reason why the Shropshire gentry later doubted his class standing though such a position for gentry was not unheard of. The chief duties of the steward were to manage the Lord's estate, lease farms, collect rents, handle the surveying of boundaries, settle tenants' quarrels, and keep accounts of all moneys received and expended. He was also expected to "superintend the cultivation of the land," keep abreast of developments in agriculture and provide legal expertise.[17] Daniel saw this position as a splendid opportunity to have access to lands he could lease out to tenants, to handle large amounts of money, and practice the arts of law and finance. Apparently his reputation for skill in these matters was considerable for he managed to fit in a few other tasks while steward. In 1651 he was a trustee for 900£ for one Anne Peck of Spixworth, Norfolk, and as trustee received "all the sums due"; when, however, the trustees did not pay certain sums, they were sued by one Warner, but Daniel retorted that "if he is troubled about it, he will sue," already a man of spirit and calculated bluff. But he seems not to have resisted successfully the demand for payment, though the case dragged on till August 1654.[18] In 1652 Daniel came into the useful position of administrator of Thomas Viscount Somerset K.B. (who died in 1651) for Sir Charles Somerset's creditors; he was to pay the creditors but the estate was "sequestered for Sir Charles' recusancy."[19]

He was evidently not present at Basing House, the Marquis' great fortified house, when Cromwell besieged it

[7]

and on 14 October 1645, captured and destroyed it, for although the aged Inigo Jones and the artist Wenceslaus Hollar were saved from its fires, a brisk young pro-Catholic royalist would not have been so fortunate. After the destruction of Basing House and the collapse of the last Catholic stronghold, the Marquis was ruined, "destitute of money," his lands sequestered by Act of Parliament and settled on Sir Thomas Jervoise and Sir Robert Wallop and, even worse, all the "deeds wrytings and evidences concerneing the premises were lost, embesselled or burnt in the late wars,"[20] the fate of many important documents of land ownership and personal title. In his need for an agent to raise money in his behalf, the Marquis appointed Daniel. Though Daniel did not neglect his own accumulation of property, his business over the next years was concentrated on the recovery of the lost deeds, mortgaging properties and houses, raising money to pay off the debts of the Marquis, until the monarchy was restored in 1660, Wallop sent packing to the Tower and his lands resequestered.

By 1647, according to William, son of George Pawlett, or Paulet, Daniel "for the most part managed the business affairs of the Lord Marquis."[21] His procedure was to borrow sums of money in the Marquis' name, for example, 700£ of one Thomas Henslowe, and sign his own name in bond for the same;[22] he entered into bond for four obligations of 2000£ apiece to Sir Thomas Jervoise,[23] a practice later to cause him much grief when the Marquis' son held him responsible for the debts and sued and arrested him. Daniel increased rent on a number of houses near the Augustine Friary in London "threescore pounds perannum," to 100£ and 120£,[24] and further used "his best means and endeavor to the Committee . . . for Removing Obstructions in the sale of delinquent lands to procure allowance of the claime of the said Lord St. John to certain Manors and Lands . . . and by his great diligent care attendance and sollicitation of the Parliament . . . procure all proceedings" on the Marquis' lands to be suspended.[25] While it may appear to have been folly on his part to bind himself for large sums of money,

Daniel was repeatedly assured by the Marquis that he would himself authorize his steward's actions and support his bonds, easing Daniel's hesitancy which he naturally felt when "he took notice that great Difficulties and Hazards would and must necessarily fall out and happen in the management of matters of soe great importance and of such nature as obtaining allowance of the claimes [to the Marquis' properties, the deeds to which were lost] and in regard that the premisses were by Act of Parliament settled on Sir Thomas Jervoise and Mr. Wallop until 1400£ or thereabouts a remaining sum of 1900£ were raised out of the forfeited premisses."[26] Apparently Daniel was to raise 30,000£;[27] in particular, we know that he was bound to Jervoise for 8000£, raised 3000£ through his friends, collected 1200£ through preemption of rents,[28] and paid 1600£ out of his own money for which he had not received reimbursement and was, as a consequence, suing the Marquis since he was being pressed for the debt and rightly wished to be "made harmless,"[29] and had borrowed of Henslowe and others 700£ and 100£ and various other sums under 200£ apiece amounting to 2427£.[30]

There is extant the "Accompt of Daniell Witcharley Gent," his chief steward's book for the years 1651 through 1655, which records with fastidious detail each sum received and each sum paid out "for and concerninge the purchase of the Estate . . . of John Marquesse of Winchester," specifically the "divers sumes of money borrowed upon mortgage of part of the Estate and alsoe other sumes . . . Imployed for the buyinge of the Estate and to prevent the Sale thereof to Strangers."[31] The money he received from mortgages, fines and fees in 1651–52 amounted to 22,060£; in 1652 to 11,235£ 18s 4d, and so forth, amounting in total from 1651 to 1655 from the Marquis' lands in "Southton," Devon, Cornwall, Wiltshire, and Dorset to 40,817£ 9s 11d. The "whole sum paid" out for that same time, entered even to the "3 shillings for a messenger that brought letters out of Chester," amounted to 40,435£ 19s 8½d, leaving the duly noted remainder, 381£ 10s 2½d.

From the beginning of August 1652 until mid-October the

[9]

steward paid out the "first moiety of the whole purchase" price of all the manors and lands he tried to recover for the Marquis; for instance, for the Manor of Abbotston, 654£ 15s 5d was paid 3 August 1652, on the whole purchase price of 1215£ 16s 8d.[32] For the Manor of Bradford, 1013£ 13s 5d was paid 1 September, the "whole purchase money" being 1818£ 15s 7d; for the Manor of Winslade, 197£ 5s of 350£ 5s 2d,[33] and so on for all the manors, Kingsclere, Froylebury, also called Frobury, and the like. The second moiety was paid out from late October till the following May, amounting in round figures to 20,500£ for all the manors and lands. Other large sums were paid directly to Sir Thomas Jervoise, for example in 1652 1000£ "in part of Six Thousand pounds being the Consideracon agreed upon for his interest in my Lord Marquesse his lands granted him [by] Act of Parliament of ye 14th of September 1649 over and above the One Thousand Eight hundred threescore and fifteene pounds acknowledged to be formerly recd by him out of ye rents & pfitts of the said land." Sir Robert Wallop received 1100£ as part of 6259£, his agreed-upon consideration over and above the 3000£ he formerly received.[34] These records, which itemize various other payments, make clear what biographer Montague Summers believed, that "vast sums of money passed through Daniel Wycherley's hands,"[35] but at the same time it seems true that, with Summers, there is "no reason to suspect him of peculation." The salary for the steward in the accompt does not approximate all the moneys Daniel apparently had available for land purchase. "My Salary as Steward for 3 yeares ending the 30th of August 1654 at 70£ pann [per annum]" is 210£. Added to this is his "Salary as Solicitor 60£" and "allowance of dyett and Chambers at 3d perdiem," 164£ 5s, for a total of 434£ 5s.[36] His salary as steward for a year and a half was 105£ and other salaries, allowances and disbursements, listed in 1655, total 267£ 2s 6d.[37] Probably one should add to that amount the "riding charges and other expenses in Keeping of Courts and letting of lands in Hampshire at Michas 1653 and in Keeping of

Courts in all Countyes where the estate lyeth at Lady Day 1654 . . . 1655,"[38] amounting to 210£, since Daniel as chief steward would normally have the duty of holding the manor courts throughout the Marquis' estates, just as later Daniel's steward, Richard Jebb, kept court in the Manor of Wem. All this income amounts to just over 911£, a good salary and allowance certainly based on 70£ per annum as steward, but not sufficient for him to deal in property for his own benefit as he did. Shrewd speculation and leasing could have, must have, made up what he lacked in real money.

When "the rt. honorable John Lord St. John of Basing Earle of Wiltshire and Marquis of Winchester," came to repossess his father's lands after the Restoration in May 1660,[39] he was greatly in debt from loss of lands by "the Usurper in those late times," and wished to sell properties to repay his debts. On 6 March 1662, Daniel, in a petition to the House of Lords, recounted his management of the affairs of the estate, his borrowing of 30,000£ and being bound for the same, and presented a letter he had received from the Marquess of Winchester and Lord St. John,

> wherein they acknowledged his services, and in part of recompense thereof by deed granted to him the office of Chief Steward of all their Courts, Manors, and Lands during his life, with all the fees and profits thereto belonging, and petitioner accordingly officiated. Nevertheless, he has lately by chance understood that a Bill has been presented to Parliament (among other things) to make void his patent and grant, without any choice being given to him, although he yet stands engaged for over twenty thousand pounds and has not forfeited his patent, which is good in law. He prays that he may have a copy of the award and deed mentioned in the Bill, and that he may be heard by counsel in order that he may not be divested of his right and freehold.[40]

The suit Lord St. John brought against "the rt hon Henry Lord Pawlett, . . . Sir Robert Peake and Daniell Wicherley gentleman . . . [who] pretend some interest in the premises" and prevent his selling them, was long and detailed, full of charge, denial and countercharge, and in

[11]

sum: his Lordship the Marquis was "indebted to several psons several great sumes of money" and prevailed with Daniel "to become bound with his Lordp to some of his Lordps Creditors," while he promised "to save harmless . . . Wicherley from all bonds."[41] Eventually, however, Lord St. John refused to be bound any further for debts and Daniel was left unprotected and vulnerable; [42] consequently "he was sued at Law by several of the Creditors of the Marquis of Winchester and Lord St. John," one of whom was George Pawlett and his wife, Sarah, who sued Daniel for nonpayment.[43] He was then arrested by Lord St. John's servants, Walter Golding, Thomas Stock and John Parry. It is probable that Daniel was imprisoned, but not for long: only "until hee gained a protection from the right honble the Duke of Buckingham,"[44] a surprising intervention, datable approximately between 1655 and 1658, from a very influential man, who became friend to William perhaps out of Daniel's allegiance to the King.

Apart from his various salaries as steward, Daniel's most lucrative interest was in accumulating properties, most of which were in these years of the 40's and 50's from the Marquis' estates. One property which has a particularly interesting history, revealing much of Daniel's range of acquaintance, influence and quality of character, is Whitchurch Farm, Hampshire, which he leased from the Dean and Chapter of Winchester in the 1640's. This lease was voided in 1649 by Act of Parliament, for Parliament was seizing all lands belonging to loyalists to the late King Charles I and would shortly take all of the Marquis' land, as well as Daniel's, which went to Sir Robert Wallop. As long as the Commonwealth continued, Wallop held the land, but he lost it in 1660 at the Restoration.[45] Immediately at the Restoration of the Stuart monarchy with Charles II, a petition was placed by "Daniel Wicherley of the Inner Temple" to the Dean and Chapter to return to him and to his brother-in-law Michael Shrimpton, the Whitchurch property. The petition is itself interesting for its remembrance of the late king:

> yor petr hath had the great honr and happiness of yor Mayties Lodging at his house when yor Royall Father of blessed memory came up with his army out of the west at which time and for many yeares together the said Mr. [William, father of Michael and Bethia] Shrimpton alsoe suffered very much (as in Duty he was bound) for his loyalty to yor Royall father in entertaining of his forces and other wayes.[46]

Although such appeals to the King's sense of obligation were common, Daniel's direct assistance to Charles I is significant for the relationship that was to develop between William Wycherley and Charles II, who was aided directly by Daniel: "out of the estate of the Marquis, Daniel remitted considerable sums to Charles II in exile."[47] These actions are illustrative as well of Daniel's readiness to pursue hazard for duty's sake and his keen sense of loyalty which he shared with the Marquis whose motto was "Aymez Loyaulté."

The property of Whitchurch which Daniel leased with Shrimpton is of continuing interest, though we are momentarily running ahead of ourselves past 1660 to follow it. In 1663, Michael Shrimpton took a lease to a part of Whitchurch, but after a few years he was unable to make the payments of 160£ per annum rent and gave over the lease— with his arrears of 500£— to Daniel who absorbed the debt handily, precisely what one would expect from his excellent business sense. But then he began cutting timber and plowing up fields and thereby brought down the jeremiad wrath of the Dean upon his head. This remarkable suit reveals not only Daniel's resolute self-confidence but his genius for inspiring violent passion in others.

> Malevolent and evil disposed persons . . . and especially the said Daniel Wycherley have lately most unjustly and maliciously and in riotous and forcible manner plowed up . . . the greatest part of this manor and ancient pasture grounds . . . and doe still threaten to plow up all the rest . . . to impaire and utterly impoverish the said farme,

and have not only fell and cut down great quantities of wood
and timber and in . . . riotous manner with wains carts and
carriages have carried away . . . expressly against the
covenants . . . But have also maliciously broken down the
gates ditches hedges . . . putting your orators agents to
great terror. . . .[48]

and so on, in language which Daniel in his response
characterized as "such manner and phrase as this court hath
hardly been acquainted with." He denied, of course, the
riotous conduct he was charged withall and insisted that he
did no plowing contrary to the lease but only of such lands as
had been plowed within 50 years of the lease, as permitted.
He readily admitted he wanted "to make what lawful
benefit" he could of the farm, and as he took the burden of the
suit from the other defendants "employed by him," he seems
to have succeeded in his wishes. In 1667 he filed a plea, which
amplified the above details, to subpoena Sir Henry Vernon
whom neither side trusted, to "make true answer upon oath
to all questions," for Vernon was threatening to charge 4£
for each acre plowed, since he was accepting the rental
income from Daniel, but Daniel's claim seemed to be solid.[49]

While most of the properties Daniel controlled were from
the Marquis' estates, exactly how much property he had in
his hands is impossible to estimate since we rely for information on law suits on property issues, and not all his lands
were necessarily under litigation. But the following certainly suggests his persistent pursuit of land in spite of a
good deal of difficulty.

He and Walter Strickland had by August 1653 bought the
estate of Harriard Grange, worth 435£ 12s 4d according to his
steward's records.[50] His connection with the property was,
however, problematic since its vicar, James Garth, could not
get the rectory's profits due him either from Wycherley or the
former owner, Sir Edmund Plowden; Daniel stalled and then
ignored the order, but presumably paid at last his share of the
demanded 50£ a year.[51] Mortimer Manor and the allied lands
in the counties of Berkshire and Hampshire were "bought by

Dan. Witcherley" from the Marquis of Winchester's properties in 1652.[52] He had in addition obtained from the Marquis of Winchester "several leases . . . of the farmes of Frobury and title of Itchingwell and Sydmountain" which, out of fear that Lord St. John would "impeach" them, he pleaded assurance under law for their possession until he had "paid and recompensed the full satisfaction" for them.[53] Daniel then purchased with an associate, John Hurding, the Manor of Bradford, Wiltshire (100 acres), and Warleigh Woods, Somerset, for 3000£, paying 1000£ on 28 February 1656, the remaining due by Easter. This property Daniel seems to have held in spite of some crafty maneuvering by its owner Henry Rogers who, after making the sale to Daniel, tried to sell the land to Sir Paul Methwin for more money, but Methwin wisely retreated from the clumsy situation. The case ran, nevertheless, from June 1656 to July 1659.[54] It is worth noting that several of the deponents for Daniel's cause were from the Middle Temple and the Inner Temple; his connections with the law profession were solidly established before he undertook formal study of law at the Inner Temple.

For some years Daniel lived with his wife and infant son in Whitchurch, and perhaps at Basing House, but we are not sure of his location from about 1645 to 1651. He probably returned occasionally to Clive, perhaps so that William could be born and christened in the ancestral environs, but he was doubtless increasingly occupied with the Marquis' affairs in and about London and Hampshire. In 1651 he took a house in London on Kings Street North in the parish of St. Paul's Covent Garden, a street which opened onto the beautiful piazza which Inigo Jones had begun building in 1631 for the fourth Earl of Bedford.[55] It must have been a fine house, with a view of St. Paul's church and the piazza bordered by a classic arched portico, for Daniel paid 17s 4d each year in the Poor Rates of the parish;[56] Sir Peter Lely, the noted portraitist, paid one pound more for his house on the piazza, and Sir Godfrey Kneller, the equally noted painter, after 1702 paid an even two pounds. One is tempted to speculate on the grand sense of importance that stirred Daniel to select this impressive address, but even without conjuring his feelings, one realizes that this residence was a considerable achievement for him. No doubt young William lived here at times before going to France to continue his education, and probably George, the second child, was born here, in 1651; it was, at any rate, the place to which William returned later to live, and nearly sixty-five years later, in St. Paul's, was brought to be interred.

Like many of his acquaintances, Daniel was identified in a number of early cases as "of Covent Garden." George Giffard of St. Martin's in the Fields, only a short distance from Covent Garden, said he often visited Daniel in 1653 and 1654 at his home in Covent Garden.[57] He kept the Kings Street house until 1657, and by 1659, Daniel was listed as "late of Covent Garden," and in 1660 "of the Inner Temple." In fact, however, he had been admitted to the study of law at the Inner Temple inn of court in November 1658.[58]

Daniel's considerable acquaintance with templars and extensive experience in legal matters over the previous fifteen years no doubt contributed to his success, for he got on well at the Inner Temple. On 27 November 1670 "Daniel Witcherley (who is to be sworn this time)" was called with several others to the bar before Sir John Heath, Sir Edward Thurland, Sir Thomas Foster, and Sir Heneage Finch.[59] He continued to sign himself "of the Inner Temple," when useful, for example in a deposition made 14 November 1671 for one Robin Adams.[60]

Though we have not "brought this Esquire to his zenith, or verticall point," as biographer Gough put it,[61] these early directions of Daniel's career provide important clues to his character and a clearer sense of his ambitions and accomplishments. Since he was perhaps the dominating figure in William's life and since he has been much maligned and misunderstood, it is important to consider him carefully even at this early stage, when his "iron resolve and indomitable will''[62] emerged as well as those inclinations which have led some to call him merely covetous and litigious. He was a more complex man than these simplicities allow, and later as we continue his life on the Manor of Wem, his character will flesh out substantially.

Chapter I
Footnotes

1. Montague Summers, *The Complete Works of William Wycherley* (New York, 1964), I, 3. See also Joseph Morris, *Genealogical Manuscripts Connected with the County of Salop and Principality of Wales*, Vol. 9, 4471. Shrewsbury Borough Library, MSS no. 4085.

2. I owe a special debt of gratitude to Mr. Frank Wycherley and his wife for their hospitality at their home in the spring of 1973, showing me the materials he has collected on the Wycherley family, allowing me to copy the fine genealogical chart he has compiled with his own family line and with the Beeston line more clearly shown than on any other. His is the best genealogical table now existing, and I gladly acknowledge his generous assistance.

3. British Museum, Lansdowne MS. 255, ff. 43–57; new paging begins with no. 32. F. 38 is placed after f. 36 though written before it. Note variant spellings of the name. *Wycherley* is the usual form, often used by Daniel and almost always by William. Variations occur on each syllable: Wi, Whi, Why; th, tch, k; ar; lie, ly, or even *Wicherl*. Thus one can find both *Whycherley* and *Wicherly* or *Whychly*. The spelling *Witherley* is uncommon and *Wetherley* is another family entirely (see C24, 799/125). Daniel was once written *Nathaniel*.

4. Bodleian Library, MS. Don. b.8. printed here by permission of The Bodleian Library, Oxford. ''The Report of Sr. William Haward Knt, Sr. William Dugdale Knt Garter principall King of Armes and Walter Chetwind Esq in Ye Case of Daniell Wycherley Esq ye Consideration whereof being referr'd to them by ye Right Honble Robert Earle of Aylesbury Deputy Earle Marshall.'' In the Papers of the Right Honorable Lord Mostyn at Mostyn Hall was found the following decision on the case, dated 24 January 1676:

> The answere of Daniel Wytherly, in the Co. of Salop, to the petition of Sir Vincent Corbet, Baronet, and eight other persons, calling themselves the gentry in the Co. of Salop, directed to James Earl of Suffolk, deputy to Henry Howard . . . with an answer to the certificate of the foure subordinate heralds, and animadversions upon the certificate of the three kinds of arms, &c . . . *Ends* ''give him a remedy answerable to his abuse and damage.''

''Biographical Data on William Wycherley and his Father, ''*Notes and*

Queries, ccxvi (January 1971), 36; my notes on this document are in error; it has nothing to do with his commission.

5. Summers, I, 6.

6. Summers I, 8: "He was never happy unless involved in some intricate and interminable law tangle." Most biographers since have accepted this.

7. Summers, I, 9: "A lover of the country and stern martinet, not to say a dour domestic tyrant, he conceived that every member of his family also was found to love and endure the routine of a country life. . . ." I believe Summers' two portraits of Daniel are contradictory.

8. Summers, I, 3.

9. B. M., Lansdowne MS 255. f.32 (new paging), answer no. 1 to interrogatories. This MS reported incorrectly that Sugar was tutor "to Richd Wicharley deceased & the said Mr. Wicharley [Daniel fils] the two sons of the said Daniel [pere]" for Richard was not brother to Daniel but was the adopted son of Thomas Wycherley of Cockshutt and did study under Sugar but did poorly, according to Gough, *Antiquities and Memoirs of Myddle* (1875), p. 84. Mr. Sugar died 1674: *MSS Calendar of Deeds and Charters*: Vol. V, no. 5097, Shrewsbury Borough Library.

10. Gough, p. 85.

11. W.A.L. Vincent, *The State and School Education 1640-1660* (London, 1950), pp. 20, 130.

12. *A History of Shrewsbury School, from the Blakeway MSS and Many Other Sources* (London, 1889), p. 176, Shrewsbury Borough Library. See also George William Fisher, *Annals of Shrewsbury School* (London, 1899), p. 210n. A confusion over entries in the school admittances of Daniel Wicharley in 1616, 1618, 1619 cannot refer to this Daniel, since he was born in 1617, nor am I convinced this is the Rev. Daniel Wycherley, D.D. whom we meet in Chapter 5. See E. Calvert ed., *Shrewsbury School Registrum Scholarium*, 1563-1653, (Shrewsbury, 1892, date of Preface), and *Annals*, p. 210n.

13. Gough, p. 85.

14. Summers, I, 4.

15. C24, 833/86, deposition of Thimebly.

16. *Ibid.*, interrogatory no. 7. Phillip Fursdon lists employments Daniel refused.

17. J. Jean Hecht, *The Domestic Servant Class in Eighteenth-Century England* (London, 1956), pp. 38-39.

18. *Calendar of Proceedings of the Committee for Advancement of Money*, 1642-56, ed. Mary Anne Everett Green (London, 1888), p. 359: 26 September 1651, 26 May 1652, 26 August; 1 August 1654.

19. *Calendar of the Proceedings of the Committee for Compounding &c.*, Cases July 1650-Dec. 1653, ed. M.A.E. Green (London, 1892), 2888:27 July 1652. Note also reference to Daniel, p. 2361; 7 July 1652 and 14 November 1654, "Marquis of Winchester's agent to have notice and no distress to be made for six weeks."

20. C24, 833/86, interrogatory no. 2.

21. C24, 874, last deposition.

22. C24, 874, deposition of Henslowe.

23. C24, 833/86, interrogatory no. 11.

24. C24, 874, interrogatory no. 8 and deposition of Edward Formen.

25. C24, 833/86, interrogatories nos. 2 and 7. In Daniel's "Accompt" book, see n. 31 below, are listed the "Charges upon ye clayme of ye Lo. Rivers in the absense of the Lord St. John before ye Comee for Removinge Obstructions," 59£ 3d (p. 5).

26. *Ibid.*, interrogatory no. 3.

27. *Historical Manuscripts Commission Report*, Appendix to Seventh Report, p. 161. See also p. 172: "Petition of Daniel Wycherley that his interest in the office of Steward of the Marquess' estates may be protected by law. The Petition is almost identical to . . . 6 March, 1662." See also Willard Connely, *Brawny Wycherley* (New York, 1930), p. 14, who refers to Gough and Perromat.

28. C24, 833/86, several interrogatories.

29. C8, 107/92, membrane no. 1. This case contains five pages, most in very poor condition only parts of which are readable. See also C24, 833/86, interrogatory no. 14.

30. C24, 833/86, deposition of Phillip Fursdon.

31. Hampshire County Council Record Office, MSS 11M 49/230.

32. "Accompt of Daniell Witcharley . . . ," p.11.

33. *Ibid.*, pp. 13, 15 respectively.

34. *Ibid.*, p. 27.

35. Summers, I, 7.

36. "Accompt of Daniel Witcharley . . . ," p. 37. Compare the salaries listed for land steward by J. J. Hecht, p. 142: 1713, 50£; 1722, 30£, 70£, 100£. Daniel's salary was indeed a good one.

37. *Ibid.*, p. 40.

38. *Ibid.*, p. 39.

39. *Statutes of the Realm*, Vol. 5, 434: 1662, "Act for confirming the estates of John Marquess of Winchester in certain Manors and Lands whereof the deed and Evidence were burnt and lost at the taking of the Castle of Basing."

40. *Historical Manuscripts Commission*, Seventh Report, p. 161, quoted from Summers, I, 7.

41. C10, 63/100 (7 Feb. 1661), and C24, 874, interrogatories nos. 2, 4, 7. As Summers pointed out, there were also suits between the Marquis and his son, some of which involved Daniel: e.g., "7 June 1660, Petition of John, Marquess of Winchester, and Daniel Wycherley. Pray for the reversal of a decree pronounced by Mr. Fountain, one of the commissioners for the Great Seal, in a suit brought against petitioners by Lord St. John"; "6 March 1661–2. Draft of an act for confirming the award made by the King's Majesty for composing the differences between John, Lord Marquess of Winchester, and his eldest son." Summers, I, 7.

42. C24, 833/86, interrogatory no. 17.

43. C24, 833/86, interrogatory no. 20, and C24, 874, deposition of William, son of George Pawlett. In another suit, 1657, "Fulke Wormelayton of Wapping in co. Middlesex distiller . . . [swore] that where the rt. hon. John Earl of Wilton and Marquess of

Winchester . . . and Walter Strickland . . . , Edward Cooke . . . , John Chicheley of Covent Garden . . . , and Daniel Witcharley of the parish of St. Martins in the fields . . . gent" had pretensions to the Manors of Frobury and Winslade and borrowed from the above 1000£ which they had not paid back as promised according to the deed of 20 July 1653 (C8, 312/168).

44. C24, 833/86, interrogatory no. 20. Walter Golding's deposition affirmed the intervention of the Duke of Buckingham.

45. *Statutes of the Realm*, Vol. 5, Charles I–Charles II, 1625-1689 (London, 1819), 318: "1661, among those to forfeit estates: Robt. Wallop." A brief history of Daniel's possession of this property with Shrimpton, before and after Wallop, is given in *The Victoria History of the Counties of England*, Vol. IV, *History of Hampshire* (London, 1914), 301.

46. State Papers, 29/13, #127. "The humble peticon of Daniell Wicherley of the Inner Temple London Gen." See also *Calendar of State Papers*, Vol. 1660–61, ed. M. A. E. Green (London, 1860), p. 251.

47. *A History of Shrewsbury School*, p. 176.

48. C10, 108/145.

49. C10, 489/157, in very poor condition, mostly unreadable. Daniel gave the state of the farm: "Shrimpton unable to pay one rent of 105£," and "much more rent long behind and unpaid," the buildings decaying, and in debt to Daniel for "moneys lent to him to start the sd farm and otherways and to pay the rent."

50. "Accompt of Daniel Witcharley," p. 16.

51. *Calendar of the Proceedings of the Committee for Compounding & c.*, Cases 1647–June 1650, ed. M. A. E. Green (London, 1891), pp. 2372, 2373; dates 23 July 1650; 13 July 1653, 29 July, 10 August; 24 February 1654, 15 March, 23 March, 23 April, 3 August, 10 October, 31 October.

52. *Calendar of the Proceedings of the Committee for Compounding & c.*, Cases July 1650–December 1653, ed. M. A. E. Green (London, 1892), p. 2533. Mortimer Manor is listed in Daniel's "Accompt" book, "last moiety pd 5th November 1652," out of a price of 1407£ 7s 7½d, (p. 24).

53. C10, 63/100.

54. C8, 75/32, 31 December 1656: "your orators did agree to pay Henry Rogers 3000£ lawful money of England, 1000£ part on 28 November and 500£ on 24 December and the other 1500£ on or before the first week of Easter term next ensuing." C8, 312/107, 11 May 1657; C24, 818/112, Michas 1657; C8, 135/96, 13 February, 24 May 1658; C3, 468/1, July 1659, in very mutilated condition.

55. John Summerson, *Inigo Jones* (London, 1966), pp. 83 ff.

56. St. Paul's Covent Garden, Poore Rates and Receipts (Overseers' Accounts) Poore Rates Ledger: Westminster City Library. In 1655 and 1656 (H. 437 and H. 439), Daniel paid 1£; assessments before and after were 17s 4d. There are surprisingly no listings in the accounts for William Wycherley, though we know he lived in Covent Garden; there seems no explanation for this lack. Michael Shrimpton had residence in Mayden Lane from about 1671 till 1675, paying 8s (H. 453 ff.). Further, there is no

reference to Wycherley in The Bedford Estates Leases, for Bow Street, nor for Kings Street North; Greater London Record Office, County Hall.

57. C24, 833/86, deposition.

58. W. H. Cooke, ed., *Students Admitted to the Inner Temple*, 1547–1660, (London, 1878), p. 372. See also F. A. Inderwick, ed., *A Calendar of Inner Temple Records* (London, 1901), III, lxxiii: ". . . Daniel was a barrister of this inn." H. H. L. Bellot, *The Inner and Middle Temple* (London, 1902), p. 142, "Daniel Wycherley, a member of our House." Both biographers Summers, I, 6, and Connely, p. 40, accept the following line as a reference to Daniel: "Orders that Wicherley be controller for the present Christmas," from "Acts of Parliament of the Gentlemen of the Inner Temple, held on the Vigil of St. Thomas the Apostle, 1662," Inderwick, p. 17. But I believe this reference is to William, that he was made controller for the Christmas; for in his introduction, Inderwick writes, "William Wycherley's father, Daniel, was a barrister of this Inn, to which the author was admitted in 1659 at the age of 19. In 1662 he was appointed controller for the Christmas. His portrait by Lely in 1668 presents him as a handsome young man" (lxxiii). The reference is clearly to William here, and it would be entirely possible for him rather than his father to be so appointed.

59. Inderwick, p. 74.

60. C24, 968/57.

61. Gough, p. 86

62. Summers, I, 6.

Chapter II

The Early Years

At the base of a high jutting hill in the village of Clive, Shropshire, stands a large house once called Wycherley Hall or Clive Hall where William Wycherley was born in May 1641.[1] It is a handsome building still today, though no longer a private home. The main street runs past this house and along the base of the hill to the left past old and new houses on either side to the parish church which now has a tall Victorian steeple and is well furnished inside.

On both sides of the church and for a short distance up the hill in back lay graves of parishioners. Some members of the Wycherley family were buried here, William's mother and father, his brother John and a sister Frances, perhaps brother Henry and others; Daniel's grave is cited by a marker on an outside wall, but the graves of other members of the family are obliterated now and the parish vicar says that no mention of the Wycherley family is given in the guidebook he prints for the parish. From the front of Wycherley Hall, only a few minutes' walk from the church at the other end of the village, one can look across broad open fields, for the land of Shropshire in this area is flat or mildly rolling, to where the village of Wem lies three miles to the right, where Daniel bought his estate, and to the left about ten miles toward Shrewsbury, the county center.

It is probable that William lived with his parents at Whitchurch, Hampshire, in his earliest years, and later at the Kings Street house, Covent Garden. Educated under the supervision of his father,[2] he was probably sent to Clive to study under the tuition of Mr. Sugar, tutor to Daniel. He attended the Royal Free School of King Edward the Sixth in Shrewsbury,[3] but it is not clear in what years. Just outside the village of Grinshill, about a mile from Clive, and directly across the road from the home of Frank Wycherley today, there is a fine old stone building known as the "pesthouse," to which students from Shrewsbury would flee in plague time in the city. Not unlikely, William escaped there during his schooling in Shrewsbury.

The education William received was an excellent one, for he was reputed a "person as highly educated as any in this County,"[4] and by his earliest biographers was known for his fine education at his father's hands[5] and for his thorough knowledge of Greek and Latin authors.[6] If he had any schooling in Hampshire, he may have experienced Catholic-oriented training for there was a large group of Catholics residing about Winchester for years.[7] If his training was entirely at his father's hands and with Mr. Sugar and the King Edward School, we can be certain that it was indeed strongly classical for his father was well schooled in the classics and the Shrewsbury schools were noted for years for their impressive classical curriculum; one of the key texts was selections from Cicero and Ludovicus Vives made by the sixteenth century headmaster Thomas Ashton.[8] Playacting was fostered there, as in a good number of schools, and so too was the study of the comedies of Terence and other writers.[9]

Daniel continued to influence decisively his son's education when, in compliance with the mode of sending a boy to the Continent for the completion of pre-university or pre-professional schooling, he sent William, at about fifteen or sixteen years of age, to western France.[10] The rationale for this petite tour to the Continent has been attributed by biographers to the disastrous state of life and learning in England under Cromwell, but this condition has been exaggerated.[11] The Long Parliament promoted educational reform which only the Restoration prevented being effected.[12] It may have appeared sufficiently calamitous to Daniel's royalist point of view, especially in view of the

[23]

decline in attendance at the Shrewsbury school during the interregnum years,[13] to insist that his first son leave for greener educational pastures, or in this case river banks, for William lived on the banks of the Charante River near Angoulême.[14] It was not, however, a radical move to send one's son to Europe to continue schooling. While we know nothing specific about William's course of study in France, there is at least a suspicion that he studied under Catholic auspices,[15] for the Catholic school system, Jesuit and otherwise, being under none of the harassment that it was in England, flourished there, and William's associates of high rank were Catholic.

Angoulême was the locus of a unique group of nobility, a second Paris as it were, where flourished in the 1640's and 1650's the celebrated school of *Préciosité*, that cultivated a self-conscious, perhaps one could say contrived, refinement of manners and language to a particular elegance of address, compliment and gesture. The center of this salon was Julie d'Angennes, daughter of the Marquise de Rambouillet whose Hotel de Rambouillet was previously the seat of elegance, visited by Balzac when he so deemed to leave his solitude in Saintonge, Voiture, noted for his mode of letter writing and for his practical joking, Capelain, correspondent of Balzac and noted for even more sophisticated letters than Voiture, and a host of lesser writers and nobility. All these hastened to Angoulême when Julie d'Angennes acceded to the ten-year courtship of the Marquis de Montausier and they were married in 1645.

It was to this provincial center that Wycherley came around 1655, shortly after Balzac's death[16]—he returned to southern France, to Montpellier, in later years to recover from illness—and he came directly into contact with Julie d'Angennes. By his own admission he had "the happiness to be in the Neighbourhood" of this Julie d'Angennes, "one of the most accomplished Ladies of the Court of France." He told Dennis years later that he had been "often admitted to the Conversation of that Lady, who us'd to call him the little

Huguenot; and that young as he was, he was "equally pleas'd with the Beauty of her Mind, as with the Graces of her Person."[17] During his sojourn in France, about four years at most, he was converted to Catholicism, no doubt at least to some extent as a result of her persuasive influence and mockery of him as a "little Huguenot." She was very persistent and persuasive, for she had also convinced her husband, three years younger than herself, to convert from Protestantism.[18] This conversion of Wycherley's has been thought to be of great moment, but it probably is not so exceptional. William's father's relationship with the Catholic Marquis of Winchester and his support of Charles I and Charles II meant that he was always closely associated with Catholicism so that his conversion was more a movement from high to higher Church than a sudden discovery of religion.

This group at Angoulême, known as *précieux* and *précieuses*, were part of what David S. Berkeley described as "at first a French and later an English fad of the seventeenth century . . . a form of ceremonious social intercourse which derived its attitudes, postures, and special vocabulary from the belief that beautiful and virtuous ladies have a semi-divine status, to which their male satellites . . . can be drawn by due worship of these ladies and the cultivation of refinement, honor, virtue, superficial learning, and a certain stereotyped wit."[19]

Charles II and his court had been exposed to this sort of manner during their exile in France before the Restoration, and Wycherley's learning the pattern was of course of definite value to him when he returned home. Certainly his mode of extravagant compliment to the proposition of the Duchess of Cleveland, which we will see later, and his discourse, even later, with the Countess of Drogheda at Tunbridge has a certain zest of préciosité. But in his plays, following the precedent of Molière's opening shot at the tissue of *préciosité* in *Les Précieuses Ridicules* (1659), and like most of his contemporaries, he satirized the mode, such as in the character of Christina in *Love in a Wood* and others, as David Berkeley points out.[20]

There was an obvious reaching for effect in the group surrounding the Marquise in the Hotel de Rambouillet. Voiture, for example, loved the ingenious prank; finding several bears in the street he brought them to the Hotel to amuse the Marquise (Julie's mother); "she saw four huge paws over her folding screen and two enormous snouts . . . She almost died of fright."[21] Chapelain was much preferred because of his "perfect tact" but even he took Balzac gently to task for his use of "ce mot de *besogne* pour *travail* ou *ouvrage*" for *besogne* simply would not do; it was base by common agreement.[22] In 1640 Julie was given a collection of poems, or madrigals, *La Guirlande de Julie, pour Mademoiselle de Rambouillet*, to which all the main poets of the circle contributed, to create one of the handsomest Moroccan-bound volumes the Marquis de Rambouillet could contrive.[23]

The exposure to this world of fragile elegance, of which the foregoing are not atypical instances, affected Wycherley in more ways than his conversion to Catholicism. It is difficult of course to ascertain what kind of impact this world, so different from what he could have known, had on him, for he would have been too young to know the visits of Queen Henrietta, wife of Charles I, to Basing House to be entertained when Inigo Jones and other artists gathered there. His knowledge of the fashionable language no doubt was indispensable preparation for encountering the nobility of post-Restoration London, though his general disposition seemed to be of the very opposite of *préciosité*. His plays only in a very remote sense seem to be striving for the establishment of an elegance of language—Congreve came closer to this in, for instance, *The Way of the World*; but for Wycherley the "heavily imaged" style of Angoulême was, as Berkeley observes, nearer false wit.[24] Personally, he used its social advantage as far as it could assist him, but intellectually he does not seem to have believed in it. Perhaps borrowing

[26]

a hint, as he did various times, from Molière, who used the Marquis of Montausier as the model for Alceste in *The Misanthrope*—a study refers to him as Un Misanthrope[25]—Wycherley may have used aspects of him for his own misanthropic Manly in *The Plain-Dealer*. Like Manly, a man of adventure, the Marquis was a soldier, Manly a sea-farer; both were inclined to be solitary and unsociable—but so too was Balzac for that matter—and fairly starchy in their manners; not necessarily virginal in their social life—one did not marry until after other adventures.[26]

Thus, these several years in France had varying impact on Wycherley; to some he responded positively, to others negatively, not toward one or the other in specifically well defined or systematic ways, but as they were useful or meaningful to him at times in his life. Nevertheless, to emerge into manhood, to meet and talk and argue with Julie d'Angennes, a woman whose like he was not to meet again, was assuredly a heady experience. When he again saw a level of social life and sophistication similar to that of Angoulême, it would be the London of Charles II, through more astute, ironic eyes.

After the death of Oliver Cromwell on 3 September 1658 and before the formal restoration to the throne of Charles II in May 1660, William returned to England. Biographer Willard Connely said that he went to Shropshire,[27] which would certainly be plausible, but we do not in fact know his travels. In October 1659, when he was 19 years old, he was admitted to the Inner Temple, one of the London Inns of Court, to study law,[28] about one year after his father had been admitted there. The suggestion of some biographers that he entered the Middle Temple seems to have no verifiable basis,[29] but there is some confusion about his law career. Summers states that Wycherley entered the Inner Temple in November 1660,[30] but this cannot be his first entrance and may mark his readmittance after a period at Oxford.[31] Historian F. A. Inderwick relates that he was appointed "controller for the Christmas" at the Inner Temple in 1662[32] and H. H. L. Bellot reports that he lived for some time as an inmate of the Temple and had chambers there, probably at the Inner Temple.[33] It seems evident that William entered the Inner Temple in 1659, then left, and returned again in late 1660, but it is doubtful that he stayed consistently even then.

Before a year had passed in the Inner Temple, he left for Oxford and took up residence there with some intention, perhaps uncertainly defined, of study. He did not matriculate into any college but in July 1660 "became sojourner in Oxon for the sake of the Public Library," and entered the Bodleian "under the name of Philosophiae studiosus."[34] He had the unusual opportunity of living with the Provost of Queens College, the famous Dr. Thomas Barlow (1607–1691), who was also librarian of the Bodleian. William's time there was spent in study, reading at the library, and in discussion with the formidable polemicist, Barlow, later Bishop of Lincoln, who had a reputation as a "great master of the whole controversy between the protestants and popists, being the uncompromising opponent of the latter."[35] Yet along with his rigid hatred of Roman Catholicism which was already of long standing when he declared his enmity to Popery and its agents, Titus Oates and James, Duke of York, Barlow was known for his talent for compromise and accommodation to new trends: he remained at Oxford during the 1648 ejectment of many clerics, stayed on after the Restoration to aid those same clergy who had been ejected, was one of the first to declare allegiance to Catholic James II at his accession, all remarkably accommodating acts. That he was a casuist requires little additional proof. Thus, it is not surprising that in his discussions with William Wycherley he succeeded in reconverting the young scholar back to Protestantism. This seemingly facile shift of allegiance suggests a lack of conviction or an undue susceptibility to environment or rhetoric; but William was never very astute politically and seems to have been persuaded in various directions by several people throughout his life. His genius did not include perspicuity in business matters or tenacity in religion. Furthermore, he was not without precedent in his conversion, though the following summation may overstate his level of religious trauma: "It cannot be said often enough that the best poets underwent grave spiritual crises early and late in the century. Donne left Roman Catholicism for Anglicanism, Crashaw and Dryden the reverse. Jonson, Marvell and Wycherley moved to Rome and back to Canterbury."[36]

Traditional views of William's life at this time maintain that he left Oxford in disgust [37] and next left the study of law with equal disgust because it was intolerably dull, and then in reaction to this tedium, threw himself onto the pleasures of the town, presumably as a preparation for playwrighting. As Gildon put it:

> he was plac'd in one of our Inns of Court, I think the *Middle Temple*, . . . But his Temper and Inclinations had taken another Bent. . . . The dry Study of the Law afforded him but little satisfaction. His free Parts soon recommended him to the *Beaux Esprits* of those Times; and he was caress'd by all the Men of Pleasure and Wit as a Person that deserv'd an universal Applause for Talents which they then call'd above the dull Plodding Way of the Men of the Long Robe.[38]

There is no reason to assume that Wycherley was not as charming as he is here presented, for charm of physique and phrase was his mark throughout life, but his presumed flight to the pleasures of the town is questionable. For one thing, he did not dislike Oxford so greatly as has been supposed, for in 1668 he sent a cup to Queens College and had his name entered in the benefactor's Liber Albus: "Gulielmus Wicherly Socio Commensalis Cantharum Argentum DD Jan A⁰D. 1667—24 oz." Possibly he sent this cup up to Oxford when his brother George went to Queens College.[39] Another consideration is that in the decade prior to the appearance of his first play in 1672, several possible activities have come to light, any one of which would indicate that he was pursuing the development of a gentleman's career in duty to the State, and not pleasure exclusively.

In the Army lists for the summer of 1662 the name "William Witcherley" appears in the Company of the Earl of Arran, "Colonel of His Majesties Regiment of Guards in Ireland."[40] While it would seem he was a very busy man if he were summering in the Army in Ireland and by December was "controller for the Christmas" at the Inner Temple, it does appear probable that he is the same man because we learn later that the Earl of Arran knew Wycherley.[41] There are very few other "William Witcherleys" who could be this man; one who had children by his wife Elizabeth in 1707, 1714, 1716 and 1725, would be too young,[42] and one who lived in Fitts, Salop, was 60 years old in 1671, obviously too old.[43] It would be appropriate for a young gentleman to serve a tour in the army for the sake of adventure as well as for the sake of the gentlemanly endeavor and exercise of courage.

There is another venture Wycherley may have undertaken, but this is less easily verifiable. On 31 January 1664, Sir Richard Fanshawe left England as Ambassador for Charles II to the court of Spain, accompanied by several staff members, one named "Mr. Wycherley."[44] Circumstances again argue that this is William, because for one thing it would have been highly appropriate for him to serve an apprenticeship in the diplomatic service; his father would have had some claim to a favor from the King, and in his role as Steward to the Marquis of Winchester, Daniel had leased houses in London to the Spanish Ambassadors, thereby giving him an acquaintance with that side of the connection.[45] William had a reading knowledge of Spanish when he set to writing his first two plays, based on the apparently untranslated plays of Calderon. Sir Richard Fanshawe was himself a man of considerable literary achievement, especially as a translator of Spanish works, though there does not appear to be any direct influence of his translations on Wycherley's works. In a study of Spanish sources of Restoration drama, Professor John Loftis expressed conviction that this traveller was William Wycherley, but verification remains tantalizingly distant.[46]

If Wycherley went to Spain, he returned to London, according to Lady Fanshawe, in February 1665, and then joined the Naval forces of the King against the Dutch in the Second Dutch War. It has been quite reliably suggested that he was in the battle in which James, Duke of York, defeated Admiral Opdam on 3 June 1665 about which he wrote his poem, *"On a* Sea Fight, *which the Author was in, Betwixt the* English *and* Dutch."[47] As is the case with many events in his life, Wycherley is almost entirely silent about his activities these early years in London. Certainly one would assume that a handsome young man would seek pleasure, but Wycherley seemed to be seeking more.

The character of the Restoration years is distinctive, in a sense unique in English history. From the distance of maturity, years and satiric perspective, Alexander Pope characterized these robust Restoration days as

> Days of Ease, when now the weary Sword
> Was sheath'd, and *Luxury* with *Charles* restor'd;
> In every Taste of foreign Courts improv'd,
> 'All by the King's Example, liv'd and lov'd.'
> Then Peers grew proud in Horsemanship t'excell,
> New-market's glory rose, as Britain's fell;
> The Soldier breath'd the Gallantries of France,
> And ev'ry flow'ry Courtier writ Romance.
> Then Marble soften'd into life grew warm,
> And yielding Metal flow'd to human form:
> Lely on animated Canvas stole
> The sleepy Eye, that spoke the melting soul.
> No wonder then, when all was Love and Sport
> The willing Muses were debauch'd at Court.[48]

These conveniently epigrammatic lines could serve as the inscription on the headstone of the Restoration era and would characterize the view of that time held by most persons, the historical image, right or wrong. It is a time credited with great change, with a decisive break with the past, with the beginnings of the modern age; it is a time too much credited with revision, as modern scholarship is steadily making clear.[49] But it is a time whose image comes naturally, for the theaters were reopened, women trooped the stage for the first time, new playwrights emerged with brilliance, and the tone of Charles II's court clashed resoundingly against the Commonwealth sobriety, as mistress was openly paraded after mistress and insolent quips amused the King and his court:

> God bless our good and gracious King,
> Whose promise none relies on;
> Who never said a foolish thing,
> Nor ever did a wise one.[50]

The masquerading which amused the court was by no means reserved for the conventions of the stage nor was it the sole device of prostitutes who were commonly called vizards or masks for their habit of wearing such signs of their trade, but it was indeed the sport of all. "At this time," reported Gilbert Burnet,

> the court fell into much extravagance in masquerading: both King and queen, and all the court, went about masked, and came into houses unknown, and danced there with a great deal of wild frolic. In all this people were so disguised, that, without being in the secret, none could distinguish them. Once the queen's chairmen, not knowing who she was, went from her: so she was alone, and was much disturbed, and came to Whitehall in a hackney coach: some say it was in a cart.[51]

Charles led the way, if such leadership was required, to seize occasion for a game of disguise; the following episode was not atypical.

> Charles agreed to go out one night with [Rochester] to visit a celebrated house of intrigue, where he told his Majesty the finest women in England were to be found. The King made no scruple to assume his usual disguise and accompany him, and while he was engaged with one of the ladies of pleasure, being before instructed by Rochester how to behave, she picked his pocket of all his money and watch, which the King did not immediately miss. Neither the people of the house,

[32]

nor the girl herself was made acquainted with the quality of
their visitor, nor had the least suspicion who he was.

When the King was about to leave, he found Rochester gone,
himself unable to pay and obliged to ask for credit till the
morrow.

> The consequence of this request was, he was abused and
> laughed at; and the old woman told him that she had often
> been served such dirty tricks, and would not permit him to
> stir till the reckoning was paid, and then called one of her
> bullies to take care of him.

The King's offer of his ring for security was rejected until a
jeweler was called to appraise it; he at once realized its great
value and recognized the King as its only possible owner,
whereupon he fell to his knees in reverence.

> The old Jezebel and the bully, finding the extraordinary
> quality of their guest, were now confounded, and asked
> pardon most submissively on their knees. The King in best-
> natured manner forgave them, and laughing asked them
> whether the ring would not bear another bottle.[52]

The masquerading and sexual sport were accompanied by
various other scandalous and extravagant activities by many
of the greatest names of the day: Sir Charles Sedley, Henry
Savile, Sir George Etherege, John Wilmot, Earl of
Rochester, and George Villiers, Duke of Buckingham. The
host of surviving anecdotes about these men jumble together
fact and fancy so that only an acute historian can disengage
them into probably correct groups.[53] The drinking, dueling,
fighting, whoring, public nakedness and profanity which
did occur hardly equalled the amount rumored. As Burnet
wrote, "The three most eminent wits of that time, on whom
all the lively libels were fastened, were the earls of Dorset and
Rochester, and sir Charles Sedley." Rochester, he said, "was
naturally modest, till the court corrupted him. . . . He
gave himself up to all sorts of extravagance, and to the
wildest frolics that a wanton wit could devise."[54] Rochester
claimed to have gone "five years together" drunk, and

Etherege and Rochester got into a scuffle with some nightwatch which ended with the death of one of their companions; Sedley was charged with exhibiting himself naked from a balcony and throwing bottles onto the crowd.

But one thing is immediately perceivable in the stories from these days of ease—the name of Wycherley almost never appears. He was not, as far as we know, involved in any duel; he did not go about beating or stabbing the nightwatch or romping half dressed in the park; he did not spend his days and nights drunk. But admittedly our sense of Wycherley's innocence derives from a lack of knowledge, and if we assume that he did not partake of these diversions, we do so without informed conviction and at the risk of denying that he would have been aware of the array of activity that flourished then and of the affairs of the most notable men and women of the day; he was almost of necessity shaped by this culture. His relatively small social and less political stature is the obvious reason why his actions were so little recorded; what the Duke of Buckingham did was history, what Lord Rochester was doing was news, but what William Wycherley, gentleman, did was not significant beyond the fringe of his friends. It is worthwhile noting here, however, that the attempts of some to make Wycherley's character ideally moral on the basis of his later satiric attacks on vice and hypocrisy do not have the evidence of life to support them, for those who know vice may be those who have touched it personally; the libertine may be at one and the same time the moralist.[55] Thus, I would not wish to wash Wycherley clean with the waters of ignorance nor dye him with the guilt of association. We shall see that he knew the town and its people, he had his affairs and a reputation to match those amours, and he had a sufficiently scurrilous mind to write *Hero and Leander*; to guess more is not of much advantage.

Wycherley's familiarity with the wits of the court and the town during the 1660's introduced or encouraged him to follow the contemporary mode of writing poetry, at least as a gentleman scribbler if not as a serious poet. He became one of the "mob of gentlemen who wrote with ease," as Pope tagged them, men like the Duke of Buckingham who was playwright as well as poet and sometime friend of Daniel and William; Charles Sackville, Earl of Dorset, patron to many writers; Sir Charles Sedley, whose genius ran to light verses; and in sharply ascending order of merit, the brilliant John Wilmot, Earl of Rochester, the best and most intelligent poet next to John Dryden in the Restoration group of poets. There were, of course, numbers of lesser poets, some competent, some would-be wits, some hacks, lesser both socially and poetically. Many of Wycherley's friends at this time were fellow Oxonians—Sedley, Sir Car Scroope, and Rochester from Wadham, Henry Guy and Fleetwood Shepherd with MA's, and Anthony Henley from Magdalen. But the real motivating force for poetry-writing in the early years of the Restoration was the King himself, for Charles was a patron of many of the arts, from gardening to the theater. He encouraged poets and loved the wit and humor of lyric and satiric verse, forgiving much for their sake, even the incredible effrontery of Rochester's comparison of his scepter to his private parts.[56]

Verse-making was a common, indeed an expected, achievement for a gentleman, especially extempore rhymes, like Rochester's invention after hearing a country clerk sing the psalms:

> Sternhold and Hopkins had great qualms
> When they translated David's psalms
> To make the heart full glad;
> But had it been poor David's fate
> To hear thee sing, and them translate
> By God! 'twould have made him mad.[57]

Wycherley, too, joined this assault on paper. Although much of his poetry is difficult to date, because none except *Hero and Leander* (1669) and *Epistles to the King and Duke* (1682) was published until 1704, a poem such as "To King Charles II *on his* Return" was presumably composed within

[35]

a year after Charles landed at Dover in May 1660. Wycherley never wrote first-rate poetry throughout his career. Much of it is in fact decidedly pedestrian in thought and feeling and often uninspired in versification or technically careless. His couplets in the poem to King Charles, for instance, tend to end-stop with too great regularity and its sentiments are not notably interesting:

> You come, Great Prince, at length Triumphant Home,
> Like Christian *Constantine* to Heathen *Rome.*
> No barb'rous Foe your Chariot-wheels attends,
> But such as All are less your Slaves than Friends.

except for the possibly sly play on "dissipate" at the end:

> So You, the long-wish'd Blessing of our Isle,
> Chase all our Fears, and make the Nations smile;
> While ev'ry Mist, that did obscure the State,
> Begins at your Approach to dissipate.[58]

By comparing these lines to the conclusion of Dryden's celebration of Charles' return,

> Oh happy Prince whom Heav'n hath taught the way
> By paying Vowes, to have more Vowes to pay!
> Oh Happy Age! Oh times like those alone
> By Fate reserv'd for Great *Augustus* Throne!
> When the joint growth of Armes and Arts foreshew
> The World a Monarch, and that Monarch *You.*[59]

one can see how far Wycherley was from a true responsiveness to poetry's rhythms. Another probably early poem, "To *an* University-Wit, *or* Poet; *who had written some ill Verses, with an ill Play or two; which, not succeeding, he resolv'd to turn* Parson," is uneasy in syntax and its lines are stuffed with fillers for the sake of rhyme or an extra syllable.

> You Wit, in your Poetic Fury have,
> Since you the Stage wou'd for the Pulpit leave:
> Will of your Wit so give us better Proof,
> Since you wou'd Starving Poetry leave off;
> And a Fat Priest, of a Lean Poet now
> Wou'd (to the best Proof of your Reason) grow.[60]

His poem "*On a* Sea Fight," datable 1665, has smoother,

more readable verse, more intense feeling and an interesting
point of view which emerges as he compares the hell of the
fight to Pluto's hell, with Pluto's fear for his overthrow:

> *Pluto* himself did tremble in his Hell,
> Pale Ghosts look'd paler, to hear new Ghosts tell
> What was in *Neptune's* Empire done above
> By Two great Fleets, that for Hell's Empire strove.
> Each Side, like Fiends, in Fire and Smoke did fight,
> And put the Dev'l himself into a Fright;
> For both dispatch'd to Hell such Numbers down,
> That *Pluto* scarce could call his Realm his own.
> And since both States to Monarchs had been Foes,
> He fear'd, betwixt them, they would him depose. . .
> For Rebels ever by their Nature hate
> The absolute Dominion of a State,
> And with the Devil himself would Right dispute,
> If He pretended to be Absolute:
> Justly he fear'd, our *English* would *rebell*,
> And knew the *Dutch* the *Dev'l* would *buy* and *sell*.[61]

Showing through the conventional images of hell is an
insight into the tumult of war and its near overthrow of all
nature and order, a concern that would occupy him further
in later poetry.

Late in the decade Wycherley turned to burlesque, a mode
brought into vogue by Samuel Butler's *Hudibras*, and in
1669 published *Hero and Leander in Burlesque*, a poem with
a crisp narrative pace and more economy and directness than
his earlier poems.

> Yet know his Praises I have not begun,
> Fine Gentleman *Leander* was his Son,
> With whose most gen'rous inclination he
> To's cost (few Fathers doe so) did agree,
> And bound him, Prentice to a worthy Barber,
> The best, not such another in the Harbour. . . .
> His Towels, like his Skin, were white and fine,
> Nought but his Face his Bason could out-shine.

Though a good deal of the verse is carried along by punning
and double entendre,

> . . . *Mercury* with his sly art

[37]

Goes the next way to steal a Maiden's Heart,
With Nature's Picklock opening Virgin Chest,
Where still the more is robb'd, the less is mist.

and at times when the subject matter threatened to become
too serious Wycherley seemed to rely on flippancy to preserve
the frolic tone,

. . . she perceived her dead Duck—dead as Herring!

. . . e're she was awar
. . . she tipt clean over
Into the Brine upon her pickled Lover,

there are genuinely amusing diversions of self-burlesque in a
Butler-Byron manner:

Now towe me, Muse! o'er to the other side,
Where most egregious *Hero* did abide;
You, sacred Dame! I mean, who once did steer
The prosp'rous Praise of great *Magnanos* dear;
If you have any time, help me ashore
With *Heros* commendation. . . .[62]

The Bookseller who reprinted the poem in 1729 thought
the poem was incomplete; he remarked that he was certain
the author was William Wycherley—there had been some
doubt—and while it was "first *Production, however
imperfect, of such a Genius*," he excused it because it was
reprinted *"from a very faulty Copy, even with Blanks and
Omissions of half Couplets in many Places."*[63] These blanks
were in fact intentional deletions which Wycherley later
supplied in an autograph copy to a friend, inscribed on the
inside leaf:

For Anthony Henly, Esq.
from
his most oblig'd and
most humble servant
Mr. Wm. Wycherley

Anthony Henley (1650-1711), the son of Sir Robert Henley of
the Grange, Hampshire, a friend of John Aubrey (author of
Brief Lives) who perhaps knew Wycherley, studied at Christ

Church, Oxford, and at the Middle Temple. He was a rather wealthy man,[64] so Wycherley's dedication to him of *Hero and Leander* may have had some self-interest attached to friendship, for Wycherley commonly contacted friends of means for assistance.

The autograph additions do not alter the poetic quality of the poem but offer an insight into Wycherley's actual composition and indicate that the copy was purposely faulty, not simply unfinished. Alexander Dyce, in whose collection of books in the Victoria and Albert Library this signed volume is found, wrote on the inside leaf: "This poem was written by William Wycherley & blank lines and amendments are throughout supplied by his own hand-writing."[65] In this volume, the following additions and changes (in italics) were hand-written in:

Mortals, whose blind Zeal so the Gods blaspheme,
Imputing to their spotless Worships shame:
Nor was her idle hand so much as put
By Sculptur to supply the place of scut.

The little Ape her son . . .
Lay at her feet, but not to hold 'um, for
She like her self Compulsion did abhor.
But good boy stood her in a stretchers stead
As when she had more need of one he did.

They'll pluck Loves Wings, and tear his Clout from's eyes,
To stop a cravening chincke 'tween maiden thighs.

But Arentine not so *the gapp doth stop*
He complaisant to Nature, and to Female,
Alloweth her no Covering, but the Male:

Mad at the sight, her blue-thin-lip she bit,
And tore her Smock from Navel down to'r Feet:
So did lay ope as large a rent
And shew'd her own, and Husbands discontent.

Note the alteration of "So shew'd" to "And shew'd."

The *Laeda* he appeared to trapan,
Who taking him but for a Goose or Swan,
Lay still like Stock; *Wherefore his wings did Switch*
And clapperclaw on each side her dull breech,

[39]

This change eliminated "till she perceived him Man," in the printed text, just as he varied the printed

With Nature's Picklock opening Virgin Chest

to

With Corall Picklock,

and also altered

. . . but kindness more than that came to
She had, he made her stand cross-legg'd, that so
Tenn inches of her slitt might lurk behind;

from the printed,

What 'twas a shame to see might lurk behind.

For her Obscenity he found a cloathing,
Causing a Flap, or Apron natural
From a paunch Half way down to her knees to fall.

And *Romans*, now who their old Gods reject,
Have seriously for him a great respect.
Nay so have those who nought like Roman will doe
But first they change their Popeish name to D—
And mortified sister of Phanatick
Will not renounce for a new opinion a p—

Not in the common way did they adore him,
But on their backs lay prostrated before him;

which was written for the printed version:

But as they should, lay prostrated before him.

Alas when I'm on fire, I must cry out
For quenching Engine of the largest spoate.

Since Wycherley's manuscript insertions and alterations are generally more indecent than the printed lines, we may suppose that the printer silenced some of the more blatant lines at his own discretion, or requested the author to delete them. Nevertheless, Wycherley reveals something of his capacity for ribaldry in writing the poem in the first place, and then in thinking that the "suppressed" reading is worth preserving for a man-to-man joke with fellow Oxonian

Henley. The poem is not improved by the revisions but they make clear his original intention.

As Wycherley looked back at the end of the decade of the 60's and took stock of his life to that point, he could see that the heritage of an ancient family, his fine formal education, and his travel and diverse experience, would enable him to choose a variety of possible careers: legal, military, diplomatic, or that least lucrative one, poetic. In London he could see his enlarging circle of friends encompassing all ranges of nobility and gentry. He was in many ways amply prepared to burst into a bright career as he entered the 70's and his thirtieth year, and perhaps he was not completely surprised at the speed with which he reached success.

Chapter II
Footnotes

1. H. P. Vincent, "The Date of Wycherley's Birth," *TLS* (3 March 1932), p. 155; the exact date given is 28 May. A subsequent letter by W. G. D. Fletcher, 10 March, accepts this date, and another by H. Ince Anderton, 17 March, is uncertain. P. F. Vernon, *William Wycherley* (London, 1965), p. 6, wrote: "William Wycherley was born in Hampshire, probably on 28 May, 1641," which is a plausible place given his parents' residence there, but no proof is given. Some sources say he was born at Clive, "though some affirm that he was born at the Trench Farm, near Wem, and others, at Wem": *The Shropshire Gazeteer* (London, 1824), p. 87. William R. Chetwood, *The British Theatre* (Dublin, 1750), p. 93, said, "born in Wem." Samuel Bagshaw (pseud. for W. Watkins-Pitchford), *Gazeteer and Directory of Shropshire* (Sheffield, 1851), p. 141: "Clive Hall, a plain substantial stone edifice in the Elizabethan style, was built by Daniel Wycherley, father of the poet . . . said to have been the birth place of the poet Wycherley, though some affirm he was born at Wem." *The Mirror* (3 March 1827), featured a picture and story of the mansion at Clive as the birthplace of Wycherley: "The house was a handsome structure, but much has been let go to decay . . . ," with a biographical sketch of usual information and misinformation, i.e., his attendance at Middle Temple.

2. Montague Summers, I, 11.

3. R. E. Davis, *Some Account of the Royal Free Grammar School of King Edward the Sixth in Shrewsbury* (Shrewsbury, 1869), pp. 54–55, listed under "Distinguished Scholars," with no dates. See notation, "his two best known plays are *Love in a Wood* and *The Plain Dealer*."

4. Gough, p. 87.

5. "Some Memoirs of William Wycherley," *Major Pack's Poetical Remains* (London, 1783), p. 182.

6. Summers, I, 11.

7. A. C. F. Beales, *Education Under Penalty: English Catholic Education from the Reformation to the Fall of James II* (London, 1963), p. 219.

8. M. L. Clarke, *Classical Education in England, 1500–1900* (Cambridge, 1959), p. 182, also p. 186n.

9. Clarke, p. 10; Foster Watson, *The English Grammar Schools to 1660* (London, 1968), pp. 322–33.

10. *Joseph Spence, Observations*, ed. James M. Osborn (Oxford, 1966), I, 33, #76.

11. Christopher Hill, *God's Englishman, Oliver Cromwell and the English Revolution* (New York, 1970), pp. 197–98: "Historians are beginning to appreciate how much the interregnum in general and Cromwell in particular did for British education and British cultural life. But the legend of the philistine Puritan, hostile to art and culture, dies hard in the popular imagination." See Summers, I, 11: "At this time education in England was at the lowest ebb."

12. W. A. L. Vincent, *The State and School Education, 1640–1660, in England and Wales* (London, 1950), p. 42.

13. *Ibid.*, p. 64.

14. E. N. Hooker, ed., *The Critical Works of John Dennis* (Baltimore, 1943), II, 409: "About the Age of Fifteen he was sent for Education to the Western Parts of *France*, either to *Saintonge* or the *Angoumois*. His abode there was either upon the Banks of the *Charante*, or very little removed from it." See *Spence*, #76.

15. Beales, Ch. IX, "The Schools Abroad," pp. 158–84.

16. *Spence, Anecdotes*, #76.

17. Hooker, II, 409.

18. Charles Louis Livet, *Précieux et Précieuses, caracteres et moeurs Litteraires du XVII siècle* (Paris, 1895), p. 42. Translation by Barbara McCarthy.

19. "Préciosité and the Restoration Comedy of Manners," *Huntington Library Quarterly*, XVIII (1955), 110. See also Berkeley, "The Précieuse, or Distressed Heroine of Restoration Comedy," *Arts and Science Studies, Oklahoma State University Publications*, 56, #19, (July, 1959), 3–21, and C. D. Cecil, "Libertin and Précieux Elements in Restoration Comedy," *Essays in Criticism*, IX (1959), 239–53.

20. *Ibid.*, p. 112.

21. Livet, pp. 29–30.

22. *Ibid.*, p. 37.

23. Amédeé Roux, *Montausier, Sa Vie et Son Temps* (Paris, 1860), p. 48.

24. Berkeley, p. 127.

25. Roux, subtitled, *Un Misanthrope à la cour de Louis XIV*. Summers, I, 13.

26. Livet, p. 41 and cf. affairs p. 40.

27. Connely, p. 28.

28. W. H. Cooke, *Students Admitted to the Inner Temple*, 1547–1660 (London, 1878), p. 372: November, 1658, Daniel Wycherley, Clive, Salop; p. 376: "October, 1659, William Wycherley (nil), Shropshire, son of the Poet and Dramatist, Daniel Wycherley a Barrister of this Inn. Died 1715." A curious inversion of facts! There are no references to William in *Middle Temple Admissions Register, Middle Templars*, or in *Middle Temple Bench Book*, nor in admissions books of Gray's Inn or Lincoln's Inn.

29. Perhaps begun by Charles Gildon, *The Life of William Wycherley, Esq.* (London, 1718), p. 4: "He was plac'd in one of our Inns of Court, I think the *Middle-Temple*"; continued by Pack, p. 182, and by innumerable others. Note however the interesting remark by Alexander Dyce: "Wycherley was at this time—1669—resident in the Middle Temple"; MSS notations inside cover of William Wycherley, *Hero and Leander*, MSS 10, 790, D.17, p. 33, from Alexander Dyce Collection in the Victoria and Albert Library.

30. Summers, I, 16: he left Oxford "for the Inner Temple where William Wycherley was in fact entered 10 November, 1660."

31. Connely, p. 33, citing Perromat.

32. F. A. Inderwick, ed., *A Calendar of Inner Temple Records*, III (London, 1901), lxxiii: "William Wycherley's father, Daniel, was a barrister of this Inn, to which the author was admitted in 1659 at the age of 19. In 1662 he was appointed controller for the present Christmas . . . ." p. 20: "Order that a committee be appointed to wait on the masters of the bench, and desire them, in the name of the gentleman this Christmas, that Ledgingham be restored to the society; and that Buggin, Powell, Hampson, Richarson, Wycherley, and Tirrell be that Committee," as ordered 10 January. This may also be William.

33. H. H. L. Bellot, *The Inner and Middle Temple* (London, 1902), p. 142. I should like to thank Mr. W. W. S. Breen, Librarian of the Inner Temple, for his assistance in tracing all available data on Wycherley.

34. Anthony a Wood, *Athenae Oxonienses*, 3rd ed. (London, 1828), Vol. IV. Note his statement: He "departed without being matriculated . . . afterwards he retired to the Inner Temple. . . ." See also Anthony a Wood, *Fasti Oxoniensis*, for same information.

35. *DNB*, I, 1145 ff.

36. Earl Miner, *The Restoration from Milton to Dryden* (Princeton, 1974), p. 208.

37. Summers, I, 16; Connely, p. 35.

38. Gildon, pp. 4–5.

39. John Richard Magrath, DD, *The Queen's College* (Oxford, 1921), II, 36n: "If the cup is from him and the date right, he must have given it long after he left Oxford, perhaps when a younger brother George came up who entered Queens as commoner, Jan. 1, and matriculated 6 March, 1668." The 1667 date is Old Style, our 1668. Battel Books for this period at Queens College do not exist; the first one extant is 1669, next is 1710.

40. "Biographical Data on William Wycherley and his Father," *Notes and Queries*, ccxvi (January 1971), 34. The summer of 1662 is my conjecture, but 1663 seems also possible.

41. *Ibid.*, a letter from Dr. John Topham to Arran, 9 September 1679.

42. *Loppington Baptisms, St. Michael's Parish Church*, October 1654–January 1859, privately typed volume by K. J. Bulmer (December 1969), Salop Record Office.

43. Exchequer Deponents, E 134, Easter Term, 1671, 12, Deponent 4, William Witcherly of Fitts, or Fitz, gent. aged Sixty Years or thereabouts.

44. *The Memoirs of Ann Lady Fanshawe* (London, 1907), p. 146: "Then went all my husband's gentlemen, and next before himself his *camarados*, two by two: Mr. Wycherley, Mr. Levine. . . "; p. 170: "On Thursday, the 19th of February [1655] went from us to England, Mr. Charles Bertie, Mr. Francis Newport, Sir Andrew King, Sir Edward Turnor, Mr. Francis Godolphin, Mr. Wycherley. . . "; p. 218: "List of household and belongings Taken into Spain Fr. Fanshawe, Chief Secretary Mr. Wycherley. . . ."

45. "Accompt of Daniell Witcherley," p. 10: "To Mr. Trevor for drawing the Assignment of the Spanish Ambassadors Lease that we might purchase the house—1£." In C10, 63/100, 1661, is a list of properties of Lord St. John, including a house used by the Spanish Ambassador in the City of London, and Daniel had control of the rents.

46. *The Spanish Plays of Neoclassical England* (New Haven, 1973), p. 121 and n. In private correspondence Professor Loftis mentioned to me that Professor David Harris searched in the British Museum and the PRO for Fanshawe materials on Wycherley to no avail. My own search through Original Letters of Fanshawe and MSS correspondence in the BM was similarly fruitless.

47. Summers, I, 17; Connely, pp. 50 ff. The poem is printed in Summers, IV, 248.

48. *The Poems of Alexander Pope*, Vol. IV, *Imitations of Horace*, ed. John Butt (London, 1961), 207–08, 11. 139–52.

49. Martin C. Battestin, *The Providence of Wit* (Oxford, 1974); Chapter I provides a good survey of relation of Augustan to prior ideas.

50. David M. Vieth, ed., *The Complete Poems of John Wilmot, Earl of Rochester*, Yale University Press (New Haven, Ct., 1968), p. 134.

51. [Gilbert] *Burnet's History of His Own Time* (London, 1883), p. 178.

52. From Theophilus Cibber, *The Lives of the Poets of Great Britain and Ireland*, as quoted by Graham Greene, *Lord Rochester's Monkey* (New York, 1974), pp. 95–96.

53. John Harold Wilson, *The Court Wits of the Restoration* (Princeton, 1948), "The Wits in Private Life," and "The Wits in Public Life."

54. Burnet, p. 179.

55. See A. M. Friedson, "Wycherley and Molière: Satirical Point of View in *The Plain Dealer*," *MP*, 64 (February 1967), 192, for the same point, well argued. For the influence of Charles on poetry, see James Sutherland, *English Literature of the Late Seventeenth Century* (Oxford, 1958), Vol. VI of *OHEL*, pp. 154 ff; and "The Impact of Charles II on Restoration Literature," in *Restoration and Eighteenth Century Literature*, ed. Carroll Camden (Chicago, 1963), pp. 251–63.

56. Vieth, p. 60.
Nor are his high desires above his strength:
His scepter and his prick are of a length;
And she may sway the one who plays with t'other.
57. *Ibid.*, p. 22.
58. Summers, IV, 214.
59. "Astraea Redux," *The Poems and Fables of John Dryden,* ed. James Kingsley (Oxford, 1970), p. 24.
60. Summers, III, 67.
61. *Ibid.*, IV, 248.
62. *Ibid.*, p. 77. All references to the poem are from this edition, pp. 75–102. Summers provides a good survey of the history of the Hero and Leander story and its many versions, with a possible inspiration for Wycherley's choice of it for his first long poem (pp. 20 ff.). Elements in this poem anticipate ideas to follow in the plays: the "Spanish Gravity" and other Spanish references are elaborated in *Gentleman-Dancing-Master*; discussions of courage, both his and hers, occur in all the plays, as do the "cabinet" references ("Keys to her Coffers," and "In Cabinet which Nature did Provide") which are metaphors for body or mind. Lines such as "Small sense with heaps of words t'orlay and smother" are like rough originals of Pope's
Words are like leaves; and where they most abound
Much fruit of sense beneath is rarely found.
(*Essay on Criticism*, 309–10)
63. *Ibid.*, IV, 253.
64. From biographical notes, J. E. Stephens, ed., *Aubrey on Education* (London, 1972), an edition of John Aubrey's "The Idea of Education." See letter from Aubrey to Anthony Henley on this tract, pp. 15–16.
65. MSS 10, 790, D.17, p. 33, Alexander Dyce Collection of MSS, The Victoria and Albert Library. After these cited lines, Dyce quoted lines from *The Plain-Dealer* of Jerry and his mother discussing law students writing plays, "plainly alluding to himself," Dyce wrote of Wycherley. He added on the next blank sheet:

From the library of the late Earl of Northington, I purchased of Mr. Payne, Bookseller, at the Mews-gate, a presentation-Copy to Anthony Henley Esqr. of Wycherley's folio volume of poems, printed 1704. Wycherley, his book lying bottom upwards, had written, on one of the end blank-leaves, the address which faces this paper; & had afterwards obliterated it with his pen. On the first blank leaf at the beginning of the book, he had written a fair presentation in the same words. From the last mentioned leaf I ascertained the MS lines, supplied throughout this book, to be the autograph of Wycherley.
Alex Dyce 9 March 1791.

The inscription to Henley on the opposite page is partly marked through, but legible.

Chapter III

The Playwright

What inclined Wycherley in the early 1670's to turn to drama is one of the persistently unanswerable biographical questions. Perhaps his success with the narrative form of *Hero and Leander* awakened his talent; perhaps his education and his experience in France had sometime earlier determined his course toward dramatic writing; perhaps too it was the influence of his associates and friends who wrote poems and plays with equal ease, and often success. But whatever air of casualness about writing he and others assumed, he was in fact deadly serious about the composition of his plays. It was his good fortune and ours that he realized his potential in comedy, for that was his true medium.

There were two main acting companies in London that would produce plays for a young playwright, the King's and the Duke's. These two were established by Royal patents almost immediately at the Restoration, when theaters, officially closed since 1642, were reopened, and they essentially dominated London theater for years, until the mid 80's when the King's company was absorbed into the Duke's and the two-company tradition was temporarily abbreviated. The King's company was developed by Thomas Killigrew, the stronger group at first, and the Duke's by William Davenant, which by inventiveness and energy soon became the stronger company,[1] and for which Wycherley wrote. With the Restoration reawakening of theater, there were several important innovations, chief of which was the appearance of women on stage to play their own roles (instead of being played by boys); the playhouse changed the open, cheap pit area into the main, and expensive, seating space; scenery and machinery for set changes greatly improved, along with other emphases on spectacle, such as entre-act song and dance acts.

The repertory of drama in those years was a combination of old plays and a steady infusion of bright new ones. From the reliable Elizabethan and Jacobean plays of Shakespeare, Beaumont and Fletcher, and Ben Jonson, among others, which were heavily utilized at the beginning of the 60's, there were added John Dryden's comedies and heroic plays beginning in 1664, the same year that Sir George Etherege's first play, *She Would if She Could*, was performed—his last, the famous *The Man of Mode*, appeared with Wycherley's last, *The Plain-Dealer*, in 1676. There were, of course, many plays by lesser authors, such as William Cavendish's *The French Dancing Master* (1662) and Sir Thomas St. Serfe's *Tarugo's Wiles* (1667),[2] the first of which sounds much like Wycherley's *The Gentleman-Dancing-Master* and the second of which is referred to in *The Country-Wife*. Such plays clearly gave Wycherley a sense of what was possible and developing on the stage, and with the influence of the Spanish and the French drama, as well as the English tradition, his dramatic predecessors were a rich source of material and inspiration.

Alexander Pope's celebrated remark on the order of composition of Wycherley's plays has not won any credence: "*Love in a Wood* he wrote when he was but nineteen, the *Gentleman-Dancing-Master* at twenty-one, the *Plain Dealer* at twenty-five, and the *Country-Wife* one or two and thirty."[3] It is remotely possible that Wycherley could have begun roughing out these plays at approximately these ages, but there are too many topical references to allow for their complete composition at any time but shortly before their stage presentation in their present order; for example, *Love in a Wood* echoes several plays of 1668.[4] Nevertheless, the problem continues to appear, especially when critics view

The Plain-Dealer with less favor than *The Country-Wife* and seek a reason in fact for their opinion.[5]

Wycherley's dramatic canon consists of only these four plays. He left no word whether he planned further plays, whether he felt his plays formed a coherent whole statement, as they in fact seem to, nor any clue to his image of himself as dramatist. He did somewhat seriously consider collaborating in a comedy with John Dryden but he withdrew from the invitation out of deference, ostensibly, to the greater poet, and nothing more seemed to come of the venture. Each of his four plays is a serious and skilled work, and since the time of their composition each has been extensively studied by critics. While it may appear somewhat out of keeping with our chiefly biographical approach to Wycherley, it may nevertheless be appropriate to spend some time in critical investigation of the four plays in order to measure the intellectual character of the plays and Wycherley's relation to the intellectual currents of the day. Accordingly, we will look not only at the literary or dramatic sources of the plays but at their conscious manifestation or reflection of contemporary political, social, moral, and philosophical ideas and trends, and as well at the more concrete topical details.

Love in a Wood was presented in March or earlier of the spring of 1671; the first quarto edition of the play is dated 1672, indicating that it was well enough received on stage to warrant the printing; later editions appeared in 1693 and 1694. Its presentation by the King's company at the Drury Lane theater was successful; it is not clear how many performances it enjoyed but it ran well and was revived in 1687 and 1694.[6]

The players for his first play were a good group of experienced performers,[7] many of whom appeared thereafter in both *The Country-Wife* and *The Plain-Dealer*—we know almost nothing about the cast of *The Gentleman-Dancing-Master.* Charles Hart, who played Ranger, also played the lead roles of Horner and Manly, and possibly Gerrard;

Richard Bell, after playing Vincent, was killed in a fire at the King's theater at Drury Lane shortly before *The Gentleman-Dancing-Master* was performed; Edward Kinnaston, who played Valentine, took the important roles of Harcourt and Freeman in the later plays; John Lacy, who often played dancers, such as in *The French Dancing Master* and *Love in a Maze* (or *The Changes,* by James Shirley), played Alderman Gripe and possibly a part in *Gentleman-Dancing-Master*; Richard Mohun was Dapperwit in the first play and Pinchwife in *The Country-Wife.* The women were chiefly Mrs. Boutell who played the main roles of Christina, Margery Pinchwife, Fidelia, and possibly Hippolita; Mrs. Knepp was Flippant, and Lady Fidget, as well as Eliza. With this basic cast of men and women, Wycherley could write on order and rely on their considerable strengths and versatility—playwrights were generally blessed with a solid corps of fine actors and actresses.

Love in a Wood, or *St. James Park* is set in the wooded park which lay west of Covent Garden; one would walk from the "city" of old walled London westerly toward the "town," the Inns of Court, Covent Garden, and then toward the park, a conveniently popular location where one could parade oneself, within the shadow of the Palace, to see and be seen among the fashionable sophisticates. Wycherley's characters are somewhat predictable ones in Restoration comedy: Ranger, Valentine and Vincent are "young Gentlemen of the Town"; Dapperwit, the usual fool who aspires to be a wit but is only a "brisk . . . half-witted fellow of the Town"; two young women, Christina and Lydia, are beloved by the first two young men; and there are assorted comic humor types, in particular, Alderman Gripe, a "covetous, leacherous, old Usurer of the City," and Mrs. Joyner, "a precise City Bawd" (p. 9). The plot is not as predictable as the character types, but is the sort of complex creation one comes to expect of Restoration comedy. In brief: Valentine who has been exiled for duelling returns to his beloved Christina who lives locked in her rooms in mourning for him; Ranger is pursuing Lydia but has trouble staying constant and veers off track after a chance glimpse of Christina; Vincent's role is to rectify misunderstandings and lead people back together; Alderman Gripe locks his daughter in her room to protect her and is, of course, outwitted in the end because of his hypocrisy and foolishness; Sir Simon Addleplot, whose name also reflects his humor, pursues in a series of farcically transparent guises (he invariably exclaims, "faith and troth!") Gripe's daughter, Martha, but Dapperwit, another species of fool, also seeks Martha and finds her willing albeit six months pregnant; Simon settles for Mrs. Flippant who with such epigrams as "Not a Husband to be had for mony" (Act I, scene i), reveals her mode of candor: "I always rail against Marriage Which is the Widows way to it certainly" (I,i). In short she has, like most of the characters, only marriage and/or money in mind, and a mask behind which to hide that preoccupation; as a result, she is to be understood by the opposite of what she says. As the play unwinds, the fools remain fools and are rewarded with foolish marriages, Dapperwit with enceinte Martha, Simon with Flippant, Gripe with mere Lucy, daughter of Mrs. Joyner the bawd. But the main characters change, or perhaps a better expression would be, develop, into stability. Ranger is laughed into constancy with Lydia ("So, the Comedy begins; I shall be laugh'd at sufficiently, if I do not justifie my self" (IV, iv), and Valentine sees the true worth of Christina; Vincent remains constant and does not in fact change since there is no pressure on him to do so in the play.

One immediately arresting aspect of this play is its Spanish source; though later Wycherley turned to Molière, he at first seized upon the Spanish comedies of Calderon to build his plays; he reworked their materials and conventions with a sureness and individuality that nothing, save his excellent education, would have foreshadowed.

From Calderon's *Mañanas de abril y mayo* he took the setting in the park, two pairs of lovers, a separation of one pair due to a duel (the Spanish duel is mortal, however), the recent return of the exile and complications between the lovers by his misunderstanding of her action done on his behalf. As Professor John Loftis has noted, "All this is in the pattern of the cape and sword play" of Spanish drama.[8] But the characters are plainly contemporary English and some of them are satirized for their contemporary excesses. In Gripe, Wycherley provides a reminder, Loftis rightly observes, "that this is a Cavalier's play, bristling with the remembered resentments of the Civil Wars, when nonconformist merchants of London took Parliament's side against the king," a memory especially close to William and his father. Mrs. Joyner too is "a caricature of merchant class calculation and hypocrisy"[9] from the "City." This merchant-and-city satire is a particularly interesting subject not only in this play but in the others as well, and very likely in Wycherley's own life, for it intimates the basic conflict of values with his father whose goals were obviously monetary and with whom the cits may have gotten on well. The persistent concern with the pursuit of money, often referred to as simply "business," and its effects and corruptions, is dramatized in this play by characters of a specific group, the cits; in the later plays the procedure is not so topically obvious but the ugliness of greed is nonetheless depicted in characters, culminating perhaps in Olivia and Vernish of *The Plain-Dealer*. Topical remarks still find their way, of course, into the plays, for Wycherley's work is full of the concrete reality of objects, places and names, but the topical references are more often related to subjects that can be translated into metaphors of deceptions, e.g., fashions in dress.

The satiric focus in this play extends beyond the topical to the larger uses of masking and deceptions, not only by the fools and lechers of both sexes, but by Ranger who deludes himself into believing "Women are poor credulous Creatures, easily deceived," even when Vincent corrects him, "We are poor credulous Creatures, when we think 'em so" (I,ii), and who characterizes love as a game or hunt, and also by Valentine who grossly misconstrues Christina almost as if

[51]

he is enamoured of his passionate jealousy. To this view Vincent's response is again important: "Open but your eyes, and the Fantastic Goblin's vanish'd [jealousy], and all your idle fears, will turn to shame; for Jealousie, is the basest cowardize." Out of the darkness of St. James Park, a symbol finally of the jealousy blinding Valentine, comes the light of comedy, a clarified vision, a stabilized society.

Wycherley seemed to like certain devices in this play well enough to use again, specifically the darkness motif which was to be central in his last play. In subsequent plays he used the device of locked doors or closets (Gripe: "I was forc'd to lock up my Daughter," I,i) as a metaphor for closed-mindedness or violated relationships. But some devices and themes he seemed to grow out of; he had developed in the Valentine-Christina plot a satire of the heroic[10] which he was not to use extensively again. Valentine's bombastic rhetoric is the stuff of heroic tragedies:

> Hunger, Revenge, to sleep are petty Foes,
> But only Death the jealous Eyes can close.(II,iv)

He relishes the resonance of these words and the stagey gestures they excite, but he certainly does not mean them in spite of his passion which led him to stab one man. Christina, for her part, cherishes her sentimental self-exile in her room. "You are grown mad," says her maid Isabel, "have put your self into Mourning, live in a dark room, where you'l see no body, nor take any rest day or night, but rave and talk to your self perpetually" (II,ii).[11] To Christina's delicately iambic anguish: "Unhappy *Valentine*, cou'dst thou but see how soon thy absence, and misfortunes have disbanded all thy Friends, and turn'd thy Slaves all Renegades, thou sure wou'dst prize my only faithful heart," Flippant counters: "Hail faithful Shepherdess" (II,ii), an appropriately ironic rejoinder.[12]

Wycherley's main thematic concerns in this play are apparent: the fascination with deception's many faces and the barriers to human relationships, the concern with language and with the meaning of wit and its relation to deception, and the concern with the qualities of society as a whole.

For his second play Wycherley once again used a Spanish source, Calderon's *El maestro de danzar*, but he relied on it less for plot than for title, calling his play *The Gentleman-Dancing-Master*. In it he ridiculed the Spanish customs affected by Don Diego, who was in comic actuality Sir James Formal, English parent of heroine Hippolita. Though Professor Loftis points out some possible actual targets of his Spanish mockery,[13] Wycherley stayed away from satire of a topical nature, embodied in a character such as Gripe in his first play, except in the Prologue which is ironically addressed "To the City" and insults the city intelligence: *"For you to senseless Plays have still been kind,/Nay where no sense was, you a Jest wou'd find,"* and in some discussions between Gerrard and Monsieur on the Dutch, the French, and rebels (I,ii). One may also see a class joke in the title which juxtaposes the class of gentry with a lowly dancing-master.[14]

The play is much simpler than *Love in a Wood* in all ways. One wonders if, in fact, the death in the recent fire, January 1672, at the King's theater of the actor Richard Bell, who had played Vincent at the King's in Drury Lane, caused Wycherley to cut a role and emphasize Hippolita; the play does not appear to be haphazardly assembled but the loss of a key player could have changed the play. Wycherley moved to a different playhouse, the Dorset Garden theater where the Duke's company played it on 6 February 1672 (not necessarily the premiere). The only actors we know of in this play are Edward Angel, who played Don Diego, and James Nokes, who played Monsieur. Whether these changes mattered substantially is not certain, but the play was not a success. Historian John Downes observed, "it lasted but 6 Days, being like't but indifferently, it was laid by to make Room for other new ones."[15] Six performances was not a bad run—two or three would have been poor—but six was

average, and Wycherley was by no means pleased with
mediocrity. Mulling his sense of failure, Wycherley referred
to himself later as a "late so bafled Scribler" (Prologue, *The
Country-Wife*). The reasons for its poor showing then and
since are still not clear; perhaps it is marked by nothing
memorable, no special scene, no character who is warmly
fascinating. It is, however, a good comedy, better by far than
its critical history would indicate, clear and direct, full of
funny dialogue and well contrived, visually energetic stage
business.[16] The play's pervasive lightness is carried by the
follies of the characters as well as by the heroine who, while
controlling events, laughs at everyone and insists that all she
does is a jest—to which the foolish agree, "I tell you all's but
a jest, a meer jest I vow and swear," says Monsieur (V,i).
Some readers see it as a farce, and perhaps it works best as a
Feaudeau-like romp, Don Diego chasing Gerrard with his
sword, Gerrard stumbling about in his "dances," Monsieur
intoning an aria to his "dear Pantalloon! dear Belte! dear
Sword! dear Perruque . . ." (III,i) as he takes off the old
man (French) and puts on the new (Spanish). Wycherley
would have had occasion about this time to see the puppet
shows at Covent Garden, the first Policinella puppet booth
appearing there in 1662.[17] According to that apt reporter
Samuel Pepys, there were six different puppet theatres in
London by 1668, three of which were near Wycherley's
haunts, at Covent Garden, at Lincoln's Inn Fields near the
Inns of Court, and at Charing Cross in St. Martin's in the
Fields Parish. Hippolita's complaint that she can never "go
to *Ponchinello*" and Prue's "nor *Islington*" (I,i), the site of
another puppet show, brings to mind the possible relationship between Punchinello and the farce within this play.
The references to "motion,"

> Don Diego: She has not been us'd to motion.
> Caution: Motion, motion, motion, de' call it? . . . I kept
>   her from motion till now, motion with a ven-
>   geance. (III,i)

recall Pepys' going to see "the Italian motion, much after the nature of what [he had showed his wife] in Covent Garden. Their puppets here are somewhat better, but their motions not at all." Though Caution's word "motion" has sexual meaning as a kind of dance, and Pepys' a somewhat different sense, there are similarities of puppet-like actions. Further, the play has many more dumb-show scenes than in other plays of Wycherley's or in most plays of the time, such as in Act II when Gerrard and Hippolita dance a courante, a pantomime-like dance, while Don Diego and Caution observe and comment from another place on stage, or in Act III when they again dance before the audience of Don Diego and Caution, or in Act IV when the black servant leads Monsieur in a dancing lesson, and so on. The Punch-like puppet-show tone provides a coherent context for the farcical episodes of the play and suggests that the play is more than a bit of farcical fluff, as some critics suspect, but rather a planned attempt to refer to a different genre of theater.

In its plot the *Gentleman-Dancing-Master* returns to the old Roman comedy formula of a young couple being forced to outwit the senex, the old man blocking character, in order to marry. Wycherley seems deliberately to abandon the Restoration conventions of wit characters—there is scarcely any mention of wit—and comic complexity of plot. Hippolita, the fourteen-year old heroine, has been ordered to marry her cousin Mr. Parris, now changed by his penchant for French manners into Monsieur de Paris, by her father who is himself altered by Spanish affectation to Don Diego; but she, playing her father's humor against her Aunt Caution's zealous self-importance, arranges visits with the far more interesting Gerrard in the guise of a dancing master, whom she of course succeeds in marrying. As before, we have father locking up daughter, hypocritical piety (Caution's "O the fatal Liberty of this masquerading Age, when I was a young Woman . . ." (I,i), the falseness of language and dress, and blindness to others. Satirizing character obsessions was nothing new in comedy, Ben Jonson being Wycherley's chief English predecessor for portrayal of

[55]

humor characters, but Wycherley seemed to have had some greater Spanish awareness in his depiction of Sir James Formal, partly from the Spanish plays he was reading and perhaps because of his first-hand knowledge when (if) he was in Spain with Sir Richard Fanshawe. Sources for the portrait of Monsieur de Paris may have been the conventions of French caricature of the time and a few direct acquaintances with fops in France and England. There is in addition at least one printed source which may have influenced Wycherley's imagination. In John Cotgrave's *Wit's Interpreter* (1655) there is a dialogue, one of a series of example-dialogues, "At the Dancing Schoole, the Dancing Master being a Frenchman," where the English language has the same ruined appearance as that of Monsieur de Paris.

	Your dance be horse play, begar, for de stable not de chambre, your ground passage never hurt de back Mounsieur, not trouble de legg much, platt il—you learn Mounsieur.
Gio[vanni].	For mirth sake as you love.
Moun.	Begar I teach you presently, dance with all de grace of de body, for your good and my profit.
Gio.	Well, let me observe your method.
Moun.	Tis but dis in de beginning: one, two tree, four, five, the Cinque pace, ailey Mounsieur, stand upright and began . . . begar de King as no two such subjects, dere be one foot, two foot, have you tree foot; begar you have more den I have den . . . One, two, you go too fast, you be at *Dover* begar, and me be at *Greenwich*, tree— toder legg . . . I teach tree hundred never forgot so much, me sweat taking paine and fidling . . . .[18]

Obviously, Wycherley's Monsieur is not the dancing master, but mutatis mutandis, the dialogue is quite similar.

Gerrard.	Well Monsieur! I'le say this for thee, thou hast made the best use of three months at Paris as ever English Squire did. . . . Well, there shall be no more said against the *French* Footmen.

Monsieur.   Non de Grace—you are always turning the
nation *Francez* into rediculè, dat Nation so
accomplie, dat Nation which you imitate so
dat in the conclusion you buttè turn you self
into rediculè ma foy: if you are for de raillery,
abuse the *Duch . . . I vill maintain, sustain,
and justifie dat one little Franch-Foot-man
have more honeur, courage, an' generosity,
more good blood in his vainee, an' mush more
good manners an' civility den all de State
General togeder* . . . . (I,ii)

In addition to such dialogues, and such as "bona roba and
Monsieur Tailleur" which recalls Monsieur's dealing with
those bona robas Flirt and Flounce, there is in Cotgrave a
verse "On an English Monsieur" which recalls more directly
M. de Paris:

> Would you believe when you this Monsieur see,
> That his whole body should speak French, not he?
> That so much scarfe of France, and hat and feather,
> And shooe and tie, and garter should come hither,
> That the untravel'd should be French so much,
> As French-men in his company should seem Dutch.[19]

Whether or not Wycherley had explicit reference to
Cotgrave's dialogues and verses, such conventional treatment of the mock-Frenchman as appears here as well as in
previous plays, such as Frenchlove in Howard's *The English
Monsieur* (1666) or Melantha in Dryden's *Marriage à la
Mode* (1672), very likely influenced his presentation of
Monsieur and contributed to his creating him in the pattern
of readily recognizable foppery. Wycherley's use of materials
and conventions that were ready at hand, turning
recognizable elements into a harmonious single play, is
probably one of his most notable achievements as a
playwright, for he combined disparate elements so that new
and more serious implications would emerge.

Ideas which Wycherley began to develop in *Love in a
Wood* continue to be examined here— the nature of jealousy,
of passion, of courage and virtue, of freedom. Jealousy was
cited in *Love in a Wood* as a serious obstruction to human

relationships. "Jealousie is the basest cowardize," for it negates the highly prized virtue, courage. Hippolita here points out that "passion un-masks every man" (V,i), that is, the extremity of its demands exposes one's weaknesses and deceptions, in this case those of her father whose passion is partly jealousy, "Ha, ha, ha, you are so full of your *Spanish* Jealousie, Father" (V,i), and partly Spanish "honor" or false-courage, as when he *"Kisses the Cross of his Sword, and runs at* Gerrard" (II,i). Hippolita explains to Gerrard the degrees of jealousy, for all virtue and vice exist by degree:

> a Husbands jealousie, which cunning men wou'd pass upon their Wives for a Complement, is the worst can be made 'em, for indeed it is a Complement to their Beauty, but an affront to their Honour. . . . jealousie in a Gallant is humble true Love, and the height of respect, and only an undervaluing of himself to overvalue her; but in a Husband 'tis arrant sawciness, cowardise, and ill breeding, and not to be suffer'd. (V,i)

Expressions as direct as this are usually reserved for maids to their ladies, but Hippolita wishes to be taken seriously; her "plain dealing is some kind of honesty . . . and few women wou'd have said so much" (V,i), for at some point she must deal plainly after using the old love-test of lying and changing her mind to test her lover.

To take for a moment a different approach to Hippolita's seriousness, we will look at Wycherley's use of language, specifically the meaning of wit which develops in *Love in a Wood* and in this play.[20] If one proceeds on the hypothesis that plain speech is preferable to the complexity of what usually passes for wit, for example, use of figures, metaphors, similes and so forth, one finds a direct correlation between the success of a character and his plainness of speech, and conversely the lack of success (indicated by satiric exposure, failure, foolishness, and the like) and a fondness for metaphoric language, since figurative language seems to be inherently variable and thus unreliable or unstable. This is the case in *Love in a Wood* when Ranger's various metaphors of love as a hunt or his pseudo-Petrarchan figures of sun-moon-shadow-mask parallel his ridiculous mispursuit of Lydia; and similarly whereas Valentine's heroic fustian identifies his foolishness, Vincent's direct speech declares his reliability. This association between character and language is even more evident in the case of Dapperwit:

> Ranger.   He has more courage than wit, but wants neither.
>
> Dapperwit.   As a Pump gone dry, if you powr no Water down you will get none out, so—
>
> Ranger.   Nay I bar similes too, to night. (I,ii)

His language is more obviously exaggerated and he is more obviously a fool. Although as has been noted, little discussion of wit and no "wit" characters as such appear in *The Gentleman-Dancing-Master*, language again identifies character. The identification is most explicit in the case of Don Diego and Monsieur de Paris; but Hippolita uses deceptions and jests for a special purpose that is not only acceptable but even necessary: after she has jested her way to victory, she turns to plain-dealing and explains to Gerrard what her scheme has been. Wycherley is as explicit in the remarks by Hippolita as he is likely to be as a playwright, but on several occasions he recorded his personal views on wit and language: "I am no Poet, since a Lover of Truth, and no Wit."[21] "Modesty is the best Proof and Aid of True Wit, as Humility is the best Sign of True Merit."[22] "As to your Excuse," he wrote to Pope, "for the plainness of your Stile. . . , I must needs tell you, that Friendship is much more acceptable to a true Friend than Wit, which is generally false Reasoning."[23]

To return then to the concepts examined in the play, we find that jealousy and passion, courage and freedom, are often linked since the first set vitiates the second. Courage is one of the key virtues, larger in dimension than facing an unsheathed sword with bared teeth and defiant epithet.

Monsieur, with perhaps inadvertent insight, lists it with honor and generosity among the three main virtues of his "Franch-Foot-man." Hippolita lectures herself on the subject: "Courage then, *Hippolita*. . . . Women formerly (they say) never knew how to make use of their time till it was past; but let it not be said so of a young Woman of this Age; . . . well then, courage, I say, *Hippolita*, thou art full fourteen years old, shift for thy self" (II,i). Courage means confronting directly whatever eventualities come along, sometimes only in the exhibition of a potential to courage rather than in overt physical acts, especially acts of heroic courage which a comedy may well lack. As Professor Ben Ross Schneider observes, there are a number of reasons why "signs of physical courage" are rare in comic characters, but since "not all courage is physical . . . the comic hero of the Restoration shows his generosity also in a willingness to take risks, to gamble," and sometimes only "in the hero's style of address."[24] In *Love in a Wood* Sir Simon does not convince one of courage by calling himself "Worthy, Noble, Brave Heroick Knight" (V,i), nor does Valentine when he draws his sword (IV,iii), but Vincent does with his preventive acts: "Vincent . . . *thrusts him back, and shuts the dore upon* [Valentine]" (IV,iii). And it is important that at last Valentine learns, "the Jealous, like the Drunkard, has his punishment, with his offence" (V,i), and "jealousie sure is much more pardonable before marriage, than after it" (V,ii), words which Hippolita in her play might have spoken. The virtue of courage in these plays, especially the variety applicable to Vincent, is that defined by Sir George Mackenzie in *Moral Gallantry* (1668): "I admire Passive Courage, as a virtue which deserves its Palms best of all others, because it toils most for them. [It] is more noble than what is active . . . for one who fights in an open Field . . . is assisted by the example of others, by hope of revenge, or victory."[25] Wycherley wrote of it: "The greatest Virtue, or Courage, and the soundest Sense . . . are most in danger of Detraction; as the best Constitutions are often a Prey to the worst Infections."[26]

That Wycherley was a moralist seems evident; a major study of Restoration drama such as Professor Schneider's *The Ethos of Restoration Comedy* makes this point indisputably clear and reemphasizes what we are prone to forget—that this was the role for which Wycherley was noted by his contemporaries.[27] Dryden, for one, cited his "most bold, most general and most useful satire."[28] Mrs. Zimbardo's warning that the "moral" approach often seems to be extra-literary is well taken,[29] but it need not exclude the literary, nor is that the intention here; rather it may point to the intellectual level of his plays as part of his literary achievement.

Moral approaches often lead to assumptions of "ideal characters" but there is no evidence that Wycherley presented ideal persons to exemplify morality. Vincent in *Love in a Wood* leads the characters to their new vision, but he is not idealized as moral agent or visionary. Christina in spite of her name is not ideal, though at least one critic believes so,[30] for her romantically darkened self-exile and decision to "see the face of no man" till her lover returns are extravagant and self-serving gestures, matching Valentine's bravado. The play works toward a conciliation of opposites, and all the characters are rewarded with what they have learned: love wins love, fools fools, and so on. Hippolita is young and iconoclastic at first but by process of freeing herself from the restraints of the narrow-minded to choose her own man, she is freed from illusions about marriage. She would agree with Ranger's remark at the end of *Love in a Wood*: "The end of Marriage, now is liberty, /And two are bound—to set each other free" (V,ii), for she states "When Children marry, Parents shou'd obey,/ Since Love claims more Obedience far than they" (V,i). As love and marriage are not ideals of liberty, but another kind of freedom-within-bounds, so none of the characters are ideal, faultless creations. Further, there is no evidence in Wycherley's other plays or poetry or personal life to maintain this severe polarization of attitude. There is a distinction and there are degrees of virtue and vice, for deception is both necessary-

[61]

good and inevitable-bad. As we continue with the last two plays, these ideas are further examined and become clearer.

If Wycherley felt himself a baffled scribbler with his wanly received second play, there is no evidence of bafflement in his brilliant next, *The Country-Wife*, the best known of his plays and with Congreve's *Way of the World*, the best known play between the Restoration and Goldsmith's and Sheridan's comedies a century later. The play was presented by the King's company in their new playhouse, the Theater Royal, Drury Lane, built after the fire destroyed the old Bridges Street theater. Thomas Killigrew's company which had begun maiden production 26 March 1674 was no doubt pleased to stage the new Wycherley comedy on 12 January the next year. We are not aware that Wycherly gained a new mistress as a result of this play as he had with his first, but he assuredly confirmed a reputation which was already well begun and which has continued, with some fluctuation, to this day.[31] The play was revived in 1683, 1688, and 1695, and was steadily played in the eighteenth century after Wycherley's death in 1715.[32]

For this play Wycherley did not borrow from a Spanish source but instead took a clue from Terence's *The Eunuch* and from Molière's *School for Wives*, but one can scarce track him in the snow of his predecessors so fully did he turn their hints into the substance of his own play. The extraordinary achievement of *The Country-Wife* has often tempted critics to find faults in the former two plays, but these first are in no way clumsy products of uncontrolled vision. The fact that one is as astonished to come from their high competence to the brilliance of *The Country-Wife* as one is to come from the undergraduate ingenuity of *Hero and Leander* to the excitement of *Love in a Wood* is one of the paradoxes of genius not really explicable. The shift in sources does not seem to have signalled a radical alteration in interests; in many ways the dramatic concerns are unchanged. But *The Country-Wife* has a boldness of conception which stamps it unmistakably. The story is enough to confuse most playgoers—one has only to listen to the pre-curtain murmur—but its lines of action are not difficult to trace. The play begins with Horner's announcing his latest deception: he will have himself advertised a eunuch (caused by "an *English-French* disaster") throughout the town in order to gain entrance to all the willing (and the willing are almost all) women of the town. Sir Jaspar Fidget gleefully allows his wife, Lady Fidget, to consort with Horner, while Pinchwife, who does not know the deception but who has just brought to town his new country wife, Margery, fears Horner's lechery. At the same time Alithea, Pinchwife's sister, has agreed to marry the fop Sparkish but Horner's friend Harcourt courts her for himself, finally succeeding when Alithea realizes Sparkish can be jealous, just as Horner succeeds in his way with Margery, Lady Fidget, Mrs. Dainty Fidget, and Mrs. Squeamish.

The play has been discussed and written about a great deal. Its peculiar form of Margery as title character and Horner as chief protagonist has led many to think of Horner as the hero—the expression is usually "rake-hero" after the Victorian assumption that all Restoration men are praised in some Hobbesian fashion for their vices—or to think of Margery as heroine, or an ideal.[33] Of course, the corollary view is that Harcourt and Alithea are dull because virtue is dull.[34] Both Margery and Horner are dramatically exciting characters, Margery as natural and artless as country life can produce, Horner as artful and cunning as his wits can conceive; their combined activity carries the motion of the play. Horner knows the ways of his world and senses that in order to have his way with women, while keeping their honor or reputation intact, he must devise a new scheme. The "Shy Husbands and Keepers" of mistresses are not, he observes, to be cheated but by "a new unpractis'd trick; false friendship," which once would have done well enough, "will pass now no more than false dice upon 'em, no, not in the City" (I,i). Horner is a scholar of deception; he knows vice, relishes it, and pursues it wholeheartedly and

[63]

successfully. Margery too knows what she wants, though she knows not yet the modes of deception or even that deception is part of the mode, and acts to gain what she desires. She cries, "I must stay at home like a poor lonely, sullen Bird in a cage" (III,i). "I was quiet enough, till my Husband told me, what pure lives, the *London* Ladies live abroad, with their dancing, meetings, and junketings, and drest every day in their best gowns" (III,i). Horner is "a proper, goodly strong man, 'tis hard, let me tell you, to resist him" (IV,ii). Though she came to London unschooled in its ways she learns instinctively the arts of deception, but at the end when she must lie for Horner ("you'l have me tell more lyes—" V, iv), she is brought sharply to see the dimensions of deception and is seemingly saddened by this knowledge. Both are lively and vital characters, but not necessarily for that reason imitable. Both dominate much of the stage business, as for example Margery's wonderful letterwriting scene where she fools Pinchwife and sends the real love-letter to Horner (IV,ii), or Horner's classic china scene where he and his ladies use china as a metaphor for sex (IV,iii). But these two characters do not provide the only focus of the play. We return again to the question of Wycherley's "ideal" characters and moral standpoint: critically there are as many who condemn Horner as who celebrate his license. There would, however, seem to be no serious suggestion that Horner is an ideal hero, unless *The Plain-Dealer* the following year is to be discounted or seen as a product of opposite, schizoid, dramatic imagination. Even recognizing Horner's role as satirist of his society, for he does expose with devastating clarity the moral prodigies of his age while exploiting them and pretending to be a railing plain-dealer, we are not confronted with the whole of Horner. Acknowledging the superiority he may have of a certain kind of refreshing candor over vicious, cramp-brained Pinchwife, or the appalling stupor of Jaspar Fidget, or the folly of Sparkish, he is still a picaresque manager of base instincts. We are as unlikely to celebrate him for Dionysiac liberty as we would honor the wisdom of Rochester's maimed debauchee who "states-manlike," "sheltered in impotence," teaches youth "to fear no lewdness he's called to by wine."[35]

If we pursue further the uses of wit[36] observed in the previous play, we find that Horner carefully organizes his language to control his world. It is often figurative: Sparkish he says may pass for a man of sense "to the short-sighted World, as a false Jewel amongst true ones, is not discern'd at a distance. . . . Such wits as he, are . . . like Rooks to the Gamesters . . ." (I,i). But he can be plain when it suits his purposes: to Lady Fidget's remark, "I'd forfeit mine [honor] for yours at any time," he replies, "No, Madam, you shou'd not need to forfeit it for me, I have given you security already to save you harmless . . ." (II,i). Nevertheless, his plain speech is not necessarily truthful of his feelings; he tells Dorilant and Harcourt, "Well a Pox on love and wenching. Women serve but to keep a Man from better Company; . . . good fellowship and friendship, are lasting, rational and manly pleasures" (I,i), to convince them he is beyond women now.

From the opening lines of the play, Horner sets out to control his world by language; he equivocates words and concepts, changing not only "nature" but the nature of words and all relationships which exist in the world of the play. "A Quack is as fit for a Pimp, as a Midwife for a Bawd; they are still but in their way, both helpers of Nature" (I, i, opening line). A midwife aids nature's process of childbirth and a pimp aids in the natural process of intercourse; there are, however, social limitations on sexual activity, for pimps sell it so it is not "natural" in the same way as childbirth. But if the distinction between kinds of natural activity is erased, any natural act becomes acceptable and society does not exist in a functional, normative way. Horner resides in this special world, knowing it works by opposites or by equivocating and levelling terms, and, in effect, creates his own language. While we cannot be certain what Wycherley meant by "nature" or what it means precisely here, it is probable that his would be the traditional view of nature: the principle of all existing things by which they attain their proper form through a process of becoming, of movement from potential to actual form. This is the Aristotelian idea of nature generally held through the seventeenth century as the causal explanation of change. To this meaning of "nature" Horner is clearly running counter, for he is involved in no process of becoming; he is rather making a situation of his own, his own nature, so to speak. As if referring covertly to himself, he complains to Dorilant: "A Pox on 'em, and all that force Nature, and wou'd be still what she forbids 'em; Affectation is her greatest Monster" (I,i). But the word "nature" is not the only one equivocated; Horner changes the nature of words themselves. The word "sign" for example no longer indicates a correspondence between object and name but between object and metaphoric sense. Sparkish introduces "sign" as he enters: *"Harry,* I must railly thee a little. . . . The best new sign is . . . in *Covent-Garden.* . . . Mr. *Horner*; he lodges in *Russel-street,* and he's a sign of a Man" (I,i). Sparkish means pretense. Alithea uses it differently when she tells Harcourt she dislikes him because he is one of the wits: "the surest sign is, . . . you are an Enemy to Marriage" (II,i). Harcourt knows both senses:

> Marrying you, is no more sign of his [Sparkish's] love, than bribing your Woman, that he may marry you, is a sign of his generosity. . . . But if you take Marriage for a sign of love, take it from me immediately. (II,i)

Margery, of course, is not quite aware of the double sense when she tells Pinchwife,

> Lord, what a power of brave signs are here! stay—the Bull's-Head, the Rams-head, and the Stags-head. . . .

Pinchwife. Nay, if every Husbands proper sign were visible, they wou'd be all alike. (III,ii)

Horner's sense of "sign" is also Mrs. Squeamish's:

And that Demureness, Coyness, and Modesty, that you see in our

[66]

Faces in the Boxes at Plays, is as much a sign of a kind woman, as a Vizard-mask in the Pit. (V,iv)

As is evident, Horner does not solely use the word, but its two senses point to the central discrepancy which separates the characters: Horner lives by signs of pretense, Harcourt by signs of meaning. The same is true of their language and the same is true of their relationships. Horner alters the friendship between Dorilant, Harcourt and himself into part of his pretense, or anti-friendship; it becomes as unnatural as the pimp's or quack's removal from natural sexuality or doctoring. Family relations are shifted out of normal structure (not only by Horner, for Pinchwife treats his sister Alithea as an enemy) as he enlists the sisters Fidget into the ranks of the virtuous gang; and of course, he permanently distorts marriages which are already somewhat angular. There are no relationships which are not altered by Horner. Even objects are changed in Horner's world, most sensationally china, which he "takes" as a metaphor for sexuality with the ladies, an especially apt one at that, as Norman Holland illustrates.[37] But any object will do, as the following exchange indicates.

Lady Fidget.	Now Ladies, . . . let us speak the truth of our hearts.
Dainty and Squeamish.	Agreed.
Lady Fidget.	By this brimmer, for truth is no where else to be found, [Not in thy heart false man.] [*Aside to* Horner]
Horner.	You have found me a true man I'm sure. [*Aside to* Lady Fidget]
Lady Fidget.	Not every way— [*Aside to* Horner]
Lady Fidget sings. . . .	
Dainty.	Dear Brimmer, well in token of our openness and plain dealing, let us throw our Masques over our heads.
Horner.	So 'twill come to the Glasses anon.
Squeamish.	Lovely Brimmer, let me enjoy him first.

| Lady Fidget. | No, I never part with a Gallant, till I've try'd him. (V,iv) |

The easy transfer of meaning from brimmer as a wine glass to Horner himself is a remarkable example of the transitoriness of language:[38] words are what they are now and may not be for long. This sort of verbal structuring happens repeatedly by the time Horner and his ladies know one another. He even suggests he prefers his art to the real; as Lady Squeamish gives him Mrs. Squeamish's picture, he says:

> Well nothing but that could bribe me, I love a woman only in Effigie, and good Painting as much as I hate them [Horner is still pretending to hate women]— I'le do't, for I cou'd adore the Devil well painted. (IV,iii)

Though ironic perhaps, these lines are not untruthful, especially when the painting is reputation or china. So effective is the manipulation of words that Margery barely catches up in time to lie into the game, and Harcourt cannot understand at all:

Harcourt.	This Lady has her Honour, and I will protect it.
Horner.	My Lady has not her Honour, but has given it to me to keep, and I will preserve it.
Harcourt.	I understand you not.
Horner.	I wou'd not have you. (V,iv)

At the last, a continued fabrication of reality is required to keep the game going.

| Horner. | Oh 'tis well you are come—'tis a censorious world we live in . . . therefore, pray satisfie these worthy, honourable, jealous Gentlemen— |
| Quack. | O I understand you, is that all—Sir *Jasper*, by heavens and upon the word of a Physician Sir— [*Whispers to Sir* Jasper] (V,iv) |

Nature or *natural* has been used here in a teleological sense, implying that by which things have proper ends to which they tend. Horner has changed the process into his own and has with his energy and prodigious imagination brought almost all the world of the play along with him. Against Horner's agility, Harcourt's considerably less mobile efforts may to some appear uninteresting, but he is not attempting to control persons and events and things, only to clarify his relationship with Alithea. No dangers threaten him, whereas Horner courts enchanting disasters throughout the play. Harcourt and Alithea are the only two who finally speak directly to one another in words which have meaning in one sense only,

> Madam, then have no trouble, you shall now see 'tis possible for me to love too, without being jealous . . . (V,iv),

and who work to establish a relationship which has a chance of continuing in normal fashion. Theirs is the only relationship which can have social sanction.

The Plain-Dealer, Wycherley's last play, appeared in December 1676, performed by the same King's company at the Theater Royal on the 11th of that month as had staged *The Country-Wife* nearly two years before. It was received with uncertainty until several of Wycherley's friends who carried the weight of reputation in town "by their loud approbation of it, gave it both a sudden and lasting reputation."[39] These "critics" were the erratic Duke of Buckingham, of whose relationship with Wycherley we shall see more; Rochester; the Earl of Dorset, who according to Matthew Prior was the chief spokesman for the play;[40] the Earl of Mulgrave; Henry Savile, Henry Bulkeley, Sir John Denham and the poet Edmund Waller. The play was revived frequently, in 1677, 1681 in Oxford and London, 1683,[41] 1685 by the request of King James himself, 1691, 1694, 1698 and 1700. On 11 March 1692, the *Lacedemonian Mercury* carried a letter deploring the "very great declension in Common Sense" in the town which caused *The Plain-Dealer* and Etherege's *The Man of Mode* to be "untouch'd and unsought for."[42]

For this play Wycherley drew the main character from

[69]

Molière's Alceste in *The Misanthrope*, but Manly is only a distant relative of Alceste, not a brother; Wycherley did not have his Manly complain darkly throughout but made him a railing scourge of society who at length was brought to conciliation with society rather than rejection of it.[43] Predictably, Wycherley's use of his source is very independent and strong-minded; he wrought the elements of Molière and various others into an uncompromisingly unique play. There are certain broad parallels to the Spanish plot of *Love in a Wood*, as well as to that play's dark-light motif, as Manly comes home from afar to find his true love but distrusts his real friend and lover, Fidelia, because he refuses to see what is apparent.

J. M. Auffret has argued that for his portrait of Manly, Wycherley used his friend Mulgrave, probably the most important person in Wycherley's life outside of his family. His reasons are biographical similarities between Mulgrave and Manly, such as: both served in the third Dutch war as ship commanders; both were misanthropic; their friendship was inviolable; both were quarrelsome, and so forth. The argument is well researched and persuasive, offering a good deal of insight into Mulgrave and Wycherley and Manly.[44] Auffret's argument agrees with much of what has been expressed thus far of Wycherley's consciousness of contemporary ideas and trends and his very frequent self-conscious reference to topical events and persons. There are, in fact, in *The Plain-Dealer* some lines which appear exactly biographical—not solely the ironically prophetic ones such as,

> Then he has shew'd Love to her indeed, in leaving her, like an old Husband that dyes as soon as he has made his Wife a good Jointure (I,i),

or the self-mocking ones such as the Widow's remark:

> there are young Students of the Law enough spoil'd already, by *Playes* (III,i),

[70]

but rather the following exchange as Manly and Freeman enter Westminster Hall:

Freeman.   Methinks, 'tis like one of their own Halls, in *Christmas* time, whither, from all parts, Fools bring their Money; to try, by the Dice. . . .

Manly.   Spoken, like a Revelling *Christmas* Lawyer.

Freeman.   Yes, I was one, I confess; but was fain to leave the Law, out of Conscience, and fall to making false Musters; rather chose to Cheat the King, than his Subjects; Plunder, rather than take Fees. (III,ii)

As we shall see, Wycherley did leave the law after serving as "controller for the Christmas," entered the army in 1672–73, and had some problem about payrolls for his troops. One suspects that Wycherley planted such special jokes for the benefit of his friends, for his plays are full of specialized remarks behind which seem to lurk extra meanings, such as the remarks on *"Ned Harcourt of Cambridge"* with his "sneaking Colledg look" (IV,i), the famous one about "the hideous *Countrey Wife*" and its "Author's want of Wit" (II,i), or the slighting references to lawyers and other professionals.

The action of *The Plain-Dealer* is not especially complicated though the play has a density of tone and atmosphere that feels complex. Manly has just returned from sea where he has, for honor, lost his ship and its valuables; though he severely disapproves social conventions he has two ideal friends, his mistress, Olivia, who has his jewels, and his trusted friend, Vernish. The inevitable happens: Olivia and Vernish dupe Manly and run off with his wealth to be married. Manly's companion throughout is Fidelia, dressed as a boy, who secretly and truly loves him. Another friend in truth, Freeman, is wheedling his way to a well-endowed marriage with the law-mad Widow Blackacre. As the play evolves, Freeman gets his rich widow; Manly exposes Olivia and Vernish, recovers his wealth, and discovers Fidelia whom he marries. This sketch conveys

[71]

none of the temper of the play, but we can see some of that in the very ironic Epistle Dedicatory, "To my Lady B . . . , the famous bawd Mrs. Bennet,

> Great and Noble Patroness of rejected and bashful men, of which number I profess my self to be one, though a Poet, a Dedicating Poet . . . You are the fittest Patroness or Judge of this Play; for you shew no partiality to this or that Author . . . for a Comic Poet, and a Lady of your Profession, make most of the other sort [not ladies of Honour], and the Stage and your Houses, like our Plantations, are propagated by the least nice Women; and as with the Ministers of Justice, the Vices of the Age are our best business.

The wry dedication takes shots at all quarters, but mainly at the sanctimonious, who fearing to be seen at such a play "like other nice Ladies" will read it in their closets:

> For what they renounce in publick often entertains 'em there, with your help especially . . . . Baudy I find, like Satyr shou'd be [kept] home, not to have it taken notice of. But, now I mention Satyr, some there are who say, 'Tis the Plain-dealing of the Play, not the obscenity; 'tis taking off the Ladies Masks, not offering at their Pettycoats, which offends 'em: and generally they are not the handsomest, or most innocent, who are the most angry at being discover'd:
>
> > Nihil est audacius illis
> > Deprehensis; iram, atq; animos a crimine sumunt
>
> Pardon, Madam, The Quotation, for a Dedication can no more be without ends of Latine, than Flattery . . . .[45]

The aggressive thrust of the play continues in the prologue, "spoken by the Plain-Dealer":

> Plain-dealing is, you'll say, quite out of fashion;
> You'll hate it here, as in a Dedication. . . .
> But the course Dauber of the coming Scenes,
> To follow Life, and Nature only means;
> Displays you, as you are . . .
> I only, act a Part like none of you;
> And yet, you'll say, it is a Fool's Part too. . . .
> For Truth is now a fault, as well as Wit.
> And where else, but on Stages, do we see
> Truth pleasing; or rewarded Honesty?

[72]

As a result of these lines and the play, Wycherley became known as the plain-dealer, an epithet he seemed willing to foster in his whimsical way. The ironic tone of the prologue, couched in the customary figure of drama as the mirror of nature and of the manners of men, has confused some viewers into believing the player and the author are the same. But his device of pretending to be the plain-dealing companion of Mother Bennet is the same kind of satiric mask employed by other satirists such as Pope or Jonathan Swift and we have managed to discriminate between Lemuel Gulliver and the Dean of St. Patrick's, between Pope, the author of "Epistle to Dr. Arbuthnot," and the person in the poem talking to Arbuthnot. It may happen of course that Wycherley's manner and the plain dealer's may correspond, and Wycherley's thoughts elsewhere may be as scornful as Manly's, but a distinction must be made to preserve the difference between author and work.[46]

The play has other more complex problems to offer than the hero-author confusion. For it is not a comedy in the usual sense of the word, not the usual humor comedy, or wit comedy, or manners comedy, or Roman new comedy, or even romantic comedy which a name like Fidelia might bring to mind. It is satire in its tone and character, and it is comedy in its movement toward a social resolution of the conflicts of characters, even while it moves contrary to the customary comic inclusion of all persons into society and has, instead, Manly accepting society on his terms. Yet it defies a single name and struggles out of the critical boxes one may construct for it. It comes close to romance at times, in its concluding rewards to Fidelia and Manly; it brushes close to tragedy more truly than any prior play of Wycherley's when the characters threaten to act on the bases of moral absolutes and leave behind the world's opinions. I have suggested that the play be called a tragi-comedy[47] but only insofar as that term be used as an entree into the play and not a critical cubicle to store it. The play will not accept an easy genre; it is dissatisfied with a name and troublesome to anyone who

[73]

tries to judge it in absolute generic terms. What will be offered here then is not another name, but a reading of the play on the basis of the meaning of plain-dealing, a term by no means entirely clear.

Wycherley had a proximate familiarity with the substance if not with the actual texts of various contemporary courtesy and morality books and was conversant with the ideas found in them which flew in the intellectual winds of the day. As we examine the term "plain-dealing," we find again his acceptance of some current meanings of the term. A. M. Friedson has pointed out:

> the term 'plain dealer' appears to have become current at the end of the sixteenth century. The first literary usage I have been able to find is in Painter's *Palace of Pleasure* (1566). . . . As far as I know, the term has never been used in a pejorative sense. In fact, it is always used as a compliment to define one who does not himself practice deceit and is, therefore, not likely to recognize dishonesty in others.[48]

This assumption about the nature of plain-dealing is, I believe, the common one, but is not entirely complete. More significantly, Professor Schneider has traced the meaning of plain-dealing from the ancients, placing it in relation to other chief virtues, in order to determine its traditional and its Restoration meanings:

> From Plato come the four virtues: Wisdom, Courage, Temperance, and Justice. These are also the main branches of Cicero's moral philosophy. Aristotle's list is considerably longer, emphasizing Courage, Temperance, Liberality, Greatness of Soul, Truthfulness, and Justice. The ethical emphases in Restoration comedy, as I derive them, are also fourfold: Liberality, Courage, Plain-dealing and Love.

> Under Temperance, Cicero takes up much that suggests what I call Plain-dealing in Restoration comedy. It is here that he discusses the concept of *decorum*, the art of being natural. . . . By following nature, we might suppose that we would all become wild animals. Not so, for *decorum* is defined as "that which harmonizes with a man's superiority in those respects in which his nature *differs* from that of the rest of the animal creation." Thus, that *decorum* which

makes our behavior *natural* derives from a deliberately imposed, hence *artificial,* discipline of disorderly appetite to prevent subhuman behavior . . . from disturbing the "natural" harmony of self and society.

When social arts, or manners, are a refinement of nature rather than a replacement of it, they can be a form of generosity. . . . Whether nature is enhanced by embellishment or by restraint, the motive may be generous. But at a certain point embellishment becomes disguise and restraint becomes formality. At this point art becomes artifice and takes the place of nature. This point, I propose, divides the plain-dealers from double-dealers in Restoration comedy.[49]

There is evidently a harmonic connection between nature and art; decorum steadies them into one character. And it is precisely this relationship which constitutes plain-dealing, not simply a frankness, a speaking of the truth.

Wycherley's contemporaries used the term frequently. *Plain-Dealing is a Jewel* (1682) was the title of a pamphlet about eliminating fears of popish intervention in England;[50] it was also, ironically, an expression of Horner's (IV,iii). *Plain Dealing; or, a Full and Particular Examination of a Late Treatise, Entituled, Humane Reason* (1675) was a pamphlet attack on Hobbes.[51] "Plain-dealing" was also a card game, as Ian Donaldson has pointed out.[52] There was even an imitation of Wycherley, Edward Ward's *The Wooden World Dissected in the Character of a Ship of War* by "Manly Plain dealer" in 1707. In 1647 Thomas Adams (1586–1665) wrote a pamphlet, *Plain Dealing, or a Fair Warning to the Gentlemen of the Committee for Union,* and about the same time produced a sermon, "Plain Dealing; or, A Precedent of Honesty."[53] While most of these uses of the term simply indicate its currency, this last work, a sermon based on the story of Jacob and Esau, bears examination for the meaning of plain-dealing it offers.

The name *Jacob* meant, the Reverend Adams wrote, *to supplant,* and twice Jacob supplanted Esau. "But Jacob did not steal away his birthright but only took advantage to buy what careless Esau was willing to sell."[54] Nevertheless, Jacob

[75]

has been "accused with fraudulent stratagems." Adams argued against these, citing Church Fathers and scholastic opinion to absolve Jacob of fraud and sin, since he acted by the Lord's counsel and his mother's advice.

> Origen says, that necessity may urge a man to use a lie as a sauce to his meat. . . . Augustine thinks Jacob spoke mystically . . . the Christian Church should take away the birthright from the elder—But one act of falsehood shall not disparage wholly that simplicity the Scripture gives him: he was a 'plain man.' . . . Yet then may Jacob stand for our precedent of plain-dealing, notwithstanding this particular weakness.[55]

In application, Adams wrote, "There are three kinds of dissimulation held tolerable, if not commendable: . . . when a man dissembles to get himself out of danger; . . . when dissimulation is directly aimed to the instruction and benefit of another; . . . when some common service is thereby performed to the good of the church." The conclusion of the sermon is a peroration to the congregation to "win you to plain-dealing" for plain-dealers, like the old patriarchs, are marked with two qualities: contempt of the world, and frugality, especially in dwellings.[56] Whatever one may think of Reverend Adams' moral and theological discriminations, his argument that plain-dealing necessitates deception is, I believe, important and by no means unique. Others seemed to think similarly. As the Marquis of Halifax observed, perhaps out of despair, "Dissimulation is like most other Qualities, it hath two sides; it is necessary, and yet it is dangerous too."[57] The King's physician William Ramesey whom Wycherley may have known, wrote in his *The Gentleman's Companion* (1672, with Epistle Dedicatory dated 15 June 1669) concerning ostentation: "A little Vanity, and Opinion, therefore, may be allowed, especially in such Natures whose Bark is ballasted with solidity, and Reason, as Fame's breath can't over-set it."[58] Though he exhorts one not to "flatter, lye, nor dissemble," his acceptance of exaggeration is important, even without use of the term plain-dealing as such. If we turn to the writings of the Spanish Jesuit moralist Balthasar Gracian, on the authority of Pope's assertion that "Wycherley used to read himself asleep o'nights, either in Montaigne, Rochefoucault, Seneca, or Gratian, for those were his four favorite authors,"[59] there we find similar sentiments on plainness and dissimulation:

> In the manner of expression one ought to have a care not to be too plain; and to speak with open heart is not always convenient in conversation.[60]

> Art corrects what is bad, and perfects what is good. The best nature without art, is but a Wilderness.

> Maxim XIII: proceed sometimes cunningly, sometimes candidly.

> Passions are the breaches of the mind. The most useful knowledge is the art to dissemble. . . .

> A compleat man must then in the first place apply himself to the subduing of his passions, and then to the dissembling of them so artfully that no spy can ever be able to unmask his thought.

> Truth is dangerous, but yet a good man cannot forbear to speak it. And in that there is need of art.[61]

Gracian's idea of the hero was characterized by "dexterity, skill, agility," or in Spanish *destrenza*: "Let this be the first skill in the art of sophisticated men, to gain the measure of a situation behind a screen of artifice. A great stratagem is to display oneself to view but not to comprehension."[62] Though Gracian did not abandon the traditional virtue of fortitude, he placed less emphasis on constancy than on seizing new ways to greatness.[63] Further, he believed "sympathy" to be the mark of the hero as well as *despejo*, translated in the English version as "the secret charm, or inexpressible somewhat; what the French call Le je-ne-sai-quoi,"[64] the Restoration definition of "manner" or pleasing air. The Earl of Carbery's advice to his son, written in 1651, likewise recommended art of a moderate sort: "There is noe Man but hath his Weaknesse; Be you true to your selfe and find it out. Having found it, Labour to remove it; if it cannot be removed then have recourse to Arte, which will eyther lessen it or cover it." For example, if one lacked courage, practice its opposite, mildness, for the "Reputation of a Gentile spiritt . . . is a signe of the best and truest courage."[65] Though he would not instruct his son "to a Spanish Counter-dissimulation," Carbery did encourage him "esteeme and practise, the Repartie, which is a quicke, smarte and pertinent Reply," for there is advantage in this at Court and women are strongly "delighted with this dexterity of witt."[66] It is interesting to compare, momentarily, the ideal gentleman presented by Clement Ellis in *The Gentile Sinner; or England's Brave Gentleman* (1664):

> He lives in the world as one that intends to shame the world out of love with itself; and he is therefore, singular in all his Actions, not because he affects to be so, but because he cannot meet with company like himself to make him otherwise. . . . His breeding has been amongst the Angels in another world, rather than amongst Gentlemen in this; . . . he is so refined from all Mixture of our courser Elements, as if he were absolutely Spiritualized before his time.[67]

This Platonic conception of man is quite the opposite of the plain-dealing man mentioned before, especially that of Gracian's hero who must respond to the real world and should never withdraw "from society in accord with traditional Christian contempt of the world"[68] (though this contempt does not necessitate isolation, at least in Pauline theology). True wisdom can only be had in the world, not in solitude. While Gracian cautioned that "what is natural must always be more agreeable than what is artificial,"[69] and while Wycherley too warned against the folly of hiding imperfections or pretending to perfect them,[70] what we recognize from these statements on the ideals of behavior and on plain-dealing itself is that art or dissimulation and pretense are necessary in life. Plain-dealing therefore does not mean speaking the truth in all cases; it means speaking the truth in the most suitable manner or altering it if circumstances necessitate such deception. As we turn to *The*

Plain-Dealer, these principles are of considerable aid in understanding Manly's behavior, both at the beginning and at the end of the play.

As the play opens, Manly lashes out at the

> *Decorums*, supercilious Forms, and slavish Ceremonies; your little Tricks, which you the Spaniels of the World, do daily over and over, for, and to one another; not out of love or duty, but your servile fear. (I,i)

Plausible insists Manly is too absolute, for these decorums are "the Arts, and Rules the prudent of the World walk by." Again Manly rejects them: "I can walk alone." And again Plausible insists, rather pointedly, "What will you be singular then, like no Body? follow Love and esteem no Body?" Manly's view—which has its possibilities certainly—is that most men are bad enough to merit ill treatment: "I speak ill of most men, because they deserve it; I that can do a rude thing, rather than an unjust thing" (I,i). Freeman, the next to meet Manly, uses the unfortunate word *ceremony*: "You use a Lord with very little Ceremony, it seems" (I,i), and Manly berates him for it. But Freeman, much in the manner of Plausible, responds: "Well . . . you are for *Plain-dealing*, I find; but against your particular Notions, I have the practise of the whole World" (I,i). Manly has, in other words, his "particular notion" of plain-dealing, that is, saying forthrightly whatever one thinks. But what one frankly thinks and believes to be honest may not be the truth; at best it may have the truth of correspondence to one's opinions, those dubious creatures of our pride. Manly has, of course, reason to scorn ceremony for it is indeed often fraudulent and a great part of the world he knows is false and hollow. But the world, for its part, merely replies that Manly is mad, and he can only rail back, admitting, "I do not, I confess," understand the world. Were we not already doubtful about Manly's "honesty," we should be persuaded by his cruel disregard for Fidelia: "I hate thy Flattery worse than Cowardise, nay, than thy Bragging" (I,i), even when

[79]

she is plain-dealing, speaking the truth of her emotions. Thus Manly who has been solitary at sea has become socially misfit, "brutish," to use the word of Gracian's fellow moralists.[71] The sympathy a hero must have is nonexistent in Manly; he has no pleasing air or manner; he believes in absolutes and ideals, not in degrees; he has only the somewhat hidden—to all but Fidelia and his sailors—virtues of courage and devotion to truth and honor (V,ii). If he is to be worth our interest and society's, he must become aware of degree in virtue and vice, of art in relation to nature, of the true nature of plain-dealing. The process of the play thus becomes the revelation of Manly's own hypocrisy as he performs every act against which he rails.

> How hard it is to be an Hypocrite!
> At least to me, who am but newly so.
> I thought it once a kind of Knavery,
> Nay, Cowardice, to hide one's faults; but now
> The common frailty, Love, becomes my shame.
> He must not know I love th' ungrateful still,
> Lest he contemn me, more than she: for I,
> It seems, can undergo a Womans scorn,
> But not a Mans— (III,i)

This blank verse soliloquy marks Manly's movement from brusque plain-dealing to gentlemanly plain-dealing, the proper kind, a movement which continues to the end of the play. Only then, at the end, does Manly acquiesce to the forms of politeness and calls Fidelia "Madam," a name he would never use before with intentional kindness; he begins to read her heart and mind correctly by believing her words to mean what they say, as Harcourt and Alithea did in *The Country-Wife*, "your blushes answer me sufficiently, and you have been my Volunteer in love" (V,iii).

Then follows a revealing dialogue and action. Manly, having regained his jewels, turns to Fidelia: "Then, take for ever my heart, and this with it; [*Gives her the Cabinet*]" (V,iii). He discovers her true fortune of money at the same time he discovers her true affections, "Nay now, Madam, you have taken from me all power of making you any

Complement on my part" (V,iii). Manly continues, exactly in accord with Gracian's urging of the hero to remain in the world:

> I wou'd quit the unknown pleasures of a retirement; and rather stay in this ill World of ours still, tho odious to me, than give you more frights again at Sea. . . . But if I shou'd tell you now all this, and that your virtue (since greater than I thought any was in the World) had now reconciled me to't, my Friend here wou'd say, 'tis your Estate that has made me Friends with the World.

He is surprisingly willing to be misunderstood by the world since it matters little after all.

> . . .Tho' I have been so lately deceiv'd in the Friends of both Sexes;
> *I will believe, there are now in the World*
> *Good-natur'd Friends, who are not Prostitutes,*
> *And handsom Women worthy to be Friends:*
> *Yet, for my sake, let no one e're confide*
> *In Tears, or Oaths, in Love, or Friend untry'd.* (V,iii)

The cabinet of jewels becomes in one sense the physical symbol of Manly's true plain-dealing heart. In much moral and courtesy writing of the period, cabinet is used as a metaphor for one's nature; for example, "Fair creature, You are that rich Cabinet wherein Nature hath lockt up all her rarities."[72] Thomas Blount typified a virtuous maid as "So rich a treasure in so pure a Cabinet."[73] The figure was extended by William Ramesey to the self as a whole, "if a Man have a Cabinet that every mans Key will open as well as his own . . . the more he aggravates his own misery";[74] and the Earl of Carbery used it as a metaphor for the memory. [75] In *Love in a Wood*, Dapperwit while pointing out Martha's house showed his acquaintance with the figure, though his motives were less than virtuous: "This is the Cabinet, in which I hide my Jewel" (III,i). The jewel image is commonly used for various virtues, such as honor as a jewel, honesty as a jewel, courtesy, plain-dealing and so on in like manner. Hippolita said to Gerrard, "I see you will part with the Jewel [her heart]; but you'll have the keeping of the Cabinet [her body] to which you commit it" (II,i). As the container of the greatest valuables, the cabinet is opposed to the china of Horner which has value only in its externals, perhaps the reason for Olivia's celebrated outburst of contrived horror at "the hideous *Countrey Wife*" and its scenes of "filthy *China*, nasty, debauch'd *China*" (II,i). In parallel sense, one should have care of one's own cabinet or soul and should not be locked away, as quite a few persons in Wycherley's plays are. Freeman draws Manly's attention to the jewel-money and jewel-virtue metaphor; "Captain, there are other things which next to one's heart, one wou'd not part with; I mean your Jewels and Money. . . . There are certain Appurtenances to a Lover's heart, call'd Jewels. . . ." Fidelia adds: "And which, with Lovers, have no value in themselves, but from the heart they come with"(II,i).

Manly's change from the railing malcontent to a true, plain-dealing gentleman becomes clear through the process of his education in the play. He assuredly is no single-dimension characterless figure; nor is he a mere fool or dupe, nor at the other extreme an ideal.[76] He has begun to merge nature and art: the ceremonies and conventions of society have a place, suspect as they often are, and honesty is not necessarily truer than convention—or even deception. Manly sees what Giovanni della Casa in *The Refin'd Courtier* (1663) meant by ceremonies and compliments: they should "either aim at *profit* and *advantage*, or are the issue of *vanity* and *ostentation*, or else proceed from *courtesie* and a *due esteem* and *regard* of those towards whom they are directed."[77] Wycherley himself had this habit of gentility and civility, which Manly is only beginning to approximate; Charles Gildon wrote, "Mr. *Wycherley* was indeed of an affable, easie, good Temper, and perfectly inoffensive to all Company, and knew how to be Civil over a glass to Mr. *Durfey* as to Mr. *Dryden*, but this was no mark of Friendship or Intimacy."[78] Wycherley could adjust his nature by the art of civility and drink with poor poet Durfey while not meaning a great deal by it. He underscored this sense of civility in a letter to Pope: "I have as much Faith in your Friendship and Sincerity, as I have Deference to your Judgment; and as the best Mark of a Friend, is telling his friend his Faults in private, so the next is concealing them from the publick, 'till they are fit to appear."[79]

It would appear from the beginning of this discussion of Manly's progress that as the play opens, Plausible and Freeman had far better understandings of plain-dealing than Manly for they disapproved his view, to some extent correctly. Both Plausible and Freeman insist that they have currency and custom on their side as proof against Manly's singularity. However, their sense of Manly places them both closer to and farther from true plain-dealing. Plausible becomes before long too supple to be a serious problem. Freeman, on the other hand, courts the widow plainly because she is not approachable through deceptive language; he does deceive her by freeing her son Jerry with the knowledge of his false minority but that too is for the end of marriage, albeit for money, her jointure. He is at the same time a good and reliable friend, whom Manly seldom chastises for his free-dealing, and a speaker of many truths. If saying the truth were the sole criterion for true plain-dealing, Freeman, and almost all others at one or another point, would qualify. But he has none of the aspiration toward civility and gentility, toward the marriage of art and nature which make plain-dealing a generous virtue. He knows the world and uses it for his ends in free and forthright ways, not, for that reason, a base fellow but rather like most of us, seeking ways of getting along, of seizing the main chance. Fidelia also speaks the truth. To Manly, she speaks through the veil of her disguise, but her plain-dealing is different from Freeman's; hers is true plain-dealing for the deception is designed as a means of giving her love to Manly in an act of generosity, not self-interest. Motive and end do seem to matter in these plays. She is thus, with Manly, a true plain-dealer, and Freeman a lesser variety. It is Wycherley's perception of the deeper veins of comedy that impelled him to foul his main characters in realities and base acts, to allow them to descend to their worst so that they could emerge with a true comic knowledge of themselves and others. Comedy sees life in all its aspects and shakes its head in sad bemusement at the paradox.

There are many other aspects of *The Plain-Dealer* which could bear fruitful examination, apart from the great conundrum of its genre: Wycherley's self-consciousness of his plays as artifice not reality, for example, in the comments on *The Country-Wife* by Olivia, or in Monsieur's joking in *Gentleman-Dancing-Master* about the players James Nokes and Edward Angel, who were probably in the play, or Hippolita's hoping some "filching" poet would not take her story to put on the stage; the remarkable correspondence between the humor names of this and other contemporary plays and the allegorical names of very different writers like Bunyan in *Pilgrim's Progress*, suggesting that humor comedy leans rather easily toward allegorical didacticism; the satire on law and the legal profession in the person of the Widow, whose caricature probably owed very little to Daniel Wycherley since the habit of litigation was hardly reserved for him in this century; the portraits of aberrant behavior in the early plays turning to the genuinely mad characters of Olivia, Vernish, and in some sense the Widow; the return to the dark stage of the first play; or the use of extra-social characters like the sailors as he had similarly used the unusual black servant in *Gentleman-Dancing-Master*; and there are others. *The Plain-Dealer* is a rich play, worth the applause of the best wits of its day. It is, assuredly, rigorous in ways that force us to abandon easy formulas of comedy and easy notions of society's structures and conventions. It is strong satire, uncompromising and unrelenting, and thus not likely to be popularly agreeable to many. It is nevertheless Wycherley's greatest play and one of the finest works of the Augustan age, comparable to Pope's and Swift's major achievements.[80]

Of Wycherley's activities during the years of his dramatic successes we have limited information. We know nothing at all of his habits of writing or his methods of composition, but he did carry on an active life while writing his plays. Tradition has it that he walked the town from the Inns of Court through the Piazza of Covent Garden, along the Strand to St. James Park observing and recording the life and manners around him,[81] and no doubt tradition has something in its favor. For his plays are filled with the actualities of places and things:

Have I not constantly kept *Covent-Garden*-Church, St. *Martins*, the Play-Houses, *Hide-Park*, *Mulbery-Garden*, and all other the publick Marts where Widows and Mayds are expos'd? (I,i, *Love in a Wood*)

—We have no Ballads.
—Then give me *Covent-Garden*-Drollery, and a Play or two
—Oh here's *Tarugos* Wiles, and the Slighted Maiden, I'll have them. (III,ii, *The Country-Wife*)

The Scene changes to the Cock *in* Bow-Street.
A Table, and Bottles. (V,ii, *The Plain-Dealer*)

He must have studied the stage, not only the business of the theater and the gossip of its personages, but the craft of staging and of maneuvering players; perhaps he played some roles himself to gain a feel for stage movement. In any case, he had an excellent sense of the uses of the stage as dramatic space; his directions keep even a reader visually conscious of the placement of actors, their entrances and exits, their movements and gestures, all of which he developed to dramatically significant function.

Enter Don Diego *walking gravely, a little Black behind him.* (III,ii)

[Lucy] *Kneels to Mr.* Pinchwife, *who stands doggedly, with his hat over his eyes.* (V,iv)

Manly *puts 'em out of the Room:* Novel *struts,* Plausible *cringes.* (II,i)

Exeunt Manly, Fidelia *on one side,* Freeman *on t'other.* (IV, i)

[85]

The last is perhaps most symbolic, though Pinchwife certainly creates an emblem of the blind man. Wycherley's confident and invariably specific handling of stage and the language of the plays is evident in all his plays and must have been part of his appeal to a large number of friends.

From the mid 1660's through the pinnacle years of his prestige until about 1677, he enjoyed the accelerating reputation of a wit and playwright quite without equal among his peers and betters. He was handsome, wittily successful and well associated with court and courtier. His letter in late summer of 1677 to his friend the Earl of Mulgrave gives us a glimpse into the pleasantly chatty, amiable relationship Wycherley held with the Earl and with, apparently, those to whom he makes reference.

London Augt
ye 20th—1677
My Lord,

At this Distance, and amongst Fanfarons You may brag as you please, but I must believe you lazy still; only by your long Letter to me it appears, (as lazy as you are) you are never weary of obliging your Friends. I received it yesterday with as much Satisfaction, as my Ld Midleton would a Billetdoux from Mrs Yard, and think your Lordship has done as much for me, as for the King of France. For the Fatigue of a long Letter at any Time is to be compared with that of a luxurious Campaigne: and Louvoy cannot be more thankful to you in the Name of his King, than I am. But G—d D—n him for his unwonted Civility; for I was in Hopes, that the Civility of the Enemy's Army, (as you call it) and the ill Usage from your own, would have made your Return more suddain than I find 't will be: But what? I forget myself, and for your Sake call the Confederates Enemies, like a false Coffee-House Brother; therefore for God's Sake, my Lord, do not stay longer with the French. For, whilst You are amongst 'em, I shall, contrary to my Coffee-house Allegiance, wish 'em well. But since, as your Lordship sais, my Ld Midleton and You are but One, I must despair of your Removal; for though You would jog on, the Midleton Side of you would hang an A—e. For his is the most invincible Laziness in the World; and he only could make it a Military Virtue, to serve him in the Place of Ambition, and make him suffer any Thing but Motion. I suppose He rides properly like a Foot-Officer, to avoid the Fatigue of pulling on his Boots, and lies rough rather than take Pains to unbutton himself; and upon a March has always the Place of Honour in bringing up the Rear: And if the whole Army were routed, would be kill'd, not to be at the Trouble of running away. In fine, if I may quibble, he is of a Young One, a very stay'd Officer; but I shall never think him capable of active Fatigue, 'till he writes me as long a Letter, as your Lordship has done, which, if it were but for the Pleasure of sitting still without Disturbance, he should do methinks. Well, to say no worse of him, he is properly in the French Army no Voluntier; and You have press'd him into that Service, whilst his Inclination would have carried him to his Brother Lazers, the Spaniards. Pray tell him, my Lord, that if the Hast of this Bearer had afforded me Time, I should have had too much Respect for him, to write to him, 'till I knew certainly he wou'd pardon a Letter, that wou'd give him an Occasion of writing an Answer; but the next Opportunity I have, (to speak in a Camp Phrase) let him look to 't; my Pen shall give him no Quarter; in the mean Time, my Lord, pray let him know, I am his humble servant.—We have no News to send you from hence, but of Your self, which seemed as false, as if it came by your Enemy's Letters, the Dutch: As terrible however as it was. I dare say your last Mistress was no more afraid than I of your being kill'd in a Quarrel by my Lord Lumley, as it was here incredibly reported. The King is not yet return'd from Plimouth, but expected to Morrow Night. This Town is now as empty, as if your Army were marching over the Bridge; and the Whores are as p—x'd, as if the French had possess'd the Town 3 Days. I have no scandalous News to send you, for Mr. Russel is out of Town, nor any Poetical News, for Dryden is in Northampton-shire. When I write to him, I will not fail to make him proud with your Lordship's Compliment, Though I am forbid drinking Wine so soon after my Waters, I cannot refrain it to your Health, which I drank lately with the Duke of Buckingham, who is now gone to Cliveden, to survey, and confound his Builders, like those of Babel; and I hope, for his Good, the Work may stand still. I had almost forgot to tell You, that, in your Absence, your favorite Plays, The King and no King, The Maid's Tragedy, and Rollo, are all torn in Pieces by a New Criticque lately publish'd by Rymer, which we intend Jack Markham shall answer. The Book is duller than his Play of Edgar, which he promises to publish as a Pattern for exact Tragedies. This last

[87]

Piece is written after the Epistolary Way of Politick Fops, directed to Mr Shepheard, I suppose from one Room to another at the George and Vulture Tavern, when the Wine was dead, and the Spirits of the Brandy too much wasted by Burning; so that it will be no hard Matter for Jack Markham's Water to inspire him with a wittier Answer in Defence of his old Friends, Beaumont and Fletcher. You may see, my Lord, I want News, since I am forced to entertain You with such: But since You confess the Conversation in a Camp is none of the wittiest, or most entertaining, I am the less impudent in keeping You so long from it. However, lest the Monsieurs grow impatient for Tatle, and my Ld Lumley for Play, I'll make an End here at the 5th Page. I will not fail to write to you by all the Opportunities I can have; and, in the mean Time, if your Lordship has any Commands for any of your Friends here, be assur'd they will not be welcomer to any Man, than to your Lordship's most humble Servant,

W. Wycherley.[82]

One notices his casual mention of Buckingham, his drinking friend; and of Dryden, with whom he was obviously on good terms for quite some time; and his rather typical sneer at Rymer, the dreadful critic. One notes also his "taking the waters," at Tunbridge Wells no doubt, to which he returned the following summer for more exciting business. It was perhaps at this time he wrote the little verse, *"To a* Friend *who had invited him to* Tunbridge," which begins,

> With Me no Water will go down,
> Not ev'n from the *Castalian* Spring;
> For Water would all Fancy drown,
> And make ev'n *Homer* cease to sing:
> Strong gen'rous Wines the Spirits cheer,
> But Water is a Murmurer.[83]

The prestige and position enjoyed by Wycherley at this point in his career had gotten off to a rather sensational start following the staging of *Love in a Wood.* We will let John Dennis tell the story, for though he is not entirely reliable on details and had a way of embellishing a little into much, he did make the episode into a good tale:

Upon the writing his first Play, which was *St. James's Park*, he became acquainted with several of the most

[88]

celebrated Wits both of the Court and Town. The writing of that Play was likewise the Occasion of his becoming acquainted with one of King *Charles's* Mistresses after a very particular manner. As Mr. *Wycherley* was going thro' *Pall-mall* towards St. *James's* in his Chariot, he met the foresaid Lady in hers, who, thrusting half her body out of the Chariot, cry'd out aloud to him, *You,* Wycherley, *you are a Son of a Whore,* at the same time laughing aloud and heartily. Perhaps, Sir, if you never heard of this Passage before, you may be surpris'd at so strange a Greeting from one of the most beautiful and best bred Ladies in the World. Mr. *Wycherley* was certainly very much surpris'd at it, yet not so much but he soon apprehended it was spoke with Allusion to the latter End of a Song in the foremention'd Play.

> *When Parents are Slaves,*
> *Their Brats cannot be any other,*
> *Great Wits and great Braves*
> *Have always a Punk to their Mother.*

As, during Mr. *Wycherley's* Surprise, the Chariots drove different ways, they were soon at a considerable Distance from each other, when Mr. *Wycherley* recovering from his Surprise, ordered his Coachman to drive back, and to overtake the Lady. As soon as he got over-against her, he said to her, *Madam, you have been pleased to bestow a Title on me which generally belongs to the Fortunate. Will your Ladyship be at the Play to Night? Well,* she reply'd, *what if I am there? Why then I will be there to wait on your Ladyship, tho' I disappoint a very fine Woman who has made me an Assignation. So,* said she, *you are sure to disappoint a Woman who has favour'd you for one who has not. Yes,* he reply'd, *if she who has not favour'd me is the finer Woman of the two. But he who will be constant to your Ladyship, till he can find a finer Woman, is sure to die your Captive.* The Lady blush'd, and bade her Coachman drive away. As she was then in all her Bloom, and the most celebrated Beauty that was then in *England,* or perhaps that has been in *England* since, she was touch'd with the Gallantry of the Compliment. In short, she was that Night in the first Row of the King's Box in *Drury Lane,* and Mr. *Wycherley* in the Pit under her, where he entertained her during the whole Play. And this, Sir, was the beginning of a Correspondence between these two Persons, which afterwards made a great Noise in the Town.[84]

Although Wycherley's something-celebrity of an affair

[89]

with Barbara Villiers, Duchess of Cleveland, lasted a few months only—she thereafter became Mulgrave's mistress for two years[85]— this "noise" Dennis refers to was perhaps more than Wycherley customarily made in his personal life, and this chiefly because men of consequence, such as Buckingham, were interested in the Duchess and looked with annoyance on Wycherley's success. She apparently would dress as a young country girl to visit Wycherley in his lodgings in the Inner Temple, just as he would try disguises to visit her elsewhere. One time he ran into the King himself, whose mistress she had been for a number of years previously:

> The King being jealous of the Duchess of Cleveland, and having intelligence by her maid that she and Mr. Wycherley lay at Mrs. Knight's, the famous singer, in Pall Mall that night, early the next morning went thither and found him muffled in his cloak upon the stair head, and then went into the chamber where he found the duchess on a bed, whom he asked what she made there, who replied it was the beginning of Lent and she retired hither to perform her devotions. The King replied, "Very likely, and that was your confessor I met on the stairs."[86]

Cleveland's notorious appetite for sex put her into a great deal of contemporary gossip and verse, and of course Wycherley's name landed in several lampoons as well. The following appeared in 1676: her lust for a better man than John Churchill (later Duke of Marlborough)

> . . . made her . . . they say,
> To the Temple so often to trudge,
> Where brawny Wycherley lay,
> Who performed the part of a drudge.[87]

Another verse (1682, ten years after *Love in a Wood* and the affair with Cleveland) speaks through the voice of a bawd about "Cleveland herself . . . when first of Wycherley bereft," and describes him:

> I ogled him and he would squint at me;
> But when his charming limbs the first time pressed
> My hectic body, ne'er was bawd so blest.[88]

Lampoons were invented to exaggerate; some people tried to be put into them, outrageous as they might be, just to be mentioned publicly in such "scandalous" form. But both these poems portray Wycherley as conspicuously strong and handsome, and available as well, and this is apparently true.

Dennis' narrative continued into several other matters, the next an immediate result of the first meeting:

But now, Sir I shall proceed to remind you of something more extraordinary, and that is, that the Correspondence between Mr. *Wycherley* and the foresaid Lady was the Occasion of bringing Mr. *Wycherley* into favour with *George* Duke of *Buckingham*, who was passionately in Love with that Lady, who was ill treated by her, and who believed Mr. *Wycherley* his happy *Rival*. After the Duke had long sollicited her without obtaining any thing, whether the Relation between them shock'd her, for she was his Cousin-Germain, or whether she apprehended that an Intrigue with a Person of his Rank and Character, a Person upon whom the Eyes of all Men were fix'd, must of Necessity in a little time come to the King's Ears, whatever was the cause, she refus'd to admit of his Visits so long, that at last Indignation, Rage and Disdain took Place of his Love, and he resolv'd to ruin her. When he had taken this Resolution, he had her so narrowly watch'd by his Spies, that he soon came to the Knowledge of those whom he had reason to believe his Rivals. And after he knew them, he never fail'd to name them aloud, in order to expose the Lady, to all those who frequented him, and among others he us'd to name Mr. *Wycherley*. As soon as it came to the Knowledge of the latter, who had all his Expectations from the Court, he apprehended the Consequence of such a Report, if it should reach the King. He applied himself therefore to *Wilmot* Lord *Rochester* and to Sir *Charles Sedley*, and entreated them to remonstrate to the Duke of *Buckingham* the Mischief which he was about to do to one who had not the Honour to be known to him, and who had never offended him. Upon their opening the Matter to the Duke, he cry'd out immediately, *that he did not blame* Wycherley, *he only accus'd his Cousin. Ay, but,* they reply'd, *by rendring him suspected of such an Intrigue, you are about to ruine him, that is, your Grace is about to ruine a Man with whose Conversation you would be pleas'd above all things.* Upon this Occasion they said so much of the shining Qualities of Mr. *Wycherley*, and of the Charms of the Conversation, that the Duke, who was as much in love with Wit, as he was with his Kinswoman, was impatient till he was brought to sup with him, which was in two or three Nights. After Supper Mr. *Wycherley*, who was then in the Height of his Vigor both of Body and Mind, thought himself oblig'd to exert himself, and the Duke was charm'd to that degree, that he cry'd out in a Transport, *By G—————————my Cousin is in the right of it;* and from that very Moment made a Friend of a Man whom he believ'd his happy Rival.[89]

Dennis exaggerated this occasion of bringing Wycherley and Buckingham together, since they had been acquainted and almost certainly on close and respectful terms since Buckingham rescued Daniel from prison.[90]

It was but shortly after that Buckingham arranged for Wycherley to become Captain Lieutenant of the Company of Foot of which he was himself Captain.

The Duke of *Buckingham* gave him solid sensible Proofs of his Esteem and Affection. For as he was at the same time Master of the Horse to King *Charles*, and Colonel of a Regiment; as Master of the Horse he made him one of his Equeries, and as Colonel of a Regiment he made him Captain Lieutenant of his own Company, resigning to him at the same time his own Pay as Captain, and all other Advantages that could be justly made of the Company.[91]

This commission, dated 19 June 1672, was followed by another on 28 February 1674 by which Wycherley was commissioned Captain of the Company of Foot. One Ferdinando Hastings was his lieutenant.[92] After only one week, however, Wycherley resigned the Commission and on 6 March the company was put into the hands of one Captain Swift Nix.[93] Dalton, the military historian, stated that Wycherley knew as much of soldiering as he learned on stage,[94] but one is obliged to doubt that view. If he did indeed serve with the Earl of Arran's Regiment in Ireland ten years before, he was well enough acquainted with basics; his letter to Mulgrave in 1677 was full of camp talk which he would not pick up from a short term as Captain. It is more probable that he was quite competent in military matters.

During his tenure as captain, there were apparently some problems with money for the troops. An entry in *The Calendar of Treasury Books* for 14 October 1673 recorded: "the Lord Treasurer directs the payment of 480£ to Capt. Wicherley out of 950£ in arrear upon the balance of Capt. George Cock's accompt. Process is now ordered to be issued against Cock if he do not speedily pay in that sum." Cock's account books had been examined on the money he had borrowed.[95] J. M. Auffret adds information to this incident but seems to draw a biased conclusion:

> Wycherley's company was part of the great expeditionary force concentrated against the Dutch, and embarked in late July 1673 only to be a few days later disembarked at Yarmouth, in the Isle of Wight, where they quartered all winter, owing to a feud between Count Shomberg, general of the land-forces, and Prince Rupert, who was both Admiral and Generalissimo. After the peace, Wycherley's company was sent to Ireland via Winchester and Chester, when the poet chose to sell his commission, as the letter to Essex shows:
>
>> London, 7.4.1674; Here hath been on Sunday last some disturbance among 2 companies commanded by Lord Mount Alexander and Captain Swiftnan the famous robber—but it seems he hath bought Mr. Wycherley's company in the Duke of Buckingham his regiment. These 2 companies coming from Winchester in their way to Chester were much dissatisfied with their officers' ill paying of them, and some ill usage about their last expedition at sea, fell into disorders, thereupon took the colours, and 85 of the whole number came away to London to complain . . . Savage, predecessor to Lord Mount Alexander, and Wycherley have not been . . . just to the soldiers. (*Essex Papers*, I, 208)
>
> Captain Wycherley embezzled his soldiers' pay, and probably brutalized them at sea![96]

Wycherley's treatment of his troops may have been unfair—one recalls with curiosity Freeman's remarks:

> Yes, I was . . . fain to leave the Law, out of Conscience, and

[93]

> fall to making false Musters; rather chose to Cheat the King,
> than his Subjects; Plunder, rather than take Fees (III,i)

but if the company was in arrears 940£ when he took
captaincy, even with government aid he would have had
trouble paying the difference, and the company, Auffret
informs us, was wintering idly without plunder on the Isle of
Wight, 1673–74. Auffret's conclusion that Wycherley
embezzled his soldiers' pay is romantic but not plausible
from the situation as we know it. If, however, Wycherley was
bringing *The Country-Wife* to final form during this long
dull winter, one can understand how a line such as
"Souldiers [are] made constant and loyal by good pay" (I,i)
got into the script.

Dennis happened into Wycherley and a collection of
friends at a pub one evening in the years following:

> I remember that about that time I, who was come up from
> the University to see my Friends in Town, happen'd to be one
> night at the Fountain Tavern in the *Strand*, with the Late Dr.
> *Duke, David Loggen* the Painter, and Mr. *Wilson*, of whom
> *Otway* has made honourable Mention in *Tonson's* first
> Miscellany, and that after Supper we drank Mr. *Wycherley's*
> Health by the Name of Captain *Wycherley*.[97]

Wycherley seemed to fancy his title of Captain and signed
himself Captain Wycherley on occasion although he was no
doubt relieved to be quit of the troublesome company and
the dull winter on the Isle of Wight. What is striking in this
incident and others is the great celebrity of Wycherley and
his easy converse with men of the highest rank. The letter to
Mulgrave identified some of those with whom Wycherley
was on good terms, who seemed as ready to enjoy his good
company as he their approbation. His friendships included,
in addition to the wits of the Court noted previously, a wide
variety of courtiers, writers and thinkers, besides the
unnamed women, horsegrooms, publicans and so forth he
mentioned in his poems. He exchanged verse letters with the
playwright Thomas Shadwell, whom we often remember
only by Dryden's sharp lines:

Shadwell alone, of all my sons, is he
Who stands confirm'd in full stupidity.
The rest to some faint meaning make pretense,
But Shadwell never deviates into sense.

(*Mac Flecknoe*)

In the summer of 1671, Shadwell wrote to Wycherley with an apostrophe to

Ale, that makes Tinker might Witty
And makes him Droll out Merry Ditty;
Ale, that much strengthens Pedlar's Back
. . . .
In Rhyme I greet my Friend in Town

The letter is full of silly business and small beer which tells us nothing in fact; and Wycherley's reply is about equally revealing, except that he is more vulgar, and observes the politics of the town, which he usually does in his letters.

For poor Whore's Lace to garnish Pinner,
You may *Tom* (if you can) get in her . . .
For F—cking she believes no sin is . . .
But stay I think you News bespoke,
Of what is done, 'mong our Town Folk.

He got at last to the news, the death of the Duchess of York, Anne Hyde ("Duke's a widdower/ But Duke's not sorry I dare swear"),[98] the playhouses reopened and so forth.

John Walkenden was a long time friend of Wycherley in various capacities.[99] In addition Wycherley knew at this time William Byrd, author of *The London Diary*, 1717–21,[100] and he sat for his portrait in the late 1670's by the most noted contemporary painter, Sir Peter Lely, who lived in Covent Garden. The other chief portraitist of the day, Sir Godfrey Kneller, did Wycherley some years later; and another artist who lived in Covent Garden, on Bow Street, was the woodcarving genius Grinling Gibbons, whom Wycherley also knew. Today a sample of Gibbons' work rests appropriately in St. Paul's, Covent Garden. In later years Wycherley knew Joseph Addison and Sir Richard Steele, of whom he wrote to Pope in 1709, "The Coffee-houses . . . are now entertain'd, with a whimsical new Newspaper, from and to the Coffee-houses called the Tatler . . . written, by one Steel, who thinks himself sharp upon this Iron Age, since an Age of War."[101] Gildon related an episode concerning Wycherley's relationship with the burlesque poet Samuel Butler, but Gildon's account is probably in some error for Butler was in Buckingham's service in the early 1670's:

> The late Duke of Buckingham was a Man eminent for his Wit and expensive Temper, Mr. Butler the Author of Hudibras wanted such a patron to take Care of him and Mr. Wycherley had made it his Business for some Time, to engage the Duke to an Interview over a Bottle, where Mr. Butler might have the Opportunity of exerting his good Qualities, and pleasant Humour, which were extreamly entertaining when he lik'd his Company. At last he fix'd the Duke one Evening at the *Cock* in *Suffolk-Street.* They met, were very pleasant, and all things seem'd to answer Mr. Wycherley's design, but of a suddain they heard the squeaking of Fiddles, and the chattering of Whores in an adjacent Room; this was a Temptation the Duke cou'd not resist, he gives them the slip, and cou'd never be afterwards fix'd to renew so noble a Conversation.[102]

The neglect of Butler has become the stuff of myth, but this meeting probably around 1675 to 1677 is perhaps more accurate for its view of Wycherley's affection for Butler than for a true account of the Duke's treatment of the impoverished poet.

Wycherley was acquainted with the philosopher Thomas Hobbes, author of *The Leviathan,* and also, rather more surprisingly, with the great philosopher John Locke.[103] The esteem with which he was held by his contemporaries is conveyed in a narrative given, ostensibly, by "a French Gentleman in London to his Friend in Paris":

> Mr. Wycherley is universally allow'd the first place among the English Comick-Poets, who have writ since *Ben Johnson.* His *Plain-Dealer* (of which he took the first hint from *Molière's Misanthrope*) is the best Comedy that ever was composed in any Language. The only Fault that has been

found in it, is its being too full of *Wit*; a fault which few Authors can be guilty of. He has also writ three other Plays, the best of which is the *Country Wife*. Mr. Wycherley is one of the politest Gentlemen in England, and the most civil and affable to Strangers, especially to those of our Nation, for whom he has an esteem; he is a little shy and reserv'd in Conversation, but when a Man can be so happy as once to engage him in Discourse, he cannot but admire his profound Sense, Masculine Wit, vast Knowledge of Mankind, and noble but easy Expression. These qualities gain'd Mr. Wycherley the Love and Esteem of his Master King *Charles II* and of his Successor the like King of Britain, as the Comeliness and Gracefulness of his Person did the hearts of several Ladies of their Amorous Court.[104]

The mention here of "several ladies," echoed by Pack,

His Company was not only Courted by The Men, but His Person was well Received by the Ladies; and as K. *Charles* was extremely *Fond* of Him on account of his *Wit*, some of the Royal Mistresses, I have been credibly Informed, set *no less Value* upon *Those Parts* in Him, of which They were more *Proper Judges*[105]

convinces one that the Duchess of Cleveland was by no means the only mistress Wycherley had, in particular during the years of his dramatic success, for keeping was, after all, the mode rather than the exception. Pack related another anecdote relative to this inclination:

One Piece of *Gallantry*, among many others, that Mr. Wycherley was once telling me They had in *Those Days*. It was This: There was an House at the Bridgefoot, where *Persons* of *Better Condition* used to *Resort* . . . for Pleasure and Privacy. The *Liquor* that the Ladies and their Lovers used to Drink at *Those Meetings* was Canary; and, among *Other Compliments* the Gentlemen paid their Mistresses, This it seems was always *One*, to *take hold of the Bottom of their* Smocks, and *pouring* the Wine *through That Filtre*, feast their *Imaginations* with the Thought of *What* gave the *Zesto*, and so *Drink a Health* to the Toast.[106]

His personality was distinguished by civility: "he was indeed of an affable, easie, good Temper, and perfectly inoffensive to all Company."[107] George Granville, Lord Lansdowne to whom Pope dedicated his *Windsor Forest*, described him in a letter to a friend:

> My Partiality to him as a Friend might render what I say suspected, if his Merit was not so well and so publickly established as to set him above Flattery. . . .
>
> My Lord *Rochester*, in his Imitation of one of *Horace's* Epistles, thus mentions this Author:
>
> *Of all our modern Wits, none seems to me*
> *Once to have touch'd upon true Comedy,*
> *But hasty Shadwell, and slow Wycherley.*
> *Shadwell's unfinish'd Works do yet impart*
> *Great Proofs of Nature's Force, tho' none of Art;*
> *But Wycherley earns hard whate'er he gains,*
> *He wants no Judgment, and he spares no Pains.*[108]

After a short digression to question the epithet "slow" as Pope did later—Rochester "is quite wrong. He was far from being slow in general, and in particular, wrote the *Plain-Dealer* in three weeks"[109]—Lansdowne went on:

> Those who would form their Judgment only from Mr. Wycherley's Writings without any Personal Acquaintance with him, might be apt to conclude that such a Diversity of Images and Characters; such strict Enquiries into Nature; such close Observations on the several Humours, Manners, and Affections of all Ranks and Degrees of Men . . . could be no other than the Work of extraordinary Diligence, Labour, and Application; But, in Truth, we owe the Pleasure and Advantage of having been so well entertain'd and instructed by him, to his Facility of doing it. . . .
>
> To judge by the Sharpness and Spirit of his Satyr, you might be led into another Mistake, and imagine him an ill-natur'd Man: But what my Lord *Rochester* said of Lord *Dorset*, is as applicable to him—*The best good Man, with the worst-natur'd Muse.* . . . In his Temper he has all the Softness of the tenderest Disposition; gentle and inoffensive to every Man in his particular Character; he only attacks Vice as a publick Enemy. . . .
>
> In my Friend, every Syllable, every Thought is masculine: His Muse is not led forth as to a Review, but as to a Battle; not adorn'd for Parade, but Execution; he would be tried by the Sharpness of his Blade, not by the Finery; Like your Heroes of

[98]

Antiquity, he charges in Iron, and seems to despise all Ornament but intrinsick Merit.[110]

Lansdowne's character of Wycherley was repeated by others as essentially true and reliable; Pack paraphrased some of it, adding,

> He was certainly a Good-Natured Man: And I reckon it as One *Great Mark* of *such* a Disposition, that He was as *Impatient* to hear His Friend *Calumniated*, as some other People would be to find Themselves *Defamed*. I have more than once been a Witness to that *Honorable Tenderness* in His Temper,[111]

before suggesting the reader consult Lansdowne for further appreciation of Wycherley. Although Rochester's remark about Wycherley's slowness prompted ready disclaimers from Pope and others, he was probably chiding Wycherley's unproductive pace rather than the relative speed of his composition, for he included Wycherley among his favorite friends and critics of his verse:

> I loathe the rabble; 'tis enough for me
> If Sedley, Shadwell, Shepherd, Wycherley,
> Godolphin, Butler, Buckhurst, Buckingham,
> And some few more, whom I omit to name,
> Approve my sense: I count their censure fame.[112]

Those who try to make a Wycherley–Manly correlation are by these accounts confounded, even though Wycherley liked to call himself Manly and Plain-dealer, as he often did in letters; Lansdowne is right in his appraisal of his character. Dryden, the final literary arbiter of the day, stated with carefully weighted critical language concerning comedy and satire,

> Many of our present writers are eminent in both these kinds; and particularly the author of the *Plain Dealer*, whom I am proud to call my friend, has obliged all honest and virtuous men by one of the most bold, most general, and most useful satires which has ever been presented on the English theatre.[113]

John Dennis, a critic of perspicacity occasionally equal to

Dryden's, defended *The Plain-Dealer* in a brilliant letter to William Congreve, whose regard for and debt to Wycherley was far greater than he ever stated; Dennis first surveyed the acclaim by great men, Buckingham, Mulgrave, Dryden, Rochester, Lansdowne and Matthew Prior, and then critically examined Wycherley's achievement in comic portrayal:

> First then, Mr. *Wycherley's* Coxcombs are really Coxcombs. And here we must observe that Fool and Wit are so far from being Terms that are incompatible or contradictory, that they are not so much as Terms of Opposition, there being several Persons who are call'd Wits, and who by the Vigour and Fire of their Constitutions are enabled sometimes to say what they call smart and witty things, who have not one grain of Judgment or Discernment to distinguish Right from Wrong, or Truth from Falshood; and that therefore the 523d Reflection of *Rochefoucault* is certainly very Just: *On est quelquefois un sot avec de l'Esprit, mais on ne l'est jamais avec du Jugement.* 'It may happen (says he) that a Man may be a Fool who has Wit, but he never can be so who has Judgment.' The Vanity of those whom they call Wits has made them pretend that there is a full Opposition between Wit and Fool, but the only true and full Opposition is between him that is a Fool, and him who is Wise. . . .Your witty Fools are very just Subjects of Comedy, because they are more troublesome and shocking in Conversation to Men of Sense, than any other sort of Fools whatsoever. Such a Fool with all his smart Repartees, as Mr. *Dryden* calls them, his snip snap, his hit for hit, and dash for dash, is but too often impertinent, impudent, insolent, opinionated, noisie, fantastical, abusive, brutal, perfidious; which shews the Solidity of that Reflection of *Rochefoucault* which is the 518*th*. *Il n'y a point des Sots si Incommodes que ceux qui ont de l'Esprit.* "There are no Fools so troublesome as the Fools who have Wit."

> Now such are Mr. *Wycherley's* Fools in the Comedy of the *Plain-dealer.* My Lord *Plausible*, Major *Oldfox*, the Widow *Blackacre*, and *Jerry*, have each of them several of these Qualities, and *Novel* has them all. He is impertinent, impudent, insolent, conceited, noisie, fantastick, abusive, brutal, perfidious. He says nothing but what a brisk Coxcomb may very well be suppos'd to say who will venture

at all, and who having a good Memory keeps the top Company in a Town over-run with Wit, as *London* was at the Time of the writing of that Comedy. What is said by him and the rest in the several Scenes in which they appear, is either trifling and superficial, or utterly and ridiculously false, or appears to be a Repetition of what the Men of Sense in the Play have said before them; whereas what *Manly, Freeman* and *Eliza* say is always sensible, and is therefore always true. . . . The Coxcombs in the *Plain-dealer* are not only fairly and justly, but vastly distinguish'd from those whom Mr. *Wycherley* design'd for sensible Characters. For *Manly, Freeman* and *Eliza* every where make it appear, that with their Wit they have Judgment, and consequently make great and important Observations.[114]

Dennis elsewhere made a too little observed judgment about Wycherley's plays: ". . . the only Man alive who has made Comedy instructive in its Fable; almost all the rest, being contented to instruct by their Characters."[115] By Fable, Dennis meant, in his neo-Aristotelian critical terminology, "plot," which he would consider central. Wycherley's plots are excellently made; they move easily and with significant progress so that there are very few occasions, even in the first plays, where characters have set pieces of talk which have no relation to the action. Dennis is one of the few to acknowledge this particular strength of the plays (we might recall that Samuel Johnson praised Shakespeare primarily for the progress of his fable), but it is an element commonly ignored in modern criticism in spite of its importance.

Wycherley wrote poems at a steady rate, mostly for occasions such as the *"Treaty of* Nimeguen, *written there,"*[116] our only evidence that he was in Holland; or *"To Sir* George Etheridge, *on his shewing his Verses imperfect,"* a rather presumptuous piece of admonition—"Be wise, and ne'er to publick View produce/Thy undrest Mistress, or unfinisht Muse";[117] or a more interesting one, "An Epistle to Mr. Dryden, *occasion'd by his desiring the Author to joyn with him in Writing a Comedy,"* written probably before 1677 when Dryden shifted to the use of blank verse in drama:

Rhimes, which with others, Reason's Fetters are, . . .
With you they guide him, and improve his Course,
In Smoothness, Measure, Majesty and Force.

His praise of Dryden is high and sustained, but not, for the
mode, excessive or false; the poem is one of Wycherley's
better and more evenly regulated compositions:

Your clear, unerring, universal Sense
Cheers like the Sun with gen'ral Influence:
New Wonders still profusely does display,
And drives the Darkness of the Mind away.
But your enlight'ning, comprehensive Mind
Cannot be to a single Sphere confin'd. . . .[118]

When the Duke of Buckingham made his speech in the
House of Lords on 15 February 1677 in defiance of the King's
power to prorogue Parliament, and the Court party in
response sent him, with the incendiary Shaftesbury, whom
Dryden tagged "false Achitophel . . . bold, and turbulent of
wit," with two others to the Tower, Wycherley wrote to his
long-time friend and benefactor: *"To the* Duke *of* B . . . ,
Imprison'd in the Tower *by a* Court-Faction.[119] The poem
has more value biographically than poetically; as a poem it
struggles tiresomely with the paradoxes of freedom and
imprisonment, and repeats "your Thought's free, tho' your
Body be confin'd," without variation or development. As an
historical document the poems show Wycherley's political
naivete, for it assuredly was impolitic to counter the King
with whom he had been so long on good terms and whose
patronage he needed to court. But this limitation seemed
always to afflict him even in familial relationships with his
father. He did hasty heart-directed things without thought of
consequence—without thought apparently that he wrote
poems on both sides of the succession question—the kind of
generosity of spirit and freedom from calculation we have
seen celebrated in comic heroes.[120] From one point of view it
is folly, from another the wisdom of generosity. Wycherley's
was an ironist's view of politics, pictured through a keen
sense of human fallibility. Another poem to Buckingham,
"a Man of a great Mind, reduc'd to a little Fortune,"

probably written in 1683 when the Duke was heavily in debt
and short on income, began with a similar kind of paradox:

> I your bad Fortune now congratulate,
> And think you in Misfortunes fortunate;
> Who can the Malice of your Fate prevent,
> And, less in Wealth and Pow'r, boast more Content.[121]

Wycherley's loyalty to Buckingham is as characteristic of
him as is his disregard of the prudential realities of politics.

In 1680 he composed a poem "To the Duke" that is to
James, Duke of York, when he was sent from the country at
his brother the King's insistence as Parliament tried to
exclude the Catholic Duke from succession by voting, on 27
April 1679, that he encouraged papists and opposed the King
and Protestants. The poem to the Duke "Written in his
Absence" is a long one, more contemporary in reference
than is usual with Wycherley. Particularly interesting is the
image of the English people as the Old Testament "Jewish
race" which parallels its appearance in Dryden's brilliant
satire of 1681, *Absalom and Achitophel*, on the attempts of
Shaftesbury to overthrow Charles with his son, the
illegitimate Duke of Monmouth, in order to prevent
Catholic James' succession. Wycherley worked out the poem
with effectively meaningful images carefully harmonized.
James is depicted as God-like in origin, virtue and office; the
occasional extravagances—"Had you not own'd a King for
Syre, you shou'd/ By Mortal *Heroes*, have been own'd a
God"—are part of the myth of order the poem develops, for
the King is by analogy God over his nation. Thus when he
suffers from the "more *Jewish* race" and is beset by "long-
Armed Monsters" who like the insurgents in heaven pull
down mountains, the threat to government and to order
itself is clearly revealed:

> Vainly seek to bring their *God's* down
> Heap'd on their own heads own Destruction.
> May all rebellious rabbles e'en so thrive. . . .[122]

The irony of this overthrow is that James, "The Noble
Driving Admiral," who "clear'd the Seas and threat'ning

Skye," is renowned for his seamanship and now holds "the tossing Government, in storms so bold." The disorders of war, shipwreck and storm are calmed by James. Wycherley builds around these images, and the allusions from the Old Testament and battle of the gods, another figure of the strong growth of a plant whose "lofty stock was shelter 'gainst all wind." The monarch-tree figure was, as Earl Miner reminds us, a richly popular one in seventeenth century writing; Sprat, for instance, portrayed the "British Oak" presiding in the "Assembly of Forest Trees" like the King in his Country,[123] and Pope, in *Windsor Forest*, fully elaborated this parallel of tree-monarch, oak-ship. And of course the oak recalled to everyone the Bascobel oak in which Charles hid himself after Cromwell had defeated his forces at Worcester in September 1650 until he could safely escape to the coast and to France; and which became a symbol of Charles, of the Stuarts, of monarchy itself, appearing years later as a secret sign of the Jacobite movement to restore the long past Stuart line. The imagery of stormy seas vs. stable land or wreck-disorder vs. safety-kingly order is developed while the light-sun-king vs. dark-evil-anarchy image supports it; and there are other images he integrates into the poem. This complexity and controlled suggestiveness show Wycherley's best poetic effort thus far and in certain ways his best overall. When he had a subject that truly moved him and that had some substance, he could develop a good poem, but many of his topics are so slight they invite redundancy. About halfway through, however, even this poem began to stray from a constant theme and took on the character of patchwork, returning at times to "curst be those Jewes by whom y'are bannished hence," and "*Whigg!* That Burlesque little paultry sound." Then musing on the poet's relation to a King,

> A Prince distrest most Honour so can give,
> In being Poets Theam, you make him live. . . .
> Who your great Name Enroles, Enroles his name.

What began as a unified poem changed into something

other, the more familiar paradox- and conceit-ridden verse which is not particularly interesting. In this poem to James are the elements which were to become in Dryden's hands in late 1681 the great satire *Absalom and Achitophel.* If Wycherley wrote this poem in 1679–80 when James was sent from the country, and not afterwards as a retrospective shortly before its publication in 1683, it would then seem plausible that Dryden had seen this poem and was moved by it before *Absalom* was composed, for Dryden was no doubt acquainted with Wycherley as early as 1677 when Wycherley mentioned him in the Mulgrave letter; by 1687 Dryden wrote to George Etherege of Wycherley's illness in words suggestive of an enduring friendship: "In short without Apoplexy, Wycherley's long sickness, I forget everything to enjoy nothing that is my self."[124]

A companion poem to "To the Duke" draws further attention to Dryden's relationship to Wycherley's poetry. The epistle "To the King" was published in 1683, but it too seems to have been written earlier, at least in part, for the poet refers several times to his exclusion from court about 1679:

> I am the only Spaniel of the Crown,
> Kick'd out, and yet must still be hangin on,
> The kinder too, for being but ill us'd,
> To baffled me, why is Court-grace refus'd? . . .
> None wretched are, who can come where you are,
> Wretch is damn'd here, who must that joy forbear.[125]

Other parts of the poem suggest the Shaftesbury–Monmouth insurrection against the King and other rebellious threats:

> When a King's Murder'd, one Man do's not die,
> Whole Nations, suffer Death in Monarchy,
> And lose their dearest Life old Liberty. . .
> To save those lives who would your power depose;
> Excess of Mercy, is self Cruelty.

Wycherley used the image of base metal stamped with the King's image, a pun on mettle-metal and an allusion to man created in God's image, "when a Prince puts the Royal stamp on Brass, /Raising the Mettles price," just as Dryden used the same image in his poem *The Medal* (1682) against Shaftesbury. Is Wycherley preceding or following Dryden? Parts of both poems treat events of 1679–80; both poems are based on images not found in Wycherley's earlier poems and which are fully exploited in Dryden's two major satiric poems of 1681 and 1682. Possibly he added to the poems after Dryden, or more probably took suggestions from discussions with Dryden on his works. In any case, the poems to the King and Duke are interesting works, comparable to his best satires written later and published in 1704.

For some reason, perhaps the illness which afflicted him in 1679, perhaps a decline in ability with age, whatever it may be, Wycherley seemed unable to conceive of a poem as a single whole process, which is by no means the case with his plays. There are sections of this poem to the King and of others which are very well done, just as some of his lyrics, both fugitive and the ones in the plays, are fine, rather Elizabethan songs; for he seemed to be Elizabethan and metaphysical in his verse, Augustan in his satire and drama. One wonders whether he could not bring his judgment to bear on the issue of poetic form or whether he did not conceive it as a problem. No doubt because the plays came quite easily to him, he had never thought through the question of form in its application to verse. For unlike Dryden and Rochester, he did not think in his poems. He put thoughts in them, thoughts picked up from playwrighting (again, the plays reflect great seriousness of thought), from reading, or from popular tracts or conversation, but there is usually no process of mental activity, except in the poem "To The Duke" and in some of the later poems on his marriage. It is, however, tedious to complain of Wycherley's poorly organized and executed verse—as Pope told him in later years, he indeed broke all the rules of couplet verse. But it may be well to note that while not all Wycherley's contemporaries were impressed with his verse, the defence by Lansdowne bears consideration, for many of his contemporaries were very astute judges and have much to teach us in the ways of understanding Wycherley's works.

> There are who object to his Versification: But a Diamond is not less a Diamond for not being polish'd. Versification is in Poetry, what Colouring is in Painting, a beautiful Orna-ment: But if the Proportions are Just, the Posture true, the Figure bold, and the Resemblance according to Nature, tho' the Colours should happen to be rough, or carelessly laid on, yet may the Piece be of inestimable Value.[126]

As we shall see, John Locke was very impressed with his poetry. And to be fair to the author, these poems to Buckingham and to the Duke of York were not seditious in content; they are rather salutations to the subject and detached commentaries on bearing life's burdens. He recognized his limitations, writing in Maxim XXXII, "The best Wits make the worst Men of Business."[127] Both in the poems to Buckingham and to the Duke of York, the emphasis is consolatory, that serenity can be in one's mind when it is not in externals. "The Brave and Just, life to himself does give." "Virtue is still the best Nobility." "He is not great who gives to others Law,/ But he whose Patience can his Passions awe." He was ready enough to expatiate to others on the ancient and ever-contemporary theme of the paradise within, but he was soon to be pressed to search deeply into himself for shreds of that paradise as the external world closed success out and introduced trials of health, finances, and love.

Chapter III
Footnotes

1. Robert D. Hume, *The Development of English Drama in the Late Seventeenth Century* (Oxford, 1976), pp. 20ff.

2. *The London Stage, 1660–1800, Part I, 1660–1700*, ed. William Van Lennep, with introduction by Emmet L. Avery and Arthur H. Scouten (Carbondale, Ill., 1965), pp. 49, 119.

3. *Spence, Anecdotes*, 78. See Summers, I, 16–17. The inversion of the last two plays also happened earlier than Pope's statement. From the

Bodleian Library, Tanner MSS. 41, f. 190, printed here by permission of the Bodleian Library, Oxford, Ralph Sheldon wrote, 19 December 1683, to answer a request of Anthony a Wood,

> I have here sent you the names of the Plays set out by William Wicherley,
>
> viz.
> 1. Love in a Wood, or St. James's Parke
> 2. The Gentleman Dancing-Master
> 3. The Plaindealour—
> 4. The Country Wife

Wood MSS, F 45, f. 301, printed here by permission of the Bodleian Library; in reply to Sheldon, 20 December, Wood wrote, among other things here omitted,

> . . . I thank you for Mr. Wycherley's catalogue—but if your occasions serve you to write me againe, I should be pleased to know from you when each of those plays were printed, and whose—for that is the method that I follow in the works of all writers in my *Bibliotheca Scriptorum Oxon.* . . .

Wood MSS F 44, f. 199, f. 200, printed here by permission of the Bodleian Library; Sheldon took time on Christmas day, at his home in Weston, to reply in gold ink no less:

> I have here sent you the dates of Mr. Wicherley's playes according to as they are in my books. I wish you a prosperous new yeare. . . .

and on reverse side:

> For Mr. Anthony a Wood Lodging over against the great gate of Merton Colledge Oxon. At Oxford
> 1. Love in a Wood, or St. James's Parke.
>   as it is acted at the Theater Royall by his Maties servants/Written by Mr. Wicherley/London Printed by J. M. for H. Hemingham at the blew Anchor in the lower walk at the Exchange, 1672.
> 2. The Gentleman Dancing Master [and so forth] . . . 1673
> 3. The Plaindealer / A Comedie . . . London Printed for R. Bentley and M. Magnus in Russell-streete in Covent-garden neere the Piazzas, 1677.
> 4. The Country Wife / A Comedy . . . London Printed for T. Dring and sold by R. Bentley and S. Magnes in Russell-street in Covent Garden, 1683.

Sheldon was a long-time correspondent of Wood (see James Sutherland, *English Literature of the Late Seventeenth Century*, p. 254n.), mentioned in Anthony a Wood's *Athenae Oxonienses* as "that most generous and well bred Gentleman Ralph Sheldon of Bealy in Worcestershire, commonly called Great Sheldon." The above inversion of the latter two plays is the apparent source of a Wood's printing Wycherley's plays in that order.

4. W. R. Chadwick, *The Four Plays of William Wycherley* (The Hague, 1975), pp. 193–95, Appendix discussion of the problem. The maturity of

The Plain-Dealer convinces me that was his last drama; it develops perfectly out of *The Country-Wife* and resonates disturbances of profound kinds.

5. *The Complete Plays of William Wycherley*, ed. Gerald Weales (New York, 1966), pp. 2–3. One should refer to editor's notes for much information not mentioned in this biography. All references to plays of Wycherley will be identified in the text by Act and Scene only; there is no complete edition of the plays with line numbers.

6. *The London Stage*, pp. 181, 360, 426.

7. For cast lists, see Weales, pp. 9, 257, 387.

8. John Loftis, *The Spanish Plays of Neoclassical England* (New Haven, 1973), p. 123. See pp. 121 ff. for complete discussion of relationship.

9. *Ibid.*, pp. 122–23.

10. I am taking exception to the excellent arguments of Cynthia Matlack, "Parody and Burlesque of Heroic Ideals in Wycherley's Comedies: A Critical Reinterpretation of Contemporary Evidence," *PLL*, VIII (Summer, 1972), 273–86. Her view of parody of the heroic is larger than mine, but I here focus on parody of an heroic character, not only lines of heroic flavor.

11. Katherine M. Rogers, *William Wycherley* (New York, 1972), p. 37, believes Wycherley meant Christina to be seriously sentimental: "Wycherley had not yet realized that sentimental heroics did not belong in the Restoration comedy of manners," a view I do not accept at all; and see prior note. For a good, close analysis of the play, see Eric S. Rump, "Theme and Structure in Wycherley's *Love in a Wood*," *English Studies*, 54 (1973), 326–33.

12. Weales, p. 118, n. 18, for discussion of relation of this remark, and the play, to Fletcher's *The Faithful Shepherdess*; also Loftis, p. 124n.

13. Loftis, pp. 125 ff.

14. C. J. Rawson, *Henry Fielding And the Augustan Ideal Under Stress* (London, 1973), p. 28. His first chapter, "Gentlemen and Dancing-Masters" is singularly interesting relative to this play, given its continued talk of dance, though Rawson does not primarily attend to this play.

15. *Roscius Anglicanus*, Augustan Reprint Society, #134, (Los Angeles, 1969), p. 32; also *London Stage*, p. 192.

16. Bonamy Dobrée, *Restoration Comedy, 1660–1720* (Oxford, 1924), p. 85; P. F. Vernon, *William Wycherley* (London, 1965), pp. 22–24; Rogers, p. 50, calls it insipid and tedious, yet, grudgingly, hilarious; Rose Zimbardo, *Wycherley's Drama* (New Haven, 1965), p. 48, "crude." Anne Righter, "William Wycherley," *Restoration Dramatists*, ed., Earl Miner (Englewood Cliffs, N. J., 1966), pp. 107–10, is much more responsive to the play, as is John S. Bowman, "Dance, Chant, and Mask in the Plays of Wycherley," *Drama Survey*, III (1963), 181–205. The careful analysis by W. R. Chadwick, *The Four Plays of William Wycherley*, pp. 47–82, is very helpful in grasping the plotting achievement of the play. Note especially Chadwick's speculations on the roles of the players Nokes and Angel, pp. 49–51.

17. George Speaight, *The History of English Puppet Theatre* (New

York, 1955), pp. 73 ff. The following information on puppets and quotations from Pepys are from this source. See also *The London Stage*, I, cxxxvii.

18. John Cotgrave, *Wit's Interpreter* (London, 1655), p. 70.

19. *Ibid.*, p. 305.

20. The following discussion of wit is summarized from my article, "Wycherley's *The Plain-Dealer* and the Limits of Wit," *English Miscellany*, 22 (1971), 47–92, which treats all four plays from the point of view of which character, in what context, uses metaphoric language, and the relation of this usage to his relative success in each play.

21. Summers, III, 13.

22. Summers, III. 7. See "Wycherley's *The Plain-Dealer* and the Limits of Wit," p. 53 for further references to similar statements.

23. Sherburn, I, 40.

24. Ben Ross Schneider, Jr., *The Ethos of Restoration Comedy* (University of Illinois Press, Urbana, Ill., 1971), p. 72, p. 86. Note his quotation from Wycherley, p. 87.

25. Sir George Mackenzie, *Moral Gallantry* (London, 1668), pp. 120–23.

26. Summers, IV, 116, Maxim LXVI.

27. Schneider, Chapter One, e.g. p. 4n., et passim.

28. Watson, I, 199.

29. Zimbardo, p. 1.

30. Virginia Ogden Birdsall, *Wild Civility: The English Comic Spirit on the Restoration Stage* (Bloomington, Ind., 1970), p. 112: "It is no doubt true, of course, that Christina represents to Wycherley some kind of ideal." With such statements of what Wycherley believed I have great reservation, since they are unprovable; nor do I accept Birdsall's contention, "The difficulty is that Wycherley never comes to grips in this play with the contradictory views" romantic idealism versus comic realism, p. 111, since it assumes an ideality. Zimbardo's view is from the opposite pole: "There are no heroes, no heroines . . . only knaves and gulls," p. 17, and is equally uncongenial to degree.

31. The Summer 1973 production at Stratford, Conn., proved its continued vitality, surprising the New York critics with its comic energy. Warren Beatty pointed to *The Country-Wife* as the source of his movie *Shampoo*.

32. *The London Stage*, pp. 227, 244, 322, 368, 440. Emmett L. Avery, "The Reputation of Wycherley's Comedies as Stage Plays in the Eighteenth Century," *Research Studies of the State College of Washington*, 12 (1944), 131–54.

33. Birdsall, p. 107: "Ideally, Wycherley felt, we all ought to be Margery Pinchwifes in character." And "Both Margery and Horner . . . belong in a 'right-way' category," p. 147. Note the extreme forcing of Hobbes into the play in Charles A. Hallett, "The Hobbesian Substructure of *The Country-Wife*," *PLL*, 9 (1973), 380–95.

34. Anne Righter, p. 79: "Wycherley cannot really bring himself to believe in them." After Norman Holland, *The First Modern Comedies* (Cambridge, Mass., 1959), Ch. 8, the best single essay is David M. Vieth,

"Wycherley's *The Country Wife*: An Anatomy of Masculinity," *PLL*, II (1966), 335–50. My discussion of "sign" below owes its origins to this essay, but mine develops in a different direction.

35. Vieth, ed., *The Complete Poems of John Wilmot, Earl of Rochester* (New Haven, 1968), p. 117.

36. See the very astute observations of Wallace Jackson, "*The Country Wife*: The Premises of Love and Lust," *SAQ*, 72 (1973), 540–46: "Wit, therefore, in *The Country Wife*, is the vehicle of desire. . . . By its nature, then, wit is hostile to marriage, and marriage and wit each postulate a concept of the relation between man and woman antithetical to the other." Harcourt must "forsake his role as true wit and accept as the *real* terms for his relation to Alithea a confidence in her virtue. . . . Such a conclusion restores Horner to the center of the play, not as moralist or as the rebuked and defeated immoralist, but as the chief actor in a game of strategies and usages, as the exponent of wit, that morally neutral thing, to which both sexes fit."

37. Holland, p. 77. See also Aubrey L. Williams, "The 'Fall' of China and *The Rape of the Lock*," *PQ*, XLI (1962), 412–25, for glass or china symbolism.

38. W. R. Chadwick points out the same change of language already present in *Love in a Wood* (p. 45): "what might be called the epic *double entendre* in which some key word is repeated so insistently that it becomes invested with an extra-literal significance. . . . Wycherley perfected the device in *The Country-Wife* with 'china.' "

39. Hooker, II, 277.

40. Rogers, p. 153, n. 32.

41. Inderwick, lxxii, on November 1. Cf. Ch. I, n. 58.

42. *The London Stage*, pp. 253, 295, 324, 497, 263, 290, 314, 316, 344, 387, 427, 514, 407, *Lacedemonian Mercury*.

43. See the important article by A. M. Friedson both for its review of critical views of Manly and its analysis of the relationship of Alceste and Manly: "Wycherley and Molière: Satirical Point of View in *The Plain Dealer*," *MP*, 64 (Feb. 1967), 189–97. A note on the source of the play is reported by Arthur Friedman, "Wycherley and 'Silvia Molliere's Memoires,' " *MP*, 75 (Nov., 1977), 186–90; Friedman includes an emendation in *Love in a Wood*.

44. "*The Man of Mode* & *The Plain Dealer*: Common Origin & Parallels," *Etudes Anglaises*, 3 (July, 1966), 209–22.

45. Weales, p. 518, notes and translation of text.

46. See Friedson for survey of this issue.

47. "Wycherley's *The Plain-Dealer* and the Limits of Wit," p. 89.

48. Friedson, p. 191, n. 10.

49. Schneider, p. 22, p. 24, pp. 104–05.

50. *Plain Dealing is a Jewel, and Honesty the Best Policy* (London, 1682): exposing "a design . . . for Introducing Arbitrary Power, Setting up Popery, Invading Liberty and Property, and extirpating The Protestant Religion Establisht by Law."

51. *Plain Dealing; or, a Full and Particular Examination* . . . (London, 1675), by A. M., a "countrey Gentleman." This work is especially

interesting for its conscious discussion of double- and plain-dealing: "we may justly suspect a double mind and some double dealings in the Author" of *Human Reason* (p. 14). He opposes the "typical and Anagogical sense of those words of the Apostles, when they are so plain and perspicuous in the litteral" (p. 66). "I am almost quite tir'd with his Similitudes. . . . For nothing can be prov'd by a Similitude; they are at best good Explications but no Demonstrations" (pp. 68–69). "I have written nothing but what became an honest Plain-dealing countrey Gentleman" (p. 164). See also *Plain Dealing, or a Friendly Reproof*, (London, 1719), *Plain Dealing, or a second Dialogue between Humphrey and Roger* (London, 1681).

52. "Tables Turned: *The Plain Dealer*," *Essays in Criticism* 17 (1967), 310. The entire essay is an important and understanding exploration of the play.

53. *The Works of Thomas Adams; being the sum of his Sermons, Meditations, and other Divine and Moral Discourses*, 3 Vols. (Edinburgh, 1861–62), I, 19–30.

54. *Ibid.*, p. 19.

55. *Ibid.*, p. 25.

56. *Ibid.*, p. 28.

57. As quoted in Holland, p. 50.

58. *The Gentleman's Companion: or, a Character of True Nobility, and Gentility* (London, 1672), p. 63.

59. *Spence, Anecdotes*, #87.

60. *The Courtiers Manual Oracle, or, The Art of Prudence. Written Originally in Spanish by Balthasar Gracian. And now done into English* (London, 1685), pp. 2–3.

61. *Ibid.*, pp. 9, 10, 92–93, 188.

62. Monroe Z. Hafter, *Gracian and Perfection: Spanish Moralists of the Seventeenth Century* (Cambridge, Mass., 1966), p. 124.

63. *Ibid.*, p. 127.

64. Gracian, p. 117, Maxim CXXVII; and see Hafter, pp. 130 ff. for analysis of "sympathy" and its relation to heroic character.

65. Virgil B. Heltzel, ed., *Richard Earl of Carbery's Advice to His Son* (Cambridge, Mass., 1937), p. 91.

66. *Ibid.*, p. 100.

67. *The Gentile Sinner; or, England's Brave Gentleman: Character'd In a Letter to a Friend.* . . . (Oxford, 1664), pp. 104–05. Ellis was a fellow of Queens College, Oxford.

68. Hafter, p. 153.

69. Gracian, pp. 113–14, Maxim CXXIII.

70. Summers, IV, 409, Maxim I: "Our Natural Imperfections are never more our Shame, than when by Art we endeavour to hide them. . . ."

71. Hafter, p. 156. As part of the discussion on solitude vs. society, the following is especially relevant to Manly: "If someone is wholly self-sufficient . . . then he must be divine; if he is unable to live with others, then he must be a beast. Gracian . . . makes specific reference to Aristotle's formula, 'To live alone, one must have either much of God or

the whole of beast,' but he subsumes it under the theme of Maxim 133: *Rather mad with all than sane alone.* . . . [but he] would modify it to emphasize his lesson that living in reasonable harmony with the community is sanity, whereas he who persists in remaining out of step is a madman" (pp. 157–58). Assuredly the possibilities of "being with God" are remote in Wycherley's world, so the solitude Manly originally seeks is anti-social and anti-human, thus a mad and impossible solution.

72. *The New Academy of Compliments* . . . , compiled by L. B., Sir C. S., Sir W. D. and others . . . (London, 1671), p. 18.

73. *The Academy of Eloquence,* 2nd ed. (London, 1656), p. 55. In the Epistle Dedicatory he characterizes a man with ability but without the means to express it as "a Cabinet keeping a rich Jewel."

74. Ramesey, p. 96.

75. Carbery, p. 85: Memory "wilbe alwayes ready to give you satisfaction, . . . if what she was intrusted with was layd up orderly, and putt as it were in the severall Boxes of a Cabbinett."

76. Holland, p. 98: "Manly is a dupe, not a hero." See Chadwick, pp. 132–80, for interesting analysis of the emergence of Manly through the plot, but an uncertain resolution of the position of Manly and others at the end.

77. *The refin'd Courtier; or, a correction of several indecencies crept into civil conversation,* trans. Nathaniel Walker (London, 1663), p. 135. He is much in favor of plain speech and opposed to "the drugs and refuse of wit; and flat and insipid quibbles and clenches . . . ," p. 200.

78. Charles Gildon, *Memoirs of the Life of William Wycherley, Esq.;* . . . (London, 1718), p. 20.

79. Sherburn, I, 82–83.

80. The discussion by C. J. Rawson, *Gulliver and The Gentle Reader* (London, 1973), pp. 100 ff. of the satiric "Catalogues" of Swift can provide important insight into Wycherley's often misread lists and catalogues in *The Plain-Dealer.*

81. Connely, p. 37, p. 59.

82. Robert J. Allen, "Two Wycherley Letters," *TLS* (18 April 1935), with historical background to the persons named, especially Mulgrave.

83. Summers, IV, 222.

84. Hooker, II, 409–10. William Ramesey had written in *The Gentleman's Companion,* p. 5: "Nay the best Wits, greatest Scholars, valiantest Captains, and most Heroick Spirits to be found in all our Annals, have been born *out of wedlock,*" possibly a source for Wycherley's song.

85. John Harold Wilson, *The Courts' Wits of the Restoration* (Princeton, N.J., 1948), p. 120.

86. John Harold Wilson, *Court Satires of the Restoration* (Columbus, Ohio, 1976), p. 22.

87. *Ibid,* p. 21.

88. *Ibid.,* p. 98.

89. Hooker, II, 410.

90. See also Eleanore Boswell, "Miscellaneous Notes," *MLR*, 26 (1931),

345, for Wycherley's connection with Buckingham in 1672. The letter to Mulgrave in 1677 also points to their friendship.

91. Hooker, II, 410.

92. Charles Dalton, ed., *English Army Lists and Commission Register, 1661–1714*, Vol. I, 1661–85 (London, 1792), 120, 170.

93. *Calendar of State Papers*, Vol. 1673–75, ed. Blackburne Daniel (London, 1904), p. 184, 28 Feb. 1674; and p. 191, 6 March 1674.

94. Dalton, p. xx.

95. *Calendar of Treasury Books*, IV, 1672–75, 201. The prior notation explains some of Cock's problem: "Mr. [Capt. George] Cock called in. The Lord Treasurer peruses his accounts and directs the Auditor to call for his cash books to see when he borrowed the money and [thereupon] by a certificate from the Exchequer of the [actual] payment [to Cock] of the orders [drawn in his name] to compute the interest [which is to be accounted only from the time he borrowed the said moneys of the bankers and others to the time when he received payments at the Exchequer or elsewhere on his said orders]: and to prepare a state of the accounts." Brackets are *sic*.

96. J. M. Auffret, p. 212. "Swiftnam" is probably Swift Nix, above.

97. Hooker, II, 410–11.

98. Summers, II, 245–47.

99. Boswell, p. 345. The horoscope of Walkenden is in the Bodleian, Ash. MS 183, f. 225, f. 375. See C5, 454/72 for depositions taken by Walkenden for Wycherley, discussed below.

100. William Byrd, *The London Diary (1717–1721) And Other Writings*, eds. Louis B. Wright and Marion Tinling (New York, 1958), p. 9: "William Wycherley . . . was also a friend of Byrd's. With literary friends such as these it is not surprising that Byrd should have developed a taste for the theater"; these others included Congreve and Nicholas Rowe.

101. Sherburn, I, 59.

102. Gildon, p. 9.

103. See letter from Locke quoted below, Chapter IV, n. 4.

104. Abel Boyer, *Letters of Wit, Politicks, and Morality* . . . (London, 1701), Letter III of "Selection of Original Letters on Divers Subjects by several Hands," p. 217.

105. Pack, p. 184.

106. *Ibid.*, p. 185.

107. Gildon, p. 20.

108. "A Letter with A Character of Mr. Wycherley," *The Genuine Works in Verse and Prose of the Right Honorable George Granville, Lord Lansdowne* (London, 1732), pp. 432–33. See a different version in "A Character of Mr. Wycherley and his Writings," in [Gildon] *Memoirs of the Life of William Wycherley Esq.; With a Character of his Writings* (London, 1718), pp. 23–26. See Vieth, ed., *The Complete Poems of John Wilmot, Earl of Rochester*, pp. 120–26, for complete text of poem.

109. *Spence, Anecdotes*, #86.

110. Lansdowne, "A Letter . . . ," pp. 433–36.

111. Pack, p. 186.

112. Vieth, ed., *The Complete Poems of John Wilmot, Earl of Rochester*, p. 126. Shepherd is Sir Fleetwood Shepherd; Godolphin is Sidney Godolphin, Lord Chamberlain to the Queen under James, and first commissioner of the Treasury in 1700 under William III; Buckhurst is Charles Sackville, Earl of Dorset and Lord Buckhurst. Dryden also takes exception to Rochester's "slow" remark in "Preface to *All For Love*," Watson, I, 230.

113. Watson, I, 199.

114. Hooker, II, 232–34.

115. *Ibid.*, I, 157, in a passage on the satire in *The Plain-Dealer*: ". . . that excellent Play, which is a most instructive, and a most noble Satire upon the Hypocrisy and Villainy of Mankind."

116. Summers, IV, 227.

117. *Ibid.*

118. *Ibid.*, pp. 155–60. The "clear, unerring, universal Sense," has the ring of Pope's "Unerring Nature . . ./ One clear, unchang'd and Universal Light," *Essay on Criticism*, 11. 70–71; as "Cannot be to a single Sphere confin'd," recalls images in Dryden's "To the pious Memory of . . . Anne Killigrew."

119. *Ibid.*, pp. 26–28.

120. Schneider, Ch. 2, "Generosity."

121. Summers, IV, 215.

122. *Ibid.*, II, 263–74.

123. *The Restoration Mode From Milton to Dryden* (Princeton, N. J., 1974), pp. 90–91.

124. Frederick Bracher, ed., *Letters of Sir George Etherege* (Los Angeles, 1974), p. 277.

125. Summers, II, 248–62.

126. *Memoirs of the Life of William Wycherley, Esq.; With a Character of his Writings*, p. 25.

127. Summers, IV, 112.

Chapter IV

Decline of Fortune

The heady years of achievement reached their pitch and began a decline with an illness which did not in itself incapacitate Wycherley but which, seen from our vantage of years, was the first of a series of bad fortunes and misjudgments leading to the dismal years of the 1680's when his prospects were most bleak. Years later, when the worst was over, he would look at a portrait he had done in 1703 engraved after the one by Lely years earlier, and select for its motto, "Quantum mutatus ab illo." Pope remembered, "he used to repeat it sometimes with a melancholy emphasis."[1] They were indeed years of great change.

In early summer, probably the beginning of June, of 1678 Wycherley became seriously ill of a fever, which Dryden called apoplexy,[2] and was bedridden in his rooms in Bow Street, Covent Garden, for nearly two months. During his illness, the King heard of his friend's distress and "gave him a Proof of his esteem and Affection, which never any Sovereign Prince before had given to an Author who was only a private Gentleman," as Dennis put it.

> The King did him the Honour to visit him, when finding his Feaver indeed abated, but his body extremely weaken'd, and his Spirits miserably shatter'd, he commanded him, as soon as he was able to take a Journey, to go to the South of France, believing that nothing would contribute more to restoring his former Vigour, than the gentle salutiferous Air of *Montpelier* during the Winter Season. At the same time the King was pleased to assure him, that as soon as he was capable of taking that Journey, he would order five hundred pounds to be paid him to defray the Expense of it.[3]

Dennis explained that Wycherley went to France in "the beginning of the Winter of 1678 . . . and returned into England in the latter end of the Spring of 1679, entirely restor'd to his former Vigour both of Body and Mind." But from another important source we find differently about his departure from London. In the fall of 1678 John Locke went to France, arriving in Bordeaux on 13 September, from whence he wrote, on the 19th, the following letter to the virtuoso collector and scientist William Charleton, addressed to Monsieur Charleton, Montpellier, a city famous for its health spa and for its physicians.

Dear Sr.,

The slownesse of my journey hither rather then of my thanks has put me in debt to you for the favour of two of your letters, one of 13th Aug. & the other of 5th instant wch brought an inclosed with it from Mr. Selapris, wch I look on as an increase of my score to you . . . And I hope by this time the raines there, as well as here, have restord the town to a very good state of health, and the air to a good temper. Sr. John Chichley writ me word of his designe to returne to Montpellier again this winter before I left Paris, & would it not be strange if we three should meet there again? I thought when I left Languedoc that we might have sooner met at Constantinople, & there togeathe [together] have drunk healths to our friends of Christendome in Sherbet & Coffé. The complement I found in yr letter from Mr. Witcherly mightily surprised me with great satisfaction, not that I think it strange that one of his great civility and good nature should remember an old acquaintance, but haveing, since I left Paris, with great concerne, heard of & regretted his death, it was altogether unexpected to heare news of him in these parts, for whatever they tell us of Old Orpheus a long time since, & though I think Mr. Witcherlys poetry as powerfull & charming as his, yet I feare that trick is lost & doe not expect that any poetry should have power enough in our days to make a man that goes underground in England rise again in Languedoc. Pray tell him I finde it much better to goe twise to Montpellier than once to the other world, & that I shall be exceeding glad to kiss his hands there.

[117]

Dear Sir

Yr most humble, most affectionate,
& most obliged servant

J. Locke.[4]

Wycherley's arrival in Montpellier was in all likelihood in mid or late August; he would then have had time to contact Charleton and convey through him his wishes to Locke in Bordeaux.

This letter establishes for the first time the long friendship between Wycherley and Locke, two men whom one would have not suspected of being friends from the evidence of their writings. Both were at Oxford, where perhaps they had first met, the "old" acquaintanceship suggesting something at least of ten years' duration. It is interesting that Locke salutes Wycherley's "great civility and good nature," as so many other contemporaries had done, apparently the chief basis of the rich friendships Wycherley had formed over the years. Equally interesting is Locke's praise of Wycherley's "powerfull & charming" poetry, rather than his plays, though the praise is couched in a fine compliment, nearly a poem itself, which accounts for some of its expansiveness. Probably the two did meet at Montpellier later, there to entertain one another with wittily wrought compliments and perhaps to discuss even such matters as the operation of the human understanding. History has so placed Wycherley in the bordello of the Restoration and Locke in the cathedral of philosophy that it takes one a moment to realize that two such intelligent contemporaries would have no reason not to be friends in spite of our attempts to isolate them into exclusive groups.

While in France recuperating, Wycherley wrote verses, perhaps the one "*To a* French Doctor, *whose name was* Le Roy, *or* King; *and who was as Generous as an* Emperour:"

We Both serve the same Saving Deity,
The God of Physic, and of Poetry,
By which, Men think to live immortally.[5]

And on the return to England he passed through Holland

[118]

where he wrote "*To the King of* France, *at the Treaty of* Nimeguen, *written there*," an agreeably cheerful poem, with some of his customary themes:

> Monarchs by War can vanquish Earth alone,
> But by their Mercy they make Heav'n their own.
> Then most above the humane Pitch they soar,
> When Justice and when Pity curb their Pow'r.[6]

He returned to London, probably in early spring, quite cured of the illness which had been so severe that Locke thought he died from it; at least in his body he was well enough to become active again and keep the attentions of the Countess of Drogheda whom he had met before he fell ill. His memory, however, was impaired—some say seriously, a terribly demoralizing blow to a man of his intellectual capacity and agility, but it is difficult to determine with certitude the extent of the damage. Pope had more to say than anyone else about his loss of memory, which

> was not by age but by accident, as he himself has often told me. He remembered as well at sixty years old as he had done ever since forty when a fever occasioned that loss to him. He lost his memory (forty years before he died) by a fever, and would repeat the same thought sometimes in the compass of ten lines, did not dream of its being inserted but just before, and when you pointed it out to him would say, 'Gads so, so 'tis! I thank you very much—pray blot it out.' He had the same single thoughts (which were very good) come into his head again that he had used twenty years before. His memory did not carry above a sentence at a time. His memory was so totally bad that he did not remember a kindness done to him, even from minute to minute.[7]

Pope's emphasis upon this loss of memory has raised suspicions in some minds that it is self-serving derogation on Pope's part,[8] but there is little in Pope's relationship with the playwright that would suggest this attitude would have any advantage, professional, psychological or other, for Pope. What Pope calls loss of memory is most usually manifest in an intermittent carelessness and confusion of mind, which did by no means typify all Wycherley's subsequent actions or his poems. The marks of the illness,

[119]

no matter whose view of them we take, were to some extent serious as Wycherley moved toward what should have been a period of great pleasure and satisfaction, the courtship of and marriage to Letitia-Isabella, the Countess of Drogheda.

The Viceroy of Ireland from 1662 until 1669 was the Duke of Ormond, whose second son, Richard, was Earl of Arran and Colonel of the King's Regiment of Guards in Ireland, under whom Wycherley perhaps served. Ormond was succeeded by John Lord Robartes, Earl of Radnor (1606–1685) who did not match either the brilliance of Ormond or his length of viceregency, for it was but one year. While in Ireland with his family, he arranged the marriage of his daughter Letitia-Isabella to Charles, Second Earl of Drogheda, son of Henry Moore, first Earl (d. 1675), and brother to Henry, the third Earl. The deed or "treaty" of marriage, a good political match for Robartes, was drawn up and signed on 28 October 1669 with the following stipulations: a portion of 4000£ should be paid; the deed was perfected "to lead to the uses of several fines and Recoveryes, where a . . . fair Settlement of the Estate was made, that is 800£ pann thereof was settled to the use of [Charles] for present maintenance during his father's life and the Lady should have 800£ pann joynture."[9] After the death of his father, Charles was to have the property for life "and then to the Sonn in Tayle Male," and in the event of no sons, to Charles' brother, Henry. The marriage and the treaty were both arranged by a relative of the Robartes, Oliver Lambert, who was a constant advisor of Letitia-Isabella and who figured importantly in the remaining life of the new bride. Their marriage was solemnized, the deed was effected, and all went well for the couple, as far as history informs us. The countess gave birth to two daughters but unfortunately neither survived infancy.[10]

The sources of information on these early events in the life of Letitia-Isabella are not invariably trustworthy because they are given by interested parties; the preceding, for instance, came from Charles' brother, Henry, who had much to lose if the 1669 deed was not properly and justly adhered to by the participants. Much of the factual information, however, has been corroborated by other sources, one of whom was Letitia-Isabella's sister Olympia. Throughout, the differences between self-interested rhetoric and verifiable information will be evident as we proceed through this complex matter, almost all of which is pertinent to the later relationship of Wycherley and his first wife.

Charles and his Countess were in London in 1676 with their retinue of servants and possessions, living probably in Covent Garden and taking occasional jaunts to Tunbridge Wells, the fashionable resort southeast of London, where one went ostensibly to take the waters of the chalybeate spring at the lower end of the curved, colonnaded promenade, or to observe the other delights which might be residing there. This journey was not their first to London, for in May 1670, Lord Robartes came to England with his daughter and son-in-law,[11] but this was perhaps their first time alone.

It is not known precisely when they arrived in London, and of their activities we have only Henry's testimony and our own sense that as titled, young and attractive provincials arriving in London, they no doubt examined the offerings of the exciting town; but of their putative debauchery only outraged and righteous Henry seemed informed. He charged the influence of "Accomplices & Friends . . . by delusions and false suggestions and insinuations" moved Charles to distrust his brother since, according to Henry, Charles was "very weake in his Judgment and addicted himselfe to noe manner of business."[12] For an unspecified reason, Charles returned to Ireland and with the aid of Oliver Lambert drew up the deed of 12 July 1677, on which all subsequent litigation turned. Whether as Henry claimed, Charles was deceived into making this deed through the machinations of Lambert and the Countess, or whether it was his own idea, the fact remains that the new deed put Henry's future in

[121]

peril. It changed the inheritance of the Moore estates from Henry, the next in line, and declared the "Fines & Recoveryes . . . a Chief & Great part of the inheritance of the sd estate [were given] to the Lady and her heires for ever," with parts to Hender Roberts, Francis Roberts, the Lady Aramintha and the Lady Olympia Roberts and her heirs, and part also to Lambert's son Charles and his heirs. When Letitia-Isabella died some years later, she made Wycherley, then her husband, her heir. One can certainly see Henry's point that the deed was neither customary nor generous, but there seemed to be no real doubt in his mind as to the strict legality of the deed. In his plea for equity, Henry played extensively on his brother's disabilities, as if he were a cripple or a madman, and accused Letitia-Isabella of driving him to distraction. Olympia, the Countess' sister, was obliged to answer his allegations, which we know only by her denial of them, and in her official answer to his charges, claimed she

> does not know if anyone by letters or discourse tried to begett ill opinions of [Henry] in the sd Earl Charles . . . And this Def[endan]t denieth that she ever told the said Earl Charles that the Compl[ainan]t [Henry] had hired any person to poyson him or to make a hole in the Vesell to drowne him as hee should come over into the Kingdom of Ireland . . . .

She did recall that the Countess of Clambrosell was once refused entrance to visit Charles in his sickness. But they worked no fraud on him;

> he was in good Apprehension Capacity and Condition to minde his owne affaires and understood very well what he did and what was the Intent of the said Deed. . . . Neither doth she believe that the Earl was so weakened in his intellectuals att or about the tyme of his Sealing the said Deed . . . or that he was threatened by the said Lady Leticia-Isabella his wife to be Shott or Stabbed if he should refuse to do the same,

that is, make over the estate, "as in the said bill is unduly and scandalously alleadged."[13] If the Countess were known for nothing else, her temper has become legend, and one is tempted to credit this charge against her, partly because of the particularity of it and partly because it confirms, one must admit, established prejudices. But Henry's allegations became more extreme as his position worsened and his desperation increased, so that by 1687 when the charges were made, their plausibility is greatly weakened into incredibility.

While Charles and his wife were in London in January 1678, having returned that fall—for Charles, whatever was stated of his senses or health, was quite ready to travel to London a few months after sealing the deed—the Countess hired as waiting-woman Sarah Barnaby.[14] Charles seemed somewhat opposed to her employment; some say his "mind and will" were against it and that the Countess "out of Kindnesse" and impressed by her seeming tactfulness placated the Earl's annoyance and doubts.[15] Barnaby herself insisted the Earl liked her very well and the Countess called her her "truest and trustiest servant."[16] Self-serving, however, is reserved to no class. Fortunately, we know enough about Barnaby to offer, in time, a truer picture of this relationship. Liked well or ill, she accepted the position with her annual wage of 10£, besides the Countess' "cast Cloathes,"[17] a customary and more than fair arrangement. We hear through Henry's testimony that Charles was once again "brought into the idle and extravagant way of Living and brought to Gaole in London, [where] not one of them would assist him with one farthing of money or creditt for his deliverance. . . ."[18] While it is difficult to doubt this astonishing fact, no other mention of prison appears, even in the testimony of Barnaby on this same period; it is an occurrence cruel enough to suit Henry's portrayal of Charles as the merest pawn in the hands of conniving relatives and thus smacks of a fabrication on his part. Yet imprisonment for debt was a quick and not uncommon turn of events, so Henry could be right.

When Charles for indefinite reasons returned to Ireland in early 1678, he left the Countess with her retinue and Barnaby

in London. She lived in Bow Street, Covent Garden, and
stabled her horses at the White Horse Inn. She waited for
money from her husband to pay her way home but none was
forthcoming. So, with summer approaching, she did not
seem to press the matter too greatly, not until December at
least, and instead drove down to Tunbridge Wells. From
there Barnaby went several times to London to the Earl's
agent to collect the 20£ weekly allowance,[19] but this was not
sufficient for the Countess' expenses. It was probably in May
that she came to Tunbridge Wells and directly into our story.
She met Wycherley there, he having gone there, as before, "to
take either the Benefit of the Waters or the Diversions of the
Place" during the "Water-drinking season," as Dennis
reported.[20] Once again, however, Dennis' eye for drama and
the challenge of rumor overpower his ear for fact; he
misdated the meeting by a year and identified the Countess as
"a young Widow, rich, noble and beautiful." Young and
beautiful, yes, but no widow, not rich, and noble only in
title.

> *Wycherley* . . . was walking one Day upon the Wells Walk
> with his Friend Mr. *Fairbeard* of *Grey's-Inn*, just as he came
> up to the Bookseller's my Lady *Drogheda*, a young Widow,
> rich, noble, and beautiful, came to the Bookseller and
> enquir'd for *the Plain Dealer. Madam*, says Mr. *Fairbeard,
> since you are for the* Plain Dealer, *there he is for you*, pushing
> Mr. *Wycherley* towards her. *Yes*, says Mr. *Wycherley, this
> Lady can bear plain Dealing, for she appears to be so
> accomplish'd, that what would be Compliment said to
> others, spoke to her would be plain Dealing. No, truly, Sir,*
> said the Lady, *I am not without my Faults any more than the
> rest of my Sex, and yet notwithstanding all my Faults, I love
> plain Dealing, and never am more fond of it than when it tells
> me of my Faults. Then, Madam*, said Mr. *Fairbeard, you and
> the* Plain Dealer *seem design'd by Heaven for each other.* In
> short, Mr. *Wycherley* walk'd with her upon the Walks,
> waited upon her home, visited her daily at her Lodging,
> while she staid at *Tunbridge*.[21]

The reference to Heaven was not exactly plain-dealing on
Fairbeard's part, but at Tunbridge it may have passed for the

same. A good story, dialogue very much like any play, and not very reliable. Wycherley was taken with the young lady and after meeting her daily at Tunbridge continued his visits to her in London.[22] The two kept the liaison discretely out of public to shield the Countess from the taint of scandalous conduct back home at Moore Abbey, the Drogheda family seat, and also to protect Wycherley's conduct from the King—not that Charles would frown upon an affair, but a serious liaison and possibly marriage with a wealthy Countess would jeopardize the King's favor, which is what happened after all. The King's approval was customarily required for marriage of important persons.

Wycherley was living at the Bow Street house at this time and there he collapsed of the fever in June, and received the generous visit and gift from King Charles. While Wycherley went to Montpellier, the Countess stayed on in London, writing to him and trying to send him gifts. She bought a gold ring set with diamonds, worth about seven pounds, and told Barnaby to take it to France to Wycherley.[23] With ten pounds travel money in her hand, Barnaby set out and went to her relatives, explaining later that she was scandalized to be party to such adultery, "it being in my Lord's life tyme."[24] And for a time she fooled the Countess, but the Countess, who was known to fly "into a passion," must have given a splendid tirade when through an exchange of letters with Wycherley, she learned of Barnaby's deception. The ring did at length reach the playwright's finger, after their wedding. The Countess also bought and paid out 5£ 12s toward "Mr. Whycherley's Picture,"[25] with the remainder paid later, probably not an original sitting but a copy of the Lely portrait; and later a silver cup (worth eight pounds) with her lover's name engraved on it. One can imagine a steady parade of little gifts and mementoes from her hand—she must have had hopes of becoming a widow—but a lack of testimony from William prevents us knowing whether he reciprocated with his own gew-gaws, though with his financial state so endemically bad, one doubts it. Their affair

[125]

began as a youthful storybook romance, passionate and carefree, but, like his illness which seemed at the time to have no great consequence in his life, it grew inexorably and at length overwhelmed his life.

Continued expenses made it clear to the Countess that she had to have money or return to Ireland. In December the Earl sent her 100£[26] to pay for some scarves and to defray the cost of the journey home. It was absorbed immediately. The accumulation of loans and debts was about to begin. After she borrowed 100£ from one Mr. Kingdom,[27] the Countess placed the management of her finances, particularly for defraying expenses and paying for the return trip, in Sarah Barnaby's hands, "as shee did all other things (as shee pleased) relating to the [Countess, who was] but young and inexperienced in such affairs."[28] Within only three weeks of their departure for Ireland, Barnaby went to Mr. Thomas Swift for 79£ for the Countess.[29] As soon as the landlady at Hatton Garden heard that her noble guest was about to leave, she "was very earnest for her rent and would seize upon all shee had," so the Countess was obliged to pay that bill; she borrowed 75£ from Mr. Allen, who was "very well content" to accept for security the Countess' coach, "not used above two or three months, which cost about one hundred pounds and other Goods that cost above one hundred pounds,"[30] besides her bond. Barnaby, who had "the keeping and disposing of all Moneys," insisted she needed more, so the Countess pawned some of her plate to Mr. Master for 46£, other plate to a goldsmith, who was probably Mr. Fowles, who accepted the pawn under the name of Francis Robartes, for 55£. The sum of 90£ was borrowed of a Mr. Spencer[31] and on the journey she accepted 36£ from Oliver Lambert and 23£ from Mr. Forster on shipboard, crossing the Irish Sea, making a total of 504£ borrowed, excluding the 100£ from the Earl. The issue which finally swept Wycherley into this morass of debt was not the amount borrowed, but Barnaby's receipts of the various moneys, her disposition of it to pay debts, and her loan of 100£ of her own money to the Countess. Since she kept no record of moneys received or disbursed, there was little that mere acrimony could do. Barnaby insisted that she receive a bond for the 79£ borrowed from Mr. Swift, although it was not her money at all; she then claimed she had to post bond for the 75£ from Allen and demanded security for that from the Countess. Swift was not deceived whose money it was, for he first went to Lambert when the entourage was at Reading enroute for Ireland for his money; when Lambert refused the bond, Swift went directly to the Earl himself, in Ireland, who gave Swift bond on 11 March 1679 for the 79£.[32] Thomas Swift was the son of the famed barrister Godwin Swift, who was uncle of the satirist Jonathan and son of Thomas (1595–1658), grandfather of Jonathan. Given Wycherley's contact with the lawyers Swift, as we shall see, he may well have met Jonathan himself.

The sentiment of biographers has always gone with Barnaby, because she appeared a poor, Pamela-like creature, beset by her betters and, at least financially, undone by them. But certain information may limn her portrait somewhat more darkly. The Countess Letitia-Isabella with Thomas Swift and Oliver Lambert, who paid all the expenses for the journey after Reading—the trip usually went from London to Reading to Coventry to Hollyhead and by ferry to Dublin, then to Drogheda to Moore Abbey or to Mellyfont—and with Barnaby and assorted servants, landed in Dublin 1 March.[33] The Earl was willing enough to grant Swift his bond but his own affairs were not going well. From what Henry said, the estate was, in spite of the ample annual allowance and Henry's payment of 4000£ for the estate of Mellyfont which was allowed him in the deed of 1677, in serious financial straits,

under a grete load of debts, a great part of which were contracted for the service of yor Royal Father [Henry is addressing the King] by yor Petrs Grandfather who was killed in his Maties Service, and yor Petrs sd Fathers estate after wards in the Usurpers time was seised sequestered & decimated . . . yor Petr hath payd and engaged to pay 11000£ Debts of his said brother.[34]

The Chancery Books of Ireland list a series of suits involving Charles so that we can trace at least some of the debts he had contracted as Henry indicated. For instance, on 19 November 1677, Charles was defendant with Lambert and five others against one Thomas Russell. On 25 November 1678, Robert and Elizabeth Parkhurst, a polemical couple, sued Charles and Edward Lord Viscount Loftus of Ely; on 10 July 1678, Charles' brother William was petitioner with his mother, Alice Countess Dowager of Drogheda, against him.[35] On 13 November 1678 Charles, his wife, Oliver Lambert, Charles Smith and Hender Roberts were petitioners against his mother, Alice, and brothers Henry and William and five others. On 19 November 1678 Charles was petitioner against the Parkhursts; and on 11 January 1679 he was defendant with eight others against his mother.[36] In March 1679 Charles was ordered to pay 300£ "being for goods bought of Christopher Lovell," to the same for a debt of some standing; the deadline was the following November.[37] Henry, the father of Charles, had been in litigation in June 1675—he lived at least until 15 June.[38] Litigation such as the above does not necessarily mean debts and payments, but in the case of Charles and his reported debts, and Lovell's unpaid bill, the many suits point toward continual financial pressure. When Charles died in June 1679, nothing was resolved and nothing would change for the better for anyone. For the Countess, newly Countess Dowager, of Drogheda, the golden apple of a fresh marriage would turn to legal ashes and death; for Wycherley it would turn to manifold debts, prison, and disheartening death all around him; for Henry, the new Earl of Drogheda, it would mean twenty years of Chancery bitterness and its companion, impoverishment.

But some profitted by the death of the Earl Charles. While she had been in London with her lady, Sarah Barnaby received all the borrowed moneys, including the 100£ from the Earl, the money for the ring, for the journey into France, for the cup and miscellaneous other items. Her functioning in this capacity was not in itself extraordinary, for a woman in her role as waiting woman had primacy over the other women servants and her duties were "dressing and undressing her mistress, arranging her hair, mending and altering her clothes. In addition she accompanied her mistress abroad and offered her companionship at home. . . . A suitable education consisted of a thorough acquaintance with the niceties of social form, an ability to read well aloud, a knowledge of the French tongue," which Barnaby apparently had since she was supposed to travel to France, "a familiarity with French modes and customs, and a real proficiency in the arts of the hairdresser, milliner, and modiste."[39] Servants were commonly given the rights to cast clothes of their mistress or master, and if such was willed at death, the right to all the clothing of the deceased. Practice varied with the wishes of the employer but was ordinarily spelled out in some form. In this position of recipient of all moneys, Barnaby did not make any accounting of her disbursements of the same; it is said only that she disbursed the money. In addition, shortly "before the journey to Ireland," Barnaby bought 20£ worth of ribbons for her use, in imitation of the Countess' purchase of similar ribbon. When Earl Charles died in June, Barnaby followed what she claimed was the "Custome that Ladyes woomen should have all their Cloathes," and took all the Countess' "rich weareing Apparell . . . poynts and Laces" and other things of the value of 800£, as estimated by the Countess, various others, and the mercer's bill.[40] Since we do not have a copy of the Earl's will, we can not be certain what provisions he made for passing on his old clothes, but Barnaby's seizure of the Countess' clothing in addition to his seems to have no precedent whatever; furthermore, she did not evenly distribute the clothing so taken among other servants, and she took a good deal more than clothing. She took the 800£ worth of clothes and took as well the Earl's clothes, worth about 100£, from his closet into which she had broken—the late Earl's footman and his wife had seen Barnaby dealing with the closet door, for servants always know what other servants do—all his clothes except "the worst of the Earl's linnen" and "a Wigg." She also took the largest share of a trunk of linen sent from Mellyfont to Lambert's house, worth about 100£; the Earl's silver watch, 9£; a "case of gold knives," 120£, a "gold tobaccoe Box value twenty three pounds," 14£ of Holland lace from the Countess, 10£ worth of pewter the Earl had ordered from England, 3£ from the pawned ring supposed to be Wycherley's, an unspecified amount for three suits of mourning dress to match the Countess' on the death of the Earl, 140£ of linen taken the day after the Earl died, though this may be part of the 800£ (as another sum of 140£ is almost certainly included elsewhere), and a bribe of "10 Guineys" to persuade the Countess to lease some land to a Mr. Butler, a Dublin tailor, by which the Countess lost 300£ per annum.[41] So much for the custom of receiving one's mistress' cast clothing—a total of well over 1000£.

And at this time, Barnaby persuaded the Countess to give her a bond, dated 16 August 1679, about two months after the Earl died, for the 79£ which Swift had loaned, and for a remaining amount up to 100£ for her "faithfull service."[42] No matter how much or little sorrow Letitia-Isabella felt at the death of her husband, and no matter how often she thought about William Wycherley whom she was to marry in a month, she did not seem to have been entirely sound of mind to give this bond to Barnaby for money Barnaby had not loaned and had no right to. The Countess seems to have been both tempestuous and timid; she tended to treat practical realities with the deliberate disregard of one who believes she deserves to be spared those cares; and Barnaby, the paradigm tricky servant, knew precisely how to play these emotions and seize remarkable amounts of goods and money. The "guift money" she demanded, at one time only 21£ and later 100£, was technically not her due, but somewhat similar to the custom developing at this time of servants' receiving tips or "vails" from visitors, a practice soon to be taken for granted and by mid-eighteenth century to cause severe strain on domestic harmony.[43]

In creating our picture of the servant, it is important too to observe the reactions of several deponents to Barnaby. John Coyle, thirty-one-year-old servant to the Countess, said Barnaby was "Master over the said Countess rather than servant and governed her as shee pleased"; he "heard her give the said Countesse several oprobrious and p'vokeing words until she hath made the said Countesse weepe." He further deposed that she had defrauded the Countess and did not deserve the "Guift Money . . . nor indeed her wages itt self." Oliver Lambert agreed with this: Barnaby "used the Countesse rudely . . . in the p'sence of this depont" and did not deserve "a penny more than her wages" because she "did defraude the Countesse." One Robert Casey Esq. added the gratuitous consideration that for her "insolent Carriage" he would have kicked her downstairs. Others' testimony corroborates the insolence of Barnaby's manner[44] and stands imposingly against the defence she makes of herself and as a clarification to the perhaps self-serving testimony of the Countess who makes her servant out to be unbearable.

The Countess' considerable, if not precisely incestuous, haste to be done with the bothersome incumbered estate and to arrange the treaty of marriage with Wycherley brought Wycherley himself to Ireland in August, perhaps shortly after Barnaby got her bond for 100£. Doctor John Topham wrote on 9 September from Dublin to the same Earl of Arran under whom Wycherley may have served twenty years before, about his acquaintance:

> Does your lordship know that Mr. Wicherley, the poet, was in this country. He landed about three weeks since and went aboard (I saw him) on Thursday last. He has been all the while in the country, but I cannot yet learn where nor what his business was.[45]

Lambert said he first met Wycherley in July 1679,[46] indicating either that he met Wycherley in London perhaps for the treaty of marriage, or, less probably, that Wycherley

[131]

was already in Ireland in July. The well-informed Doctor, of whose relationship with Wycherley we have no other information, spotted Wycherley's coming and going but significantly had not yet caught the hint of the coming marriage, which they wished to keep from the general public eye. Wycherley's three-week stay to complete arrangements for the wedding concluded, and he returned to London the first week of September, having promised to meet his Countess at Northampton when she came later that month.

Letitia-Isabella's journey to London by way of Dublin, Hollyhead, Chester, Coventry, Northampton and Barnett began 17 September 1679. She had no money to pay her way and so borrowed 113£ from Barnaby. Barnaby figured accounts according to a singular arithmetic: to the 79£ of legend and bond she added enough to make 97£, and that added to the said 113£ made the even sum, she claimed, of two hundred pounds![47] For this 200£ Barnaby demanded of the Countess two separate bonds of 100£ with penalty of 200£ each, which the Countess gave her on the road, again, one is inclined to think, irresponsibly. Barnaby at this juncture depicted herself as generously aiding her importunate mistress; her mistress depicted her as "very Clamorous and Scurrilous . . . to the amusement of the whole house or Inn [with her] threatening . . . indecent speeches."[48] Without undervaluing the irascibility of Letitia-Isabella, the evidence does not favor Barnaby's position. She was obviously a remarkably high-handed and ingenious woman with a fast, well-schooled tongue. When they reached Northampton and found Wycherley was not there to meet them, the Countess became incensed at both him and Barnaby, and seizing the bonds burned them. She feared Barnaby had told Lord Radnor of her intended marriage "whereby . . . Mr. Wycherleys meeting of her was prevented,"[49] for the match was a poor one in Radnor's eyes, though Daniel Wycherley encouraged it. The Countess and Barnaby continued their rancorous way and met Wycherley at Barnett, where the Countess accepted his excuses for accidentally failing to meet her at Northampton; she did not inform him of all the events of their travels but kept him ignorant of them for some time.

With Barnaby pacified by his promises to present new bonds after the wedding, Wycherley and Letitia-Isabella arrived in London and were married in the evening of that day, Michaelmas, 29 September 1679.[50] The couple lived in London in the delightful peace of being at last together, and within a few months when Barnaby began to drop large hints about the bonds, Wycherley tried to preserve that peace by settling the matter with finality. He called to his home his friend John Walkenden to take down "from her own mouth in a paper all . . . that could be due her." She began with the list of expenses for 83£ 3s 4d of 11 September at the beginning of their journey from Ireland, and added to that another list of expenses totalling 113£ 6s 10d, from which was to be deducted 15£ for John Bucston, 10£ 17s 6d due John Rogers, 1£ 10s due Mr. Taylor, totalling 27£ 7s 6d. To this she added 20£ due for her wages till next Christmas, and the total was 105£ 19s 4d[51] she had loaned the Countess and was due her. Further Barnaby continued to demand the bond for 100£ gift money and for Swift's 79£. She recalled later having left off Walkenden's list sums of 1£ 18s and 1£ 12s 6d which Wycherley paid at once. But as he examined her accounts he found her charging for sums for which others were also charging—for example, Forster for 30£ and 6£ 15s—and Wycherley for his part demanded the 40£ received for plate from Mr. Fowle the goldsmith, which Barnaby had not accounted for. The peace Wycherley thought he could enjoy was even further remote than settling Barnaby's claims. The Countess' compulsive borrowing led her to take money from almost anyone: five guineas from Jane Bucston, a maid, six from her cook, thirteen guineas from her footman. And curiously, the Countess admitted that the Earl "by his will set aparte Seaven or Eight hundred pounds per annum upwards as shee has heard . . . towards the payment of his Debts," but she would not "intermeddle with his Estate so

[133]

setled." There were "his Cloathes & horses . . . and some gold plate worth about 60£ which the Earle said was hers . . . if he died before her.[52] Whatever was happening to all this money one certainly wonders, for Barnaby's proper debt of 113£ was indeed a small one for Wycherley to pay, since she chose to ignore the goods in excess of 1000£ she had recently taken. Perhaps, like Jacob of old, Barnaby thought she was not stealing but only taking what others were so willing to part withall.

She stayed with the Wycherleys until he finally dismissed her from service about the beginning of February; she nevertheless persistently demanded the bonds for her gift money and Swift's money until the day she visited them at Epsom. His patience did not outlast her persistence; "he on a suddaine fell into a great rage and passion . . . and most grievously beat and wounded her soe that she was under the Chirurgeons hands for a good while afterwards."[53] Exasperated by her resistance to what appeared to him to be just payment, he refused thereafter to speak to her and threatened to go to Ireland "there to resyde & dwell where hee shall be free from [her] prosecution."[54]

Wycherley might also have been anxious to flee to Ireland to look to the execution of Charles' will and the release of the money due his wife. But there was yet another reason. He wished to avoid London. Immediately upon his return from recuperation in France, King Charles met him with warm greetings and offered him the generous and accommodating sinecure of tutoring his seven-year-old son, the Duke of Richmond, born of one of Charles' mistresses, Louise de Querouraile, the Duchess of Portsmouth. The opportunity was an undoubted honor to his intelligence, learning and integrity, and the excellent salary of 1500£ per annum was an astonishing mark of the King's esteem, even without the pension attached to it. Dennis cited the King's words, "when the Time came that his Office was to cease, he would take care to make such a Provision for him as should set him above the Malice of the World and Fortune." But Wycherley spurned the offer, chose instead malice and inconstancy, and marriage with the debt-dowered Countess, an action Dennis claimed was by command of his father,[55] perhaps because Daniel misguidedly believed she was profitable in real and personal estate; but it was an action clearly in violation of all principles of decorum in relation to the King's right of sanction. When Wycherley stayed away from the Court, unusual under normal circumstances, he committed "an Affront to the King"[56] and the longer he stayed away the more impossible the relationship became until explanation became too tardy, too futile. *The Epistle to the King* was a kind of tentative knock upon the palace door to ask whether he might be acceptable again. No one answered during Charles' reign.

After plucky Barnaby recovered from her beating which convinced her Wycherley was not about to give her those bonds, she filed suit. In March 1680, she opened the case with an affidavit on 31 March that the Countess had burnt the bonds, her account of the expenditures, a brief of their relation so far, a request for new bonds for the alleged debt of 200£, and a subpoena to the defendants to appear to answer her.[57] But already she was worried they would run off to Ireland, so on 19 May she swore affidavits that "she hath very frequently beene credibly informed that the Deftes intend speedily to remove into Ireland . . . to avoyd the debt due by the pett. . . . She knoweth not of any estate or Interest they have in this Kingdome whereby to Answr her Demand."[58] Acting upon this concern, she filed on the twenty-first of the month a "ne exeat regnum" because they were planning to leave England and had no property there.[59] The answer of Letitia-Isabella and Wycherley was sworn on 24 May, a very long and detailed response, most of the details of which have been presented above concerning amounts borrowed by the Countess, amounts handled by Barnaby without any accounting, loans actually made by Barnaby and amounts not yet received from her by the defendants. Whether or not Wycherley took his wife to Ireland in June is

[135]

uncertain, but by December they were there.[60] Barnaby filed her reply on 14 December to their bill of complaint; thereafter depositions in Barnaby's favor and in the defendant's favor were taken and filed, the latter at "the Feather Tavern in Castle Street, Dublin, 25 May 1681."[61]

In April 1681 an affidavit was entered which provides important new information to our understanding of William's relations with his father. "Lawrence Breres gent maketh oath that he being ymployed by Daniell Wycherley Esqr. to looke after a cause depending in the High Court of Chancery betweene" Barnaby and William Wycherley and his wife, had particular instructions to go to Ireland to draw up the interrogatories for witnesses on the defendants' behalf, and then to find the witnesses. But he reported that several could not be found, especially one Richard Foster, "a most materiall witnesse in this cause . . . haveing beene Agent for the said Countess in all her Affaires in Ireland.[62] What this tells us, besides the unfortunate lack of a key witness, is that Daniel was by no means ignoring and neglecting his son in his business but was actively involved in aiding him. In fact, Daniel was himself in Ireland in March 1681, perhaps with Breres, to see about the progress of this suit: Humphrey Perry had looked for Daniel in Clive on 11 May, but was "credibly informed yt . . . Daniell Witcherley about two months sithence went into ye Kingdom of Ireland & yt hee is not since retorned to his usuall habitacon."[63] He was in Ireland in October, having either stayed there or returned on a separate trip, presumably for the same purpose of tending to this suit.[64] One further incident at this point will help clarify Daniel's relation to his oldest son, a rather paradoxical reaction at that, but nevertheless telling. In a case later to be discussed involving William's brother George, Daniel had been asked to pay off George's large debts but did "Absolutely refuse the same, the greate trouble and charge hee had suffered soe lately for being bound with the Complt's Eldest Brother being so fresh in his Memory."[65] We have, on the one hand, Daniel being highly agitated at William's extravagance during the summer of 1682—Daniel borrowed 500£ in May 1682 possibly for this purpose[66]—yet going only one year before to great pains to hire legal assistance and to travel to Ireland probably more than once for his son; yet such strong, different responses by Daniel are far more typical than uncharacteristic. This "greate trouble and charge" Daniel fretted over was almost certainly his payment to Barnaby to end the suit, an amount according to the Court of 304£ 13s 4d. The suit does not appear to have continued beyond the middle of 1682 nor was the sum listed in the Fleet Prison charges against William.[67]

Prior to the conclusion of the case, Wycherley stayed out of reach. On 7 February 1682 one Phillip Reeve was sent by the Court to serve an order to Wycherley, pursuant to the court order that he pay the judged amount. The messenger went to the parish of Farringham, Surrey, "about 14 miles from London to the house of Christopher Steward," of whom nothing is known except that he was obviously cordial to Wycherley and his wife. Reeve stated on his oath that he went to serve

the Deftes with an order made in the Cause the third day of February . . . butt this Depont saith that soe soone as this Depont came at the said house a younge man that belonged to the said house . . . came out to this Depont & imediately cryed out to some that was in the house to shutt the doore & when this Depont asked to speake with Mr. Witcherley or the Countesse of Drougheda he denyed that they lodged there although this Depont was informed by agent that he mett a little before he came at the house that Mr. Witcherley & his Lady had their habitacon there And this Depont saith that he would have left a Coppy of the order with a woman who he saw in the said house butt she refused to open the doore or to receive the same whereupon this Depont left the said Coppy by the younge man who was at the out side of the said doore (he alsoe refuseing to receive the same) & desired him to give the same to Mr. Witcherley or his Lady.[68]

This hiding-behind-the-door ploy was not particularly

original—William may have learned it from the old practitioner Daniel—and no one was fooled.

One notices that while Wycherley was thought to have lived in Covent Garden fairly continuously, he did in fact move about a good deal, possibly to alleviate the expenses of the Bow Street lodgings but also because he and his wife were frequently moving to avoid messengers like Mr. Reeve and were traveling to Ireland, not necessarily as Barnaby put it, "absconding themselves" for fear of her, but to settle the late Earl's will.

The suit in Ireland, which ran concurrently for a time with that of Barnaby and has been confused with it, began on 17 November 1679 with a suit by Letitia-Isabella Countess Dowager of Drogheda, two months after her marriage with Wycherley and four months before Barnaby initiated her suit, against Henry Earl of Drogheda and Thomas Russell, defts.[69] Shortly thereafter her father, Lord Radnor, reacted favorably to her request for assistance, and, no longer opposing the marriage, petitioned the King, who on 6 February 1680 sent his letter to the Marquis of Ormond:

> I have been applyed to by my Lord Radnor in behalfe of his daughter, the Countess of Drogedaugh, in some concernes of hers in Ireland. I do therefore desire you would be as favorable to her in her pretensions as farr as law and justice will permit.[70]

What the outcome of this petition was is not known. The documents of the suit in Ireland have not survived except for the answer of Olympia Roberts in 1692 and Henry's plea to the King and Parliament for aid in 1687, but the Chancery Bill Books reveal the case evolving and the participants involved. The first bill was amended in January 1680, but until 19 April 1681, everything seemed to be quiet except for a bill filed against the late Charles (19 November 1680) by Walter Burrowes Baronett, answered by Henry on 16 February,[71] presumably for land or debt. In April William Wycherley and his wife—their attorneys were Godwyn Swift and John Forster who were at least as busy as Lambert and who frequently appeared (sometimes with Robert Casey who had advised kicking Barnaby downstairs) in Irish cases at this time—filed against Henry and a host of forty-one others, probably all landholders of the Drogheda estates or agents.[72] Answers came in from May through November but there is no way to know the upshot of this suit. On 14 November 1681 Wycherley et ux. filed against Henry, the Parkhursts and twelve others who were not in the prior case,[73] and on 21 November he filed against Hellen Wall of whom nothing is heard before or after.[74] Then he filed another suit on 6 December, with his wife and Thomas Henshawe and Elred Hyes against Henry, Alice, the Parkhursts and four others, even while answers to the prior cases were forthcoming.[75]

Henry began to return in kind on 3 May 1682 against the Wycherleys, Letitia-Isabella's four brothers and sisters and Oliver Lambert; to this they replied on 21 November,[76] no doubt in Ireland. Their frequent appearance to file suits in 1681 and 1682 obviously made awkward the attempt to deal with the Barnaby suit, quite apart from the strain of expense from continued travel. On 25 July one James Hamilton Esqr. (a relative; the third Earl was Henry Hamilton-Moore) filed against Henry, Viscount Loftus and the Wycherleys, again for unknown cause but probably because they were all claiming property Hamilton believed rightfully his; Henry answered 22 February 1683, the others on 4 June.[77] Though Henry's problems did not abate—Elnathan Lunn (or Lumme) sued him in June[78]—Wycherley's were not decreasing either. On 29 November 1683, he and his wife sued the Lord Mayor of the City of Dublin, among others, who answered 24 January following.[79]

The suits dated during the first years of the 1680's indicate that Letitia-Isabella was actively engaged in the affairs of law in Ireland and in London, and it is not until 1686 that her name is conspicuously absent. Her death has been accepted for years, even without evidence, as occurring in 1681, but that date is no longer credible. It is now clear that she died in 1685. Her sister Olympia testified that "the said Lady Leticia Isabella dyed in or about the month of July 1685."[80] In the *Index to Prerogative Grants* in the Ireland Public Record Office is the following entry under the date 1685: "Droghedaugh, Countess Letitia-Isabella," apparently a commission to an incumbent to take an oath of an executor or administrator.[81] She died in the last week of June or first week of July of unknown causes, probably in Ireland, and was probably buried with the rest of the family at St. Peters, Drogheda, but no further details of her demise are known. William himself, in a distressed letter he wrote from prison,[82] did not tell us more than that she was in fact dead.

The misery he expressed at her death does not seem to tell the whole story, and the state of their relationship might be worth looking into for a moment. From what we have observed of her alleged dealings with her husband the Earl, which are partially plausible if not true, of her explosive temper at Northampton when Wycherley failed to appear, of her generally precipitous and insensitive behavior, we have little difficulty believing the tales Dennis related of her jealousy during their residence in Covent Garden. Whenever Wycherley went down to the Cock Tavern with his friends, she insisted he leave the window of their Bow Street lodgings open so she could check periodically on his activities, and of course she would be, Dennis said, "in a downright raving Condition" if he had the temerity to speak with some ladies, though he obviously would speak with the many he had met in the course of his years thereabouts. Dennis also reported in a curiously knowing way that her experience did not find "his manly Prowess" as great as she anticipated.[83] Very likely she had heard about his sexual energy some time before marriage, when Wycherley's reputation and talents were highest. His sexual failure, to a minor extent attributable to his illness, was chiefly due to disenchantment with his wife; for the financial security he anticipated and frankly married for he did not get. The terrible ironies that inevitably drifted out of Wycherley's plays into conscious reality, the jokes about lecherous widows, the fantastic goblin of jealousy, the falseness of humoring wives, or trusting friends and painted exteriors, and innumerable other perversities he had once mocked must now have returned to choke him; the cabinet of his self and his jewels had been cheaply sold and he would himself be soon locked away. The bitterness one assumes he felt to have had so lovely a wife turn into so uneasy a companion, compelling him to futile appeals and defenses in England and Ireland, to pleas from his father and finally his loss of almost everything, can be plausibly supported by a poem he wrote to the Lord Chancellor of Ireland, Michael Boyle (d. 1702), for kind assistance in the *"Suit depending before Him"* concerning the late Earl's will, not as some have thought Barnaby's suit. The poem is redundant enough to make us realize that Wycherley's weakened memory and sense of artistic control may have made him a disagreeable and trying companion for the Countess as well, for it is easy to exaggerate or caricature her rash temper and jealousy and to forget that his gentility no doubt failed him when the pressure of his physical, financial and artistic limitations grew extreme. The poem to Boyle dallies at unnecessary length on nevertheless perceptive distinctions between Custom in law and Reason in law; the latter, which is the Chancellor's noble strength, would benefit Wycherley against local custom which favors the richer but legally weaker causes:

> At least, in *Ireland*, it was ne'er thought, that
> Good Sense had Title to a Good Estate;
> For, where'er Fools, or Knaves, most numerous
> Are found, their Right, Poor Men of Sense must lose.[84]

At the end, the poet moves to more interesting matter for there he argues,

> Since 'twas an Estate, which in my Case,
> Consideration of my Marriage was,
> Your Court, (since 'tis a Court of Conscience) shou'd,
> By right, my Title to me now make good . . .
> Give my Claim (as a Chancellour) Relief,
> Or me relieve (as a Bishop) from a Wife,
> End my Law-Suit, or my Domestic-Strife.

[141]

The divorce Wycherley is requesting appears to be the kind possible when one party broke the contract and thus made the marriage void or voidable. Another kind of divorce possible at the time was based upon the revelation of a prior contract or upon the grounds of having been forced into marriage against one's will, a situation not precisely Wycherley's, unless the condition upon which the marriage was based was in truth her wealth and thus spurious.[85] It is interesting to compare Wycherley's view of custom with those of another somewhat earlier writer on divorce, John Milton: "Error supports custom, custom countenances error; and these two between them would persecute and chase away all truth and solid wisdom out of human life." One can almost see Wycherley murmuring, as he wrote to Boyle, these words of Milton: "He that marries intends as little to conspire his own ruin as he that swears allegiance," and agreeing that the covenant of his marriage was no longer what it was when he and the Countess were first married.[86] From any point of view, this poem to Boyle is a remarkable confessional poem, exposing deeply felt emotions which, with due caution of taking the poem as pure biography, convey a straightforward desire to be either married with the estate or not married at all.

In London it was still 1682 and, though Barnaby was a name now possible to forget, debts there continued to mount from various quarters. In Common Pleas Court on 11 November, Wycherley "late of the parish of St. Pauls Covent Garden" was summoned by Richard Newport to pay the 536£ which he had borrowed the previous August, and 20s damages. But the summons was in vain; the debtor did not pay.[87] On 15 July 1683, one Thomas Fowle, possibly the same goldsmith to whom Letitia-Isabella had pawned some plate, summoned Wycherley in Common Pleas for a loan of 50£ "which he owes him and unjustly detains." This loan was of long standing, having originated at St. Mary le Bow in May 1680, and carried a penalty of 100£ if not paid fifteen days later. As in the prior case, Wycherley's defence was not presented in person but through his attorney and was in fact no defence at all. One more Common Pleas case against "William Witcherley of the parish of St. Pauls Covent Garden" concerned a debt of 373£ 40s from 1681, and once more the pattern of response was the same. Wycherley was "solemnly summoned to give reason why he has not paid and he does not come"; the sheriff reported "the aforesaid Wycherley has nothing in his bailiwick and [is] not found in the same." At each summons he stayed away. At length, the Court in Easter term 1684 gave "the execution of the debt and damages" to Henry Beatley "by default of the same William." Although the cause of these debts is not revealed, from what we know of the Countess' mode of living and Wycherley's endemic financial distress and disinclination for the practical, the debts must have been the combined result of her prior debts, their expensive habits and the continual travel to and from Ireland—and one evident reason why he failed to answer summons was that he was expending time and effort in Ireland in that potentially more lucrative enterprise and allowing these relatively minor debts to run their legal course. The inevitable end of this cavalier reaction to the sober and serious Court was debtors' prison, the Fleet.

Some biographers believe that he was first in Newgate prison, then had himself transferred to the more commodious Fleet, but there is no available evidence for this nor any to suggest this as even possible. Gildon's assertion that "Newgate was the first scene of his confinement . . . From thence he removed himself by a Habeas Corpus to the Fleet where he continued seven years in close Imprisonment,"[88] is at least half wrong: he was not in prison for even one full year, although Dennis in 1717 still believed Gildon's version.[89] Much of their entire story becomes questionable as a result of this huge error. For as Professor W. R. Chadwick has pointed out, if Wycherley could not be found by the sheriff during the Common Pleas cases, he must not have been in prison, for when he actually was there he was called to the bar to defend himself. The Fleet Prison Committment Book records Wycherley's incarceration as follows:

> William Wycherley was committed to the prison of the Fleet on the seventh day of July in the first year of the reign of our Lord James II present King of England etc. by the court of the said Lord King's Bench by virtue of a writ of habeas corpus directed to the sheriff of Hertford.[90]

From all available evidence this would appear to be his first imprisonment, for he was brought there, not from Newgate, but from Hertford by the sheriff of the county. Wycherley was still moving about a good deal, from Bow Street, his predominant residence, to Epsom, to Farringham, to Ireland, to Hertford, and elsewhere, The Fleet imprisonment was on account of eleven charges of debt totalling 1590£ 12s 9d, a great deal more than the 1009£ of the three Common Pleas cases, and than the 700£ for which Wycherley had supposedly been jailed according to early biographers.[91]

On the day after he was placed in the Fleet in a state of deep depression and confusion, he wrote a letter to a hoped-for patron whom he may have known during his service in the Navy, Baron of Dartmouth, George Legge, master general of the ordnance, 1682–88, associate of diarist and naval secretary Samuel Pepys, and "an active & understanding Gent in sea affaires."

> I am now the most unhappy man living, my wife being lately dead, and I frustrated of all my expectations from her estate unless I can prevail by your lordship's interest with some one in Ireland who has the honour to be employed by your lordship to keep possession for me of an estate in Dublin, of which she has levied fines to my use, so that if I had any friend there I could be sure of I might secure that estate; but if that be not to be done, I am the most miserable man in the world, and cannot secure myself of a friend in the world, unless your lordship's great generosity and goodness shall take pity on a man eternally lost in the world since frustrated of my only hopes in the world, if your lordship can think of any agent you have in Ireland, perhaps by his means I may prevent my total ruin.[92]

[144]

Dated July 9. From the Fleet Prison. Signed, Captain Wycherley. The letter's despairing tone stands in sharp contrast to the jocund youth of those earlier letters to Mulgrave and Shadwell, and to the soberly argued plea, only a short time before, to Chancelor Boyle. Wycherley was free of his wife but not of the legal entanglements and impending ruin which lurked nearby and which filled his letter almost to the exclusion of mourning for the dead Countess. After a few months, he wrote again from the Fleet, in a much quieter tone but still pleading assistance, this time of good friend Mulgrave.

Fleet Prison
Oct. 24, 1685
My Lord,

Tho', amongst great Courtiers, the Congratulations of little and unfortunate Men are thought Compliments out of Interest, and rather a kind of giving Joy to their miserable little selves, than to their great, and successful Patrons; they give them Joy, to give themselves Hopes; felicitating themselves rather than those they compliment; yet I assure you, my Lord, I congratulate your Lordship without any End by it, than appearing grateful to One, to whom I am so much oblig'd, so much oblig'd [sic], not only by your Lordship's first Obligations on me, but by your Lordship's doing more for me, that is, to believe, that it is my Misfortune, and not my Fault, that I have not yet return'd the Debt I owe your Lordship; I mean, the Money Debt; for to the great Debt of Obligations I owe your Lordship I can never make any Return, however vainly I may endeavour it, as long as I live. In the mean Time I cannot help congratulating, in Imagination, the King's good Fortune, rather than your Lordship's: For, in the Preferment of the Meritorious, Kings rather honour themselves, than those they confer Honours upon, and do themselves more Kindness by Favours they confer on the Deserving, and have more Interest in giving to such Subjects, than in receiving from all the rest. In fine, my Lord, I think it is the King's Honour, more than your Lordship's, that You are Master of his House enough to reconcile me to that Place, which has been so severe to me: But since your Lordship is now the Second Master of it, I should have the Confidence to hope, (if ever) that I might

[145]

have now a Wellcome in that House, whom your Lordship
has always so much oblig'd in your own. But, my Lord, tho'
Congratulations are generally Introductions to Petitions, I
have no other to make to your Lordship, or to beg any Place
of You, but that I may still preserve the best in your
Lordship's Gift, a Place in your Lordship's good Opinion,
which if your Lordship shall be pleas'd to do for me, You
would do more than I would ask of the King, which Place (if
ever I was so unhappy as to lose) 't is the only Place in Court I
would be ambitious to be restor'd to, who am, tho' out of
Waiting,

> My Lord,
> Your Lordship's
> Most Obliged, and
> Most Obedient
> Humble Servant
> W: Wycherley.[93]

The phrasing is unmistakable Wycherley, but compared to
that brisk report from the summer of 1677, that of a very
changed man. Mulgrave had been but recently appointed
Lord Chamberlain (July 1685) by King James, and while
Wycherley acknowledged the 500£ loan Mulgrave had made
him, his intentions were not without self-interest, and in fact
Mulgrave eventually aided his release from prison.

Another composition from prison, also unmistakable
Wycherley, is a poem *"In Praise of a* Prison, *call'd by its*
Prisoners *their* College; *and written there."*[94] Though ironic
and detached, the poem shows clearly the sharp sense of
disillusion:

A Man, in thee, may study best, Mankind,
And the true Knowledge of the World may find;
The most hard, and most useful Knowledge, which
The World can least teach, least known, by the Rich. . . .

Thus, we have Sense, Peace, Quiet, Safety here,
He who has nothing, nothing has to fear;
Within thy Walls, so Hospitable *Fleet!* . . .

For Love, more to my Grief, Plague, Infamy,
Has more than Debt, caus'd my Captivity. . . .

A Prison is, from Marriage, a Reprieve,
To keep Men from, Hanging themselves, alive,
About the Neck of a Kept Whore, or Wife. . . .

The poem considerably advances the sexual disgust and bitterness at his marriage that we saw in the poem to Boyle; there is even a viciousness toward his wife, or women in general, which is a far cry from his much acclaimed civility of manner, which returned after a few years.

King James II was one of the first persons to come to the financial assistance of the playwright, though it was a friend, Colonel Brett, who persuaded the King to attend a performance of *The Plain-Dealer* which had been arranged to be performed at Court on 14 December, perhaps the handiwork of Mulgrave in his position as Lord Chamberlain. James' pleasure at watching the play prompted him to ask about the author, and hearing he was in the Fleet, sent the Earl of Mulgrave, certainly the best choice he could have made, to learn the particulars of the debt. However, out of embarrassment, Wycherley told him the debt was only 500£ rather than the true amount.[95] The King therefore on 22 March signed out of the Secret Services accounts 500£ to "William Wycherley, bounty, to enable him to pay his debts to redeeme him out of prison."[96] With this amount he could begin to pay some debts and with the promise of a pension of 200£ from James he could manage to live reasonably well after prison whether the estate in Dublin came to him or not. In the beginning of 1686, he was examined for release from these debts and one by one they were paid. According to Dennis, Wycherley was confined "almost half a year longer" after Mulgrave's visit, supporting the time of dismissal from the Fleet as April or May, "till his father was at last prevailed upon to pay the rest—between two and three hundred pounds."[97] Other payments were made through the 500£ loaned him by Mulgrave[98] and perhaps through gifts from Colonel Grahme to whose generosity over a two-year period Wycherley graciously alluded in a letter of 1688.[99] It is evident that he

[147]

was no longer in the Fleet in April for his name is absent from the Fleet rolls; and in May, Fowle had his attorney notify the Court that he "recognizes that satisfaction has been made to him concerning the debt . . . therefore the aforesaid William Wycherley is to be quit of the debt."[100]

Thus Wycherley was freed from the Fleet about ten months after he was summoned from Hertford. As he walked out a free man, his world was changed. His wife was dead; King Charles was gone, 6 February 1685; Rochester and Butler were dead too. The promised pension from King James would not materialize when James was removed from the throne and sent from England in 1687 to make way for the Protestant William of Orange. Though his money debts were temporarily gone, his greater debts of gratitude toward many friends remained; his health and humor were weakened—one person looking upon him remarked that his once sprightly conversation and gaiety were destroyed by prison—[101] though that loss was not permanent. The suit in Ireland proceeded with no immediate sign of solution despite his pleas; and at home in Wem, a bitter fight was growing, not with his father, annoyed as he probably was to have twice to pay his son's debts, but between his father and brothers Henry and John against brother George, who was already in prison when William came out and would soon be transferred to the Fleet where in lonely conclusion to sordid family quarrel he would die. Though these affairs in Wem seem to have little direct bearing on William, they run in uncanny parallel to his rising and then sharply declining fortunes, and thus reflect the tendency of the family as a whole, not only of George, to start with great ambitious promise and then to go awry. Finally, too, it fell to William to bury his brother George in the churchyard at Wem.

Chapter IV
Footnotes

1. *Spence, Anecdotes,* #77.
2. Charles E. Ward, ed., *The Letters of John Dryden* (Durham, N.C.

1942), p. 27. Katherine Rogers' belief that his illness was probably encephalitis (p. 99 and n. 11) is possible; I have found no information that would clarify the nature of the illness.

3. Hooker, II, 411.

4. Autograph file, John Locke to William Charleton, 19 August 1678. Reprinted here by permission of the Harvard College Library. From the notes to the transcript we find that Locke misdated the letter "19 Aug. 78" whereas other sources verify he arrived in Bordeaux in September, as seems also to be evident from Locke's words, "the other of the 5th instant" apparently 5 September. The notes also observe that "Wycherley was close to Shaftesbury (and so to Locke)." Letters of Charleton I have read in the British Museum collection (B.M. MSS 3962) offer no further information on this relationship with Wycherley, but there are others between Charleton and Locke.

5. Summers, III, 239.

6. Summers, IV, 227.

7. *Spence, Anecdotes,* #90, #91, #96.

8. *Ibid.,* notes to #91.

9. Petition of Henry Earl of Drogheda, D21, 912, reprinted here by permission of the Council of Trustees of the National Library of Ireland, Dublin.

10. Anne Moore, Countess of Drogheda, *The History of the Moore Family* (Belfast, 1902), p. 79: "Charles . . . married the Lady Letitia-Isabella Robartes, daughter of the Earl of Radnor . . . and by her he had only two daughters, who died in infancy. . . . His wife and her relations behaved very cruelly to him, and finally forced him to make a Will leaving all the Drogheda estates to them, instead of to his brother Henry, who succeeded him. This Will, signed on the day he died in 1679 in a very trembling hand, remains, and was the occasion of much litigation . . . ." This account does not agree with information to be presented following.

11. *Calendar of State Papers,* Vol. 1670, ed. M.A.E. Green (London, 1895): "19 May 1670, Coventry. Ra. Hope to Williamson. Lord Robartes arrived yesterday from Ireland, accompanied by Lord Roscommon, and [Charles, Lord] Moore, son of the earl of Drogheda, who married [Lady Letitia, Lord Robartes'] daughter. They are gone to the Countess of Southhampton's, a mile hence, and from there to Northampton." Brackets as in text.

12. Following quotations from Henry's Petition, D21, 912 noted above.

13. C8, 435/23: The Several Answers of Lady Olympia Robartes, one of the defts to the Bill Complt of rt Honble Henry Moore Earl of Drogheda . . . , jurat primo Aprilis 1692.

14. C5, 96/93. She had been employed by the Spencer family in Lancaster and received from them a parting gift of 100£, which reappears in the story.

15. C5, 583/78.

16. C5, 96/93.

17. *Ibid.* According to J. Jean Hecht, *The Domestic Servant Class in Eighteenth Century England* (London, 1956), pp. 145–46, the salary for Lady's maid was in the first half of the century, from 5–10£. And

arrangements for cast clothes were common; see also Dorothy Marshall, *English People in the Eighteenth Century* (New York, 1956), p. 177.

18. D21, 912.

19. C22, 324/39, Demonfryett, deposition #7; C5, 96/93: "to receive the first of the said twenty pounds" of Mr. Lun.

20. Hooker, II, 411.

21. *Ibid.*

22. *Ibid.*

23. C5, 583/78; see Eleanore Boswell, "Wycherley and the Countess of Drogheda," *TLS* (28 November 1929), pp. 1001–02, in response to W. G. Hargest, *TLS* (21 November 1929).

24. Boswell, "Wycherley and the Countess of Drogheda."

25. C5, 96/93.

26. C22, 324/39, Demonfryett, deposition #7; "100 pounds Sterl, was recd by [Barnaby] to the Countesses use and returned out of Ireland"; Coyle, #3; and Lambert #3: "about December 1678," and #7. See C5, 454/72 for Countess' statement.

27. C22, 324/39, Lambert's deposition #7; also mentioned as Kindom.

28. C5, 454/72, Countess' statement.

29. *Ibid.* C5, 96/93. All expenses listed here are verified by more than one source; thus C5, 96/93 is Barnaby's account; C5, 454/72 the Countess' and Barnaby's accounts; C22, 324/39 contains depositions, as also C24 1053/10 and C24 1061/148; see also Boswell, *TLS.*

30. C5, 454/72.

31. C5, 583/78.

32. C22, 324/39, deposition of Godwin Swift, father of Thomas, the prominent Irish lawyer who died January 1680.

33. C22, 324/39, Lambert's deposition #5.

34. D21, 912.

35. Since the Ireland PRO was burned in 1922, the cases do not exist, but the *Chancery Bill Books* allow one to follow the progress of suits and the persons involved, but no information about the nature of the case is revealed. *Chancery Bill Books,* 1677–1682, pp. 5, 56, 59 respectively. Ireland PRO.

36. *Ibid.,* pp. 65, 70, 77.

37. D21, 910, National Library of Ireland, printed here by permission of the Council of Trustees.

38. *Index to Exchequer Bill Books,* 1634–1676, p. 142. Ireland PRO.

39. Hecht, p. 61. See also pp. 115 ff. for discussion of cast clothes.

40. C22, 324/39, Lambert's deposition #9.

41. *Ibid.,* various depositions. Lambert said the loss was 600£, deposition #10, the arrangement taking place prior to the Countess' trip to England in September.

42. C5, 96/93.

43. See Hecht, pp. 159 ff. for discussion of vails.

44. C22, 324/39, respective depositions.

45. "Biographical Data on William Wycherley and His Father,"*N&Q,* ccxvi (January 1971), 34.

46. C22, 324/39, deposition #1.

47. C5, 454/72, Barnaby's account and arithmetic.

48. C5, 454/72, Countess' account.

49. C5, 96/93.

50. See Boswell, *TLS*, for information on the marriage license.

51. C5, 454/72; Barnaby's list of expenses is the first sheet of this case. Walkenden is also mentioned in C5, 583/78, with similar accounting of expenses.

52. C5, 454/72, Countess' account. The salary for a chambermaid would be probably under a pound per annum; for a cook not more than six pounds; for a footman, less than six pounds; see Hecht, pp. 144–47.

53. C5, 96/93.

54. C5, 454/72, Barnaby's account.

55. Hooker, II, 411.

56. *Ibid.*, p. 412: "as soon as the News of it came to Court it was look'd upon as an Affront to the King and a Contempt of his Majesty's Offers." The King had approved, however, the elopement of Rochester with his wife, irregular as that would appear: Graham Greene, *Lord Rochester's Monkey*, p. 67.

57. C5, 454/72.

58. Register of Affidavits, C41, 23, Easter Term, #264; same as Chancery Affidavits, C31, 49, #269.

59. Hargest, *TLS*, and Boswell, *TLS*.

60. Connely, p. 176.

61. C22, 324/39. C41, 23, Hilary Term, #52, concerns an order made 15 December, a response to Barnaby's answer, delivered to Barnaby's counsel.

62. C41, 23, Hilary term, #484.

63. C41, 23, Easter term, #226.

64. C6, 66/82, the suit of Arthur Dunn and Daniel concerning cloth goods: "about Michaelmas last" Dunn asked Daniel for payment, but he "was absent in Ireland or in other parts remote."

65. C6, 253/88: Daniel is in this statement presenting himself as a wronged father, so I am inclined to doubt the authenticity of his annoyance here, contrived as it at least partly is.

66. C6, 565/169, Richard Clayton supplied Daniel "with the sum of five hundred pounds about the month of May 1682."

67. W. R. Chadwick, "Wycherley: The Seven Lean Years," *N&Q*, ccxvi (1971), 32–34, for Fleet Prison records. Boswell, *TLS*, for 304£ 13s 4d. See C41, 23, Hilary term, #341, William Horsley on 21 February left copies of orders of 2 and 9 Feb. with Clerke for defendants.

68. C41, 23, Hilary term, #208. See Connely, p. 177n.

69. *Chancery Bill Books*, 1677–83, p. 132. Ireland PRO.

70. "Biographical Data on William Wycherley and his Father," p. 35. On 26 December 1685 "to Letitia Isabella Countess Dowager of Radnor, bounty of 750£ was paid for undisclosed purpose: *Moneys Received and Paid for Secret Services of Charles II and James II*, for 30 March 1679 to 25 December 1688, ed. John Y. Akerman (Camden Society, 1851). This is Letitia's mother.

71. *Exchequer Bill Books*, 1680–1682, p. 41. Ireland PRO.

72. *Ibid.*, p. 114. All names of persons involved are given and the dates of their responses to the charge; amendments are indicated by date only.

73. *Ibid.*, p. 229.

74. *Ibid.*, p. 239.

75. *Ibid.*, p. 256.

76. *Chancery Bill Books*, 1677–1683, p. 296. Ireland PRO.

77. *Ibid.*, 16 June 1683–26 May 1687, p. 10.

78. *Ibid.*, p. 62.

79. *Ibid.*, p. 82. I could not find any information on this case in histories of Dublin.

80. C8, 435/23.

81. *Index to Prerogative Grants, 1595–1810*, Vol. C–E. My thanks to Deputy Keeper of the PRO Ireland, Breandan MacGiolla Choille, for information on the meaning of the entry. Further searches for her will or details of her death have not been successful.

82. "Biographical Data on William Wycherley and his Father, " p. 35, to be quoted in full below, n. 92.

83. Hooker, II, 412: "Whether this outragious Jealousy proceeded from the excess of her Passion, for she lov'd her Husband with the same Violence with which she had done her Lover, or from the great Things which she had heard reported of his manly Prowess, which were not answer'd by her Experience, or from both together, Mr. *Wycherley* thought that he was oblig'd to humour it."

84. Summers, III, 195–96. See his poem *"Upon the Tyranny* of Custom," III, 138–40:

Custom is Right, by Popular Accent;
Right, by Succession, and Example too,
Will Right by Precedent, not Fancy, do;
Most pow'rful Law of Nature, since to it,
Men against Law, Sense, Nature, Faith, submit,

for similar expression of his intense feelings against the lawlessness of custom which destroyed the possibility of law working effectively and fairly.

85. David Ogg, *England in the Reigns of James II and William III* (Oxford, 1955), p. 78.

86. "The Doctrine and Discipline of Divorce," in *John Milton: Complete Poems and Major Prose*, ed. Merritt Hughes (New York, 1957), pp. 697, 700. The editor points out that "Milton's attacks on custom . . . continue a tradition among Protestant Reformers. . . ."

87. W. R. Chadwick, "Wycherley: The Seven Lean Years," pp. 30–34; all information of these debts and the imprisonment is from this source. My thanks to Professor Chadwick for sending me copies of various primary source materials, particularly the Common Pleas documents.

88. Gildon, p. 7.

89. Hooker, II, 121.

90. Chadwick, p. 32.

91. *Ibid.*, for sum of actual debt; Hooker, II, 411 for 700£.

92. "Biographical Data on William Wycherley and his Father," p. 35.
93. Robert J. Allen, "Two Wycherley Letters," *TLS* (18 April 1935).
94. Summers, III, 272–75.
95. Chadwick, p. 32.
96. *Moneys Received and Paid for Secret Services of Charles II and James II*, for 30 March 1679 to 25 December 1688, p. 120. Manuscript of this volume is in the Bodleian. On the previous 29th September, 200£ bounty was paid to Sir George Etherege, p. 112.
97. *Spence, Anecdotes*, #791.
98. Hooker, II, 230.
99. Quoted in full, Chapter 5, n.79.
100. Common Pleas, 40/3016, m.1092.
101. Gildon, p. 8.

Chapter V

The Manor of Wem

After his success as steward to the Marquis of Winchester during the Commonwealth, and his apprenticeship in the practical, as well as theoretical aspects of the law as steward and as student in the Inner Temple, Daniel Wycherley, whose career we now resume, was well prepared to take the next step, the purchase of a single large estate. He already had possession of Clive Hall and adjoining properties as his inheritance from his father, and he maintained that as his main residence.[1] He had apparently been compelled to give up many of the leases to his diverse holdings of the Marquis' properties,[2] and he wished now to continue and consolidate his acquisition of land. His purchase in June 1665 of the Manor of Wem and Loppington, Shropshire, where the family had originated, gave him the lordship over several hundred tenants of the Manor, the advowson to the parish church of Wem (shortly to pass into the hands of son George) and claim to a title, Lord of the Manor, Lord Wycherley, a dignity which pleased his middle class sense of achievement.

The new beginning which the purchase of the manor marked did not, however, sever all ties with the past, nor, as we shall see, did it insure a steady mounting to the hoped-for heights of success. His stewardship with the Marquis continued to bind him to suits for some years. In 1657 one James Knight, whose family had leased Frobury Farm from the Marquis of Winchester since the days of Queen Elizabeth, asked Daniel, who was steward to the Marquis, to take over the lease and sublet it to him again since he was

[154]

"infirm . . . and used Crutches" and was too old to pay the rent or to purchase more as he had planned. In June of that year they reached agreement for 20£ a year and 340£ fine for the adjacent Dayryhouse Farm. So "Daniel Wycherley of the Inner Temple London gent" took over Frobury Farm, made over 100£ worth of repairs to the buildings and let Knight rent Dayryhouse Farm. But after Knight died several years later, his widow, Anne, sued Daniel for having tricked her husband into the agreement, for failure to turn Frobury Farm back over to her, and for demanding the 340£ without proper papers. He agreed to be content with 30£ and the old rent if she would pay 30£ per year, 20£ toward rent and the remainder toward the fine. But she failed to do so, and in 1661 he tried to eject her. At length on 10 December 1667, the court decreed that Daniel "should be quieted in enjoyment of Frobury Farm and that the said Anne should pay him the arrears of 30£ per annum incurred in her husbands life time," and Daniel was to rent part of Dayryhouse Farm worth 20£ per annum to her. The Court ratified this decision 10 January 1668. Nevertheless, son William Knight sued while yet a minor; interrogatories were still being taken in 1678 on behalf of both sides, but the depositions were clearly in Daniel's favor and his agreements stood under time and test. Not many persons were so dogged or wrongheaded as Anne Knight and William in fleeing an agreement to which they were bound, but such gad-fly suits about a wide range of properties occupied Daniel needlessly.[3]

There were, for example, miscellaneous suits, such as the one which ran from 1661–1664 involving the true claim to a piece of property—almost all the cases seem to revolve about this issue—in Lincolnshire,[4] and several suits concern houses in London, leased from the Marquis' properties. The historian Gough reported that "Wicherley parted with all the leases which he had of the Marquesse's lands and what houses he had in London,"[5] after the suit brought against him by Lord St. John; but Gough was misinformed. Daniel had, for instance, possession of the Whitchurch Farm,

[155]

Hampshire, which he had from his brother-in-law Shrimpton, as late as 1667, and he probably held it longer for there
was no indication in the suit concerning that property that
he must or would sell it.[6] In a deposition Daniel gave for a
friend John Hawes on 14 November 1671, his address was
given "of the Inner Temple, London," which suggests that
he may have retained quarters in the Temple, as William
apparently did, for his use, or which may have been used
only for the effect of status in the case.[7] He certainly could
have used a residence in London, for he became involved in
1682 in an argument over property he owned in St. Peter the
Poor Parish in London.[8]

Daniel did not, quite obviously, place all his property into
one holding but kept several well-placed rentals, perhaps
more than we are presently aware of, if they did not become
subject to law suits. He gained a position of some prestige in
1663 when he was named one of the Commissioners for the
King in Shropshire. *The Statutes of the Realm* list his
appointment and yearly recommission from 1663 till 1680,[9]
but this may not have been a constant service, for in 1675 the
list of Commissioners was amended "with the omission of
. . . Danl. Witcherly of Clive," although the 1674–75
listing included "Danll. Witcherly of Clithe."[10] A document
which may clarify this question contains "a list of the
Justices of Peace put out of commission since your Lordship
had the Seals," at the end of which we find: "Daniel
Wicherley Salop, May, 1675, per Lord Newport with counsel
hearde."[11] Daniel had been made Justice of the Peace,[12]
though it is not certain when, in addition to commissioner
for collecting taxes and so forth, and several justices wanted
him out; they presented their case and, as Gough reported:
"The King rising up said to the Lord President, 'I thinke wee
must putt him out,' to which all the rest agreed, and it was
done."[13] He lost the commission for a time and may have
been later reinstated,[14] but he apparently lost the Justice
position conclusively.

In June 1665 Daniel purchased the Manor of Wem and

[156]

Loppington from Sir William Playters and Richard Onslow and several others, trustees of Thomas Earl of Arundell. Loppington is a little village about equal in size to Clive and forms the western-most point of a triangle with Wem and Clive. The purchase price of the Manor is not known though Garbet mentioned that Daniel owned estates "to the amount of 560£ per annum exclusive of this Manor of Wem and Loppington,"[15] and one might guess its price to be at least 7000£, based on the resale price.

Daniel's career as Lord of the Manor was not a smooth one, for several major issues rose during that time: a suit by 43 tenants against him, a great fire in Wem, his son George's disastrous clerical career and a plethora of lesser concerns in and out of the family.

Hardly ten years had passed in Daniel's lordship when there were unmistakable signs that a serious breach between lord and his tenants—copyholders, boroughholders, and freeholders—was developing. Already in 1667 George Chambre and his widowed mother, Mary, defended their purchase of freehold lands from Playters, but Daniel wanted to see proof since he said the land was copyhold not freehold and they owed him rent. The crux of the question rested on how the court rolls actually described the nature of possession, where the court rolls were and who would or would not reveal them; these issues recurred countless times. Daniel said the tenants would not show the court rolls; they said they had them and would show them and he could look at them himself for certitude.[16]

In a parallel suit to that of Chambre in November 1669, Daniel charged that his chief steward, Richard Jebb, who had been steward under Arundell for twelve years, held a number of court rolls for properties in the manor but would not show them to the manor lord, particularly those which were said to be freehold. When Daniel purchased the manor, Jebb continued as steward and retained all of the court rolls of the manor; in addition, he had the continuing right to accept surrenders of properties or grant admittances to the

[157]

same by new tenants; set and take fines and enroll all changes of tenant in the court rolls and manor books as well as enroll all acts of the manor court. The key to this case is once again the precise contents or conditions of the deed and its whereabouts. In this case, however, Daniel admitted that the Jebbs "had anciently within the manor several copyhold lands and lands called boroughhold lands and . . . hath of late times purchased the freehold of some part of the copyhold lands . . . But the certainty thereof is unknown to your orator," that is, Daniel.[17] The implications of the suit became clearer when Daniel insinuated "the said Jebb by combination with several other persons yet unknown to your orator . . ," suggesting conspiracy, which by the time all this business of copyhold is over seems a reasonable notion. Jebb's reply set forth each of the plots of land of which he had freehold or copyhold and the tenants who were now living on or farming each plot, that is, twenty of them. He refused to show the deeds to Daniel "to give him an occasion to impeach this defts title," and relied on the court's judgment upon his evidence.[18]

Daniel apparently had no fear of alienating his closest allies when he sued his own steward, Richard Jebb, who obviously knew the manor and its ways far better than Daniel, who repeatedly claimed that as a new purchaser he was ignorant of many of the customs of the manor. Jebb was during this time, as presumably before Daniel's lordship, in charge of the manor courts; these court records were kept in a cryptic Latin: "curia Baron, Daniel Wicherley gent Dm manor pd ibn tenta sep die Augustii regm Dom nos Car Secundi dei gratia Angl Scoc Franc et Ebur Regis fidei defendor . . . coram Richard Jebb senll." The court was held frequently, 7 August 1665 as above, 10 October, 9 November, 30 November, 21 December, 1 February, 5 April and so forth; and from it a good deal of revenue flowed into the Manor lord's coffers, over 400£ in 1670.[19]

The case of the tenants against the lord of the Manor was building year by year. In 1672 William Allenson was sued by

Daniel for refusing to hand over "several of the court books" which he had "gotten into his hands"; and Allenson on his part declared that many of the papers were destroyed when his father was in Shrewsbury with a garrison for the "late majesty King Charles I in his late unhappy wars" which was plundered by the "rebellious forces," but he knew minute details of the properties and was willing to hand over some papers even though there had never before been any question of his holdings.[20] Richard Higginson came into a fairly similar suit with Daniel almost simultaneously and once again supplied minute details of land holdings; Daniel sued for several fines and rents and herriots due him, according to the court rolls which Higginson "contrives with others to conceal," but in reply Higginson claimed to have purchased the leases from Playters "which the complt viewed and thereunder subscribed viz. DW 26 Augusti 1665," apparently close to the purchase date of the manor, and brought the deeds to Daniel, but his bailiff refused them in demand for "more money for rent than this deft knows to be justly due to him."[21]

Allenson and Higginson, with William Felton and "others the freeholders Burroughholders and copyholders of the Manor of Wem," tried again in May 1672 to charge Daniel, but he effectively parried their suit by pointing out that the complainants were "not particularly named" and there were "above a hundred burroughholders and copyholders . . . besides freeholders" who were obviously not all being bound.[22] By the next year they had the suit properly prepared and in Michaelmas term the following forty-three tenants sued Daniel:

William Allenson, William Felton, William Menlove, Lewis Bevan, Richard Higginson, Richard Allen, George Tyler, John Tyler, William Tyler, Adam Tyler, William Moody, Samuel Skeynton, John Pay, Rowland Dirkin, William Forgahan, James Forgahan, Samuel Barnes, Edward Barnes, Ralph Barnes, Robert Higginson, John Higginson, Robert Hotchkiss, Roger Chidloe, John Hotchkiss, Roger Hussey, Randle Hanmer, Peirce Roderick, Richard Pidgen, Richard

Wells, Allen Sherrat, John Wood, Richard Jebb, Arthur Colcott, John Davyes, John Holgate, Richard Gibbons, Roger Sythe, Arthur Hincks, William Adderley, Margt Adams widow, Anne Adams widow, Mary Barnes widow, & widow Harwood.[23]

The basic purpose of these suits was to test the customs of the Manor, for the Manor of Wem, like others, had many customs which regulated the daily financial, social, and legal affairs of the lord and the tenants, fixing such costs as the payment of rent, inheritance fines, purchase fines, exchange fines, penalties for breaking the peace of the manor—so many pence for an "affray" and so many for a "blood" when the tenants got into pub fights—and controls on the lord as well. Thus the suit of 1673 reexamined the customs which were of long standing and was generally understood by everyone on the Manor to ascertain whether Daniel's alterations were justified or not, whether his actions which so greatly annoyed the tenants were, in truth, in accord with those customs. In their abortive suit of 17 May 1672, Allenson, Higginson and Felton enumerated at least sixteen separate customs to be tried, and they laid at Daniel's feet a dozen violations of custom, some of the chief of which were: he conceals the manor customs so they cannot be examined; assesses unreasonable fines for admittances when these fines are to be absolute and unchangeable (one of the key issues); seizes lands until payment is made, contrary to due process; sits in his own manor court, when the steward is in charge, and returns his own juries, which of course intimidates jury and judge and destroys the legal process; makes his servants rather than a disinterested party assessors of property values; "exacts Rents & Herriots from poore men where none are due"; and conceals the court rolls which indicate the property and agreement of possession, when such must be available for concerned parties to examine.[24] The customs were later reduced for the convenience of trial to six: a fine must be paid when a whole, not part of an estate is surrendered; a tenant could sublet his lands without surrendering them; if a man married a woman who held property, he would retain it after her death; a wife would hold all lands of her husband after his death; a tenant could cut and sell timber from his leased lands; set penalties were to be paid for nonappearance at manor court.[25]

To sketch out the progress of this suit, which is painful to read in its length and cruel destruction of many of the participants, we will rely on the Exchequer Decree of 9 February 1682, a document of nearly 4000 words which rehearses dispassionately the actions of the case; other documents provide the human element.[26]

To the suit brought to Court by the forty-three tenants, Daniel admitted, under subpoena, to some of the charges and denied others: he did take the Court rolls to his own house "about a mile and a halfe from the Mannor," meaning Clive, in order to protect them from Richard Jebb; he declined to accept the expected fine upon admittances because the amount of the fines was at his discretion and not absolute; he did not sit in court and so forth. He then filed his cross-bill in Hilary term, the beginning of the year 1675, asking the court to subpoena several of the now defendants to answer his queries and present some of the Court rolls. Thereafter, depositions were taken on both sides and the Court set a trial date for 3 December,

on which day upon hearing Mr Attorney Generall Mr Sollicitor Generall Mr Sergeant Baldwin Mr Sawyer & others of Councell with ye said Complts in ye first suite & upon reading of severall of ye deposicons taken on ye part of ye said Complts in ye same suite & of an aunctient parchmt Roll or writeing produced by Lord Newport entituled a booke conteining ye Customs of ye Mannor of Wemm And alsoe one other pchment writeing entituled a presentmt Roll of a Jury of a Court of Survey taken in ye yeare of our Lord God 1564 & of severall aunctient Copyes of Court Rolls on ye behalfe of ye said Complts in ye first bill & upon hearing Mr Serjeant Maynard Mr Serjeant Calthrop Sir John King Mr Serjeant Pemberton Mr Lechmere & others of Councell with ye said Daniel Wicherley And upon reading a Decree made in ye late Court of Wards in ye 20th yeare of ye reigne of Queene

Elizabeth . . . [and upon reading of several other documents on the issue] And upon long debate of ye matter by Councell on both sides this Court seeing noe Cause to depart from ye said Decree were of opinion & soe declared that ye matters in ye said Decree in ye Court of Wards being so delib[er]ately & upon serious consideracons made as it appeared to bee wherein the fynes aswell upon Admissions as upon Surrenders are declared to bee Arbitrary & at ye will of ye Lord . . . It was then ordered by this Court that ye said Defendant Daniel Wycherley be quieted & Settled in ye possession of his said Mannor of Wemm and of Assessing & takeing fynes upon Admittances according to ye said Decree of ye Court of Wards.

Nothing, however, was finished, appearances to the contrary. Daniel, in his customary abrupt fashion, seized the lands of one William Mather for refusing to pay a fine upon admission after the death of his predecessor, and Mather sued him for trespass in Michas 1677, with Richard Higginson taking the case for Mather who was still a minor. A Shropshire jury awarded in favor of Mather, thus overthrowing the previous verdict and granting Daniel nothing more than 95£ costs and a prohibition against taking any fines until the case was settled—that is, if no further cross bills or exceptions were made. But Daniel refused to accept the verdict by the Shropshire jury and demanded in February 1678 a trial by a jury of "an Indifferent County." The court approved his request, the tenants not objecting, and on 6 June a trial was announced for the following 23 October before a jury of Lincolnshire, but the tenants not appearing, the trial was reset for 20 November, when they again did not appear. Daniel brought an action against Mather to try the custom again, and the Court noted that "if the deft did pay Nynety five Pounds costs for ye former tryall that a new tryall should be had in Michas Term following by a Jury of the County of Hertford." Daniel missed the payment date but managed to pay the original costs besides an additional 5£ by 21 June 1680. George Tyler for the tenants brought an action against Daniel, which was tried at length on 28 April 1681, reaffirming that the fines should be "one year at ancient Copyhold rent & noe more," that is, absolute and not at the will of the lord. Thus the verdict would stand unless the defendant Daniel should demand new trial, "and accordingly the said Daniel Wicherley did instruct his Councell for ye said tryall," and in Hilary term, 27 January 1682,

said issue was tryed at ye barr of this Court by a speciall jury of ye said County of Hertford where after a long & faire hearing of what could be alleadged on either side And upon full Evidence given on either side ye Jury did give their verdict for ye deft Daniel Wicherley . . . This Court was fully satisfied by ye proofs made by ye said deft Daniel Wicherley at ye tryall aforesaid And with ye verdict thereupon And unanimously declared that ye fynes payable to ye Ld of ye said Mannor of Wemm upon Admission of any Copyholder to any lands held of ye Mannor either upon descent or upon surrender of any such Copyhold lands have bene from tyme to tyme whereof ye memory of man is not to ye contrary & still ought to be Arbitrary uncertaine & at ye will of ye Ld of ye said Mannor It is therefore this present day that is to say on Thursday ye nynth day of February . . . adjudged & decreed that ye said Daniel Wicherley his heires & Assignes Lords of ye said Mannor of Wemm from henceforth bee & are hereby established & quieted in ye possession of such Arbitrary & reasonable fynes by him already assessed & leavyed according to ye Custome aforesaid upon any of ye Tennts of ye said Mannor who are parties to theise suites for any lands by them respectively held of that Mannor.

The decree was made on 9 February 1682, but once again the tone of finality in these words is deceptive: there was yet more. The case had been begun under the names of Allenson, Higginson, and Felton, but Mather became specially involved and Higginson with him, with the action of trespass against Daniel; George Tyler filed depositions in behalf of Mather before he too became more deeply implicated.[27] Thus, various persons presented specific cases but the issue was always the customs of the Manor. Tyler and Wycherley had met before at the bar under better, though somewhat farcical, circumstances. Tyler had leased some property on the Manor from a Thomas Payne, who upon admitting Tyler, was to pay the Manor lord a fee, called a herriot, for admittances according to the Manor customs. Payne delayed, and when Daniel said he wanted a black mare worth 9 or 10£, he delayed further, saying he wanted to buy the mare back. Daniel agreed but meanwhile, "then needing to go to London and no coach being available,"[28] he sent his servant to Payne to get the horse saying he would sell it back to Payne later. Surprisingly enough, after Daniel had trotted off to London, Payne, being unable to get the horse, sued Daniel. He in return made an offer of sale to Payne, who refused. Then Daniel refused: no sale! Tyler must have sat on his land watching this Keystone cops escapade, glad he was not part of that sort of legal circus.

In 1680 the cost of supporting this suit now stretching out to Jarndycean length was bearing heavily on the tenants, in particular those who were paying the major costs. According to the House of Lords papers of 27 November 1680, "two several sums of 95£ were taxed" on the trials "to be paid by the Petitioner," who was Wycherley. "William Felton, the principal plaintiff with several others (who had disbursed all or most of the money in the suits), having applied to Petitioner for a final agreement, Petitioner paid them the two sums of 95£, and obtained discharges therefor. Notwithstanding this, one George Tyler, named a plaintiff, and others (who expended little or no money in the suits), obtained an order in the Exchequer against Petitioner to pay the one 95£, then and there, and the other 95£ on the last day of term, or in default be committed to the Fleet."[29] Daniel protested but the Court would not interfere. Tyler continued into 1684 to test some of the customs and did in fact appear to win some, such as the absolute right of tenants to cut and dispose of timber from their lands;[30] but the case of Felton is particularly interesting for the light it throws on Daniel and on his methods of dealing with his tenants. The House of Lords report of 27 November annexed the following:

The Appellant [Daniel] finding Felton displeased with the

[164]

Respondents for having employed another agent [this is Tyler] being unable to defray his extravagant expenses, obtained a fraudulent release from him, or by means of fair promises, contrary to the trust reposed in him by the rest of the tenants, who have paid Felton 1,400£ for his expenses, for which he refuses to render an account. The Appeal is merely to weary out Respondents, who have lost some 23,000£ in the late fire at Wem. Appellant has his proper remedy against Felton at Common law; though in fact he never actually paid the two sums of 95£ to Felton at all, but took the release as a consideration for enfranchising his copyhold estate. As to releases from other of the Respondents, they were gained, if at all, from indigent tenants, who were forced to seal them to avoid imprisonment for debt. . . .[31]

In Easter term, 1682, Wycherley asked Felton to accept a subpoena as a favor in case Daniel might need him to answer some questions which would supposedly protect Felton from additional charges of the other tenants; Felton agreed and did nothing but wait the arrival of the promised copy of the bill, until he was suddenly charged with failure to appear and was haled into court "to come into London being about 130 miles distant from the same." This was not the first time Daniel had duped another and Felton's testimony is revealing. The reasons, he said, why Daniel had to go to other counties for a fair jury was that his "litigiousness caused an ill report to be of him and most did absent themselves from his company." Further, his refusal to pay the 95£ costs was, Felton claimed, purposely designed for "the utter ruin of the tenants" for he had "prevailed for a protection under the Marquess of Winchester to stop any proceedings at law against him." Felton "should have been admitted to a copyhold estate within the said manor upon the surrender of Richard Higginson . . . for the reimbursing and indempnification of this deft of a deed of 500£ paid and engaged to pay by this deft for the use of the said Higginson." Consequently, he exhibited his bill in the Exchequer for Daniel to admit him to his lands but Daniel "prohibited the steward from acompting of any surrender or admittance unless they would first come into composition

[165]

for their fine at an unreasonable rate contrary to the custom and verdict . . . passed thereupon." Felton was in short pressured to extremes: he was "greatly out of purse and in debt for several sums of money," yet Daniel would neither pay the costs nor admit him to his lands. "At the most wicked and unreasonable demand of the complt . . . [he signed] a release that he would not further prosecute him for the aforesaid 95£."[32] And from the House of Lords records we know to what extent Felton was out of purse. It is an action such as this Garbet had in mind when he wrote, "Mr. Wycherley's last resource was corruption. He found means to bribe Mr. Felton the plaintiff's agent, to betray them,"[33] and thereafter Tyler was appointed, as noted above, much to Felton's displeasure. Garbet also pointed out that, by the last trial, "thirteen of them had been bought off by Mr. Wycherley; some had been ruined or undone by the great fire, others by the bankruptcy of Mr. Smith; and what was worst of all they could not recover their most material writings and evidences":[34] Felton, we might add, to complete this dismal winding down of the legal process, found himself in November of the year 1683, in Fleet prison: "a prisoner in Exemcon in his Mayties Prison of ye Fleet for considerable sums of money." Daniel had apparently arranged his stay there, for the deeds in question are "at ye Defts owne house scituate in Clive."[35] He was still in the Fleet the following February, dodging a law clerk who was demanding payment of 8£ 3s 4d court costs: the clerk met Felton in the Fleet but being unsure who he was asked him where Felton was; Felton said he would "goe & see," and quietly went off to another corner of the Fleet and "came not backe."[36]

Charles Dickens wrote in 1851 about the legal creature of London, and much of what he said about it would have been familiar to Felton and endless other suitors and to Daniel as well:

> This is the Court of Chancery; which has its decaying houses and its blighted lands in every shire; which has its worn out lunatic in every madhouse, and its dead in every

churchyard; which has its ruined suitor, with his slipshod heels and threadbare dress, borrowing and begging the round of every man's acquaintance; which gives to monied might the means abundantly of wearying out the right, which so exhausts finances, patience, courage, hope; so overthrows the brain and breaks the heart; that there is not an honorable man among its practitioners who would not give the warning, "Suffer any wrong that can be done you rather than come here!"

. . . Another ruined suitor, who periodically appears from Shropshire, and breaks out into efforts to address the Chancellor at the close of the day's business, . . . can by no means be made to understand that the Chancellor is legally ignorant of his existence. . . . (*Bleak House*, Chapter 1)

It is almost as if he had in mind one of the tenants from the Manor of Wem, Shropshire, in 1684.

During the decade of 1675 to 1685, Daniel Wycherley was extremely busy with a number of important matters simultaneously with the suit with his tenants: the great fire of Wem in 1675, referred to several times above (see Appendix I); the debts of his son George; the several concerns of William which we have already seen; and a miscellany of at least a dozen unrelated suits. Little wonder that at the end of this decade, much of his power was dissipated, though assuredly not his life or spirit. Of these matters, the short sad career of son George is no doubt the most important.

The second son of Daniel and Bethia, George was born in 1651, ten years after William, possibly at the Kings Street house in London. Destined by his family to take orders in the Church and educated at the schools of Wem and at several public schools[37] to prepare him to attend the University, he went down in December 1667, to Oxford to Queens College and "by the advice and direccon of that Reverend Devine Doctor Barlow then Provost of Queenes . . . [was] putt under the tuterige of one Master Crossthwait a Fellow of that College."[38] It soon became apparent that his family's intentions and his inclinations in no way corresponded. That is not to say he failed to take a degree, for after

[167]

matriculating on 6 March 1668, he took his BA in 1671 and his MA in 1674, but almost by inadvertence rather than by his full effort. By the time he was to leave Oxford, he had avoided his tutor for a good two years, had sold all his books, had "disposed of his bead from under him" to pay his debtors, and had run into "a great debt to the Colledge and severl psons to the sum of one hundred and forty pounds." And this in spite of a parental allowance to him as commoner of 40£ a year, somewhat more than he was to pay his curates a few years later, and the not infrequent gifts from his father and, more covertly, his mother.[39] In Daniel Wycherley's view, George had "lived verry badly much addicted to play and kept verry idle Compenny." He was, in imitation of the Prodigal Son, the very pattern of the young man from the Provinces who came to the City, or University, and spent his portion in loose living, in gaming, and in what is usually called riot, following the stereotypical progress of youth in its moral decline, a very popular topic in eighteenth century moral literature and painting from Defoe to Hogarth. But George had only begun to show his potential for prodigality. After his father had paid his debts in Oxford, except for that of a mercer, George came back to Wem to be presented on 12 April 1672, as Rector of the Church of Wem, the advowson to which Daniel had attained when he purchased the Manor of Wem. The Parish of Wem was at that time a very well managed and profitable organization, divided into four sections or quarters, Ashton, Wem, Edaston or sometimes Cotton, and Horton, each with its complement of three church wardens and an exact accounting system.

At least one of the clerics who preceded George is of special interest. When in May 1670, Master Rees Hughes died, leaving the rectorship vacant, his successor was Rev. Daniel Wycherley, D.D., minister from 21 July to 16 November 1671.[40] This Daniel may have been a remote relative of the Clive Wycherleys, for he was brought to the parish "ad pntacionem Danielis Wicherly de Clive als Cliffe in com. Salop generosi,"[41] or as elsewhere expressed, Daniel

"presented one of his own name Doctor Wycherley . . . during the minority of" George,[42] apparently
out of kindness to this man who had been dispossessed on 1 June 1644 of his living in Queens College, Cambridge, after being charged by ten witnesses on a series of
eleven "notoriously false" charges, e.g., not known to have
taken Solemn League and Covenant, slack in getting
signatures of others, bargained for tithes, and so forth.[43] He
was one of those dispossessed when Dr. Barlow was finding
means of surviving similar purges in Oxford. From this 80£ a
year post, Wycherley wandered to Hereford in 1649 to wait
out the Puritan interregnum, and was attached as prebend
there in 1660. In June 1670, the King granted him his D.D.
degree which he "by his loyalty" had been prevented from
taking,[44] and on 21 August of that year a warrant was signed
for him to hold the rectory of Wem, along with that of
Withrey, Herefordshire.[45] By 1672, the Bishop of Worcester
was petitioning the King for a *mandamus* for the canonry in
the Cathedral Church of Hereford for Wycherley, which the
King granted on 15 September.[46] He had matriculated in
1622 at Queens College, Cambridge, had a long, arduous but
honorable career, passing near the more famous family of
Wycherley almost by accident, before going south to end his
days at Hereford Cathedral.

He left Wem 14 November 1671, as George was about to
reach his majority, but George's accumulation of years had
so little corresponding increase of money or prudence that as
in his first twenty-one years, he continued to live off his
father. One is tempted to speculate on causes for George's
hapless ways, perhaps a collapse in the shadow of the very
visibly successful older brother, perhaps a victim of the worst
aspects of desire for gain and the easy life, at least to some
extent inspired by Daniel, perhaps simply a weak and
doomed character. When his father compounded for the
First Fruits on 11 November 1672, Daniel paid the money
therefor to the King, just as he had paid the 30£ for George's
installation into the Rectory. Almost simultaneously

[169]

George became involved in two separate but crucial situations. On 1 April 1674 a former incumbent cleric in the parish, Andrew Parsons, who had been "outed for scandalous words preached against" the King, tried to eject George from the Parsonage; the verdict went in the defendant's favor and the "Attorney's bill of about fourscore pounds" was paid by Daniel. In October of 1674, George would find it necessary to borrow "money to defraye the Charges of Collecting and gatheringe in the sd. Tythes," and approached Charles Charleton several times for loans of 100£ and later for 50£ more for "some debt which he owed att Oxford and some other disbursements."[47] Thus began the process of George's short life of assuming his father would pay his bills while he himself borrowed heavily. It is not possible from available evidence to determine why George went into debt so far so fast—though he burned up 5£ worth of tobacco in six weeks, if that is any clue—for he lived in his father's house for about two years where he and his servants had their lodging and food, before taking possession of the Rectory;[48] the Rectory of Wem was ordinarily worth 500£ per year in rents, though estimates ran from 400£ to 700£; his marriage around 1679, to a woman named Dorothy (against his father's wishes) brought a portion of 500£ "besides plate";[49] and his prior debts in Oxford had been paid by his father (though his borrowing from Charleton suggests further debts there). Nevertheless, between 1674 and 1682 when the sheriff seized his property and bore him off to Wem prison, he had amassed a debt of 1500£.[50]

After a few weak denials, George did not protest the fact of his debts but went to his father to beg assistance. Daniel's refusal to pay should not be viewed as cruelty even though the imprisonment and subsequent events stimulated the acrimonious family quarrel which ended only with the death of George in 1688. For Daniel realized full well his son's financial and constitutional inability to repay anything, and he had little money himself. His trial with the tenants was, by 1682, reaching a climax and its expense was very great (3000£ for the tenants,[51] scarcely less for Daniel); he had been actively assisting William, with the "greate trouble and charge hee had suffered soe lately for beinge bound with [George's] Eldest brother beinge so Fresh in his Memory,"[52] an allusion to his paying the debt to Barnaby; and son Henry in 1680 matriculated at Christ Church, Oxford, where, Connely maintains, he ran up "rather amazing College bills"; while there is no evidence for this, he may well have followed his brother George's bent;[53] and under any circumstances the expense would have been a significant additional burden on Daniel.

After George was locked into Wem prison on 7 April, Daniel worked out a solution and presented it to his son to be sealed on 3 August 1682: it was a trust which empowered brothers John and Henry Wycherley, Thomas Teague and Robert Smith to take control of all the properties, buildings, and lands, except for two rooms in the Rectory for George and his servant, for nine years, under the supervision of Daniel, who would himself keep control of Trench farm for his own benefit, to gather all the tithes of the Rectory of Wem and "with the rentes and profitts of the said Rectory and premises pay or cause to be paid all such debtes as [George] doth now owe . . . untill all his just debts . . . with the lawfull interest thereof shall be fully satisfied and paid together with all such summes as the said Daniel Wycherley [and the four trustees] shall expend . . . in gathering of the said tythes."[54] Inevitably, in such family arrangement where the soundest trust would create animosity and bitterness— Daniel admitted trusts were "certaine troubles"—this one shortly became a source of great rancor. Whatever one may think of Daniel's inflated sense of importance, he was a generous man to his own family, and to others in distress— until he was crossed. Then, when the spirit vanished and the letter took charge, he was unsympathetic, tenacious, exacting. George was of course unprincipled; he spent money with incredible abandon, and he had a genius for the very worst choice: he christened his infant daughter, on 17

December 1680,[55] Letitia-Isabella in obvious adulation of his brother's glamorous Countess wife. The poor child died even before her father. Yet for all his frailty, it is quite likely that he was in some measure treated unfairly by the trustees, although one is placed in the position of judging his various distortions of the situation, just as was the case with Henry, Second Earl of Drogheda. His plea, "he wanted to buy bread and drinke and hath been forced to drinke water," sounds melodramatic.[56] Yet, his testimony on his father is quite damning; "Daniell by cunning practice and contrivance had of and fraudulently detained from your Orator George Wycherley all the residue out of your Orators Estate by the hands of one of your Orators Tennants whom the said Daniell Wycherley most wrongfully disseized and dis-possessed of what hee held from your Orator." He is equally harsh on his brothers, claiming that he entered the trust with "Confidence that the Obligation of Nature would have been sufficiently prevalent to have disposed the said John and Daniel Wycherley to doe your Orator comon Justice which indeed was more than your Orator (who Knew theire temper) could expect from their Generosity and principles,"[57] but this was preceded by an obvious distortion, and later he cried he had been forced into the trust. Daniel, for his part, was understandably incensed that his son married against his wishes, that George allowed parishioners who were homeless after the fire in Wem to use the large parish house for only a short time and then "forbad [my and others'] comeing to or troubleings his house which [I] thought verry Ill requitall,"[58] that he himself had paid 90£ for a suit brought by sixty parishioners in 1674 against George to detain paying tithes and was never paid back even though he travelled to London three times over three terms to defend George,[59] that George ignored his advice to be prudent with money and retorted "he was past his Pupillage," and later that he "used such expressions against . . . his Father not fit to bee repeated much less to bee used by a man of his profession."[60] Nevertheless, it is a fact that Robert Mathews, whom George had selected to officiate at the parish church in his stead, had to bear slanderous insults from the trustees concerning his proper ordination and was denied his 30£ yearly salary by the trustees in his third and fourth year (1684 and '85) until he besought the Chancellor of the Diocese of Lichfield and Coventry to sequester tithes for payment.[61] In February 1686, three defendants submitted sworn answers to the trustees that "1200£ of the debt yet remains,"[62] which under any reckoning is an extremely slow reparation of debt by the trustees, though one person believed that after paying for labor done, the trustees had little or no money left over.[63] The accusations against Henry and John, who had very few endearing qualities about them and who seemed much more taken with greed than with fraternal piety or principle, and those against Daniel, that they did not discharge their part of the trust properly to pay debts but kept undue amounts under the guise of expense, repair and so forth, apparently have real basis, for little true communication occurred between the disputants except through charge and countercharge. George did not pacify matters when he had Teague and some others arrested (Smith fled the country) because they had signed bonds for his debts and refused to pay for them, Teague for 800 or 900£;[64] and then he had his tithe barns locked and forbade his parishioners to cooperate with the trustees.

Throughout these family quarrels one has the impression that Daniel dominated almost entirely, but his wife was in fact actively involved as well, although we happen to know relatively less about her. Bethia appears to have been a strong woman, not agreeing with her husband in principle or act, and inclined to hand her children, to George at least and probably to the others, money under the table. Several witnesses affirmed that Daniel was "much discontented" with his wife's "intermeddling" with the trust. She had ordered servants to sell grain from the tithe barns for George's benefit[65] just as she had independently sent servants to Oxford with money for George. She pawned house plate and sold it for him and borrowed money for him, contrary to Daniel's wishes, and another time she apparently sent "a piece of silk and at another time six silver spoons as a token" of good will to Charleton until full payment was made to him of George's debt.[66] But Daniel held great respect for her, and when he was in London, she took over the official running of the Manor; "all her time in her husbands absence except for about two years before her death," which was three years after Daniel's demise, she managed "the sd Daniels housekeeping and servants . . . and received monies coming from the profits of the farm . . . and paying servants wages and workmen."[67] There is no reason to suppose she did not perform these operations with authority and skill, for otherwise Daniel would have employed his steward or one of his agents to handle business or continue to entrust it to his brother John, after whom his son was named, who was "sojourning at Clive at the sd Daniels house," and who usually "looked over Daniels business and gave orders and directions for management of the same.[68] Though we know unfortunately little of her character,[69] one senses in her a great capability which had relatively small scope for expression. It would be strange to think that she was not deeply pleased with William's successes in London and proud that some of her firm character showed through in his works. One wonders in fact to what extent she was responsible for Daniel's paying William's several debts and in other ways softening her husband's reaction to their first son's financial ineptness.

The cross purposes of George and the trustees resulted in a near collapse of the trust; the debts were being tardily satisfied, the rectory buildings were falling into ruin, and the trustees completely relinquished their function to Daniel.[70] By 1687 the disaster was nearly accomplished. One Thomas Prichard claimed that the

> trustees do not aid in the managing of the said Trust but suffer the Corne gathered last year & for the tithes of the said Rectory to be eaten by vermine And that he hath seen the dore

[174]

of the barne where the same Corne is lodged carelessly lye
open & swine eating the said Corne, And yt the walls
belonging to the said Farme are become ruinous . . . .[71]

Another saw "mice and Ratts" eating the tithe grain, "to ye
loss of ye sale of ye Corne & it would have gotten a very good
price this last winter. And last 18th of May . . . the tithe
barnes were locked as formerly."[72] George's decision to lock
his barns was profitting him nothing, except to gratify his
spite. He had Thomas Teague arrested as well as "divers
other persons . . . for acting under the said trustees and for
serving them in that affair," and would have arrested Robert
Smith had he not fled England.[73] His reasons for not
arresting John and Henry were perhaps because they had
loaned him as much as 500£—John said his debt was
270£[74]—and Daniel was bound for 100£.[75] But what George
did was to press to have the trustees changed; John said he
was agreeable if his money were repaid. By the beginning of
1686, the court ordered that the trust be transferred,[76] though
it was Michas 1687 when John testified that he received

a note inscribed with the names of Ed. Kinaston, C. Sankey &
Wm Hanmer thereby giveing notice to this dept that [they]
were there att Wemm & did require this dept in psuance of an
order of ye 7 of July last past to transfer the trust & deliver to
them the poss[ess]ion of the barnes & corne belonging to the
Rectory.[77]

So the trust failed to solve the 1500£ debt. The case dragged
on, year and year, term after term, affidavit after deposition.[78]
George, who was supposed to be granted 100£ a year for his
expenses, complained he had "very little to maintaine
himselfe his Child & curat,"[79] and in 1685 that daughter, that
Letitia-Isabella, died, uncannily close to the death of her
namesake. In 1688, George was transferred to London and
committed to the Fleet prison, still groaning under a debt of
near 1000£.[80] His stay was short. Death relieved him. It was a
stroke of all too appropriate irony that William, not long out
of the Fleet himself, had to beg the money to bury his brother
George. We have his letters on this matter: he sent one to

Colonel James Grahme, who was Privy Purse to the King, but that first letter went astray to his brother Fergus, at Levens Hall, Westmorland; thus the pointed notation "Not Mr. Fargus" on the first letter extant.

> To Col., the Hon'ble J. Grahme, Whitehall, and not Mr. Fargus.
>
> December the 27th, 1688.
>
> Being, Sir, in the last distress for ten pounds to bury my late poor deceased brother in prison, I took the confidence to have recourse to him who has so generously (without solicitation) supported me these two years last past. You know I can mean none but yourself. But however, your brother has mistaken the direction of my letter, as he does the sum mentioned in it, for he tells me he has not twenty pounds in the office, which I did neither ask twenty pound or twenty pence from him. But I had the confidence to hope and beg it in this my present distress for my deceased brother. I might have found so generous a friend as you have been to me to have had the charity (on such an occasion) to have supplied me with ten pound (and not twenty) which I would and I hope could have repaid in some short time.
>
> To rectify therefore Mr. Fargus his mistake, not mine, you are troubled with this, from Sir,
>
> Your most obliged faithful humble servant,
>
> W. Wycherley.

Wycherley's appeal was in vain, not because Grahme was poor, which the writer was ironically observing when he wrote in the following letter, "if you want ten pounds," but possibly because Grahme who had "supported me these two years past," had tired of charity, or because with James II driven out of the country in November by a Parliament bent on a Protestant King, William III, he no longer had the King's benefits to dispense. At any rate, the second letter, following, which begins with the "courtier" reference similar to that in the letter to Mulgrave from prison, substituted any true hope for assistance for an ironic, circumlocutory wit.

> You courtiers, Sir, seldom cease to be friends but you begin to be enemies, and it is a double unkindness as it is a double

unhappiness for the miserable deserted man, which I beg
your honour and justice will secure me from. For as I got at
first your kindness without deserving it, so have I lost it too,
without deserving it. And I protest before God, if we were not
of late very much given to change, I should a little admire at
yours.

And (if I may be believed) I am more concerned for the loss
of such a friend than for the loss of his assistance, because the
first is a secret upbraiding me with the want of merit to keep
his friendship longer, the other but an upbraiding me with
the want of good fortune, which often attends the most
meritorious.

But I must consolate my want by yours, for if you want ten
pounds, I may the better bear the want of such a sum, so you
have, as 'twere, relieved my want in telling me you have not
wherewithal to do it. But yet, though you want money for
your friend, I hope, Sir, you will not kindness, for the less
assistance you can afford him, you should allow him the
more pity, the want of which and your good company would
have him yet more miserable, if it were possible for him to be
so.

But however, Sir, I may of late have deserved from you, I
hope you have charity enough left to pardon the trouble
given you by him whom no want of a new obligation can
make forget an old one. Let me not be so miserable at least as
to lose your kindness, for your love's a million, in the
opinion of.

Sir,
Your most obliged humble servant,
W. Wycherley.

To James Grahme, Esq.[81]

It was in Christmas week apparently that George died in the
Fleet. William's attempt to beg the burial fee having failed,
he took George's body home to Shropshire and buried him at
last at Wem.[82] Whatever happened to his wife, Dorothy, we
do not know; his most noticeable legacy was his debt which
came back to Shropshire with him to haunt the family.

Through these years of the 1680's, not only George, with
his inglorious fall and death, and William, but all the
members of the Wycherley family were undergoing critical
difficulties which created divisions, some perhaps permanent, between wife and husband, father and sons, brother

and brother. Even with due caution not to overemphasize these crises from the information we have, there is little to suggest that the state of the family or its relationships would improve substantially. Specifically, the steadily multiplying expenses Daniel incurred pressed him further to pay his just debts, quite apart from maintaining that standard of living in which the family had settled.[83] We have seen him borrowing 500£ from Richard Clayton in May 1682, which was probably to pay William's bills to Barnaby, but this loan became more troublesome when Clayton died and his widow, with Thomas Ireland, a long-time Wycherley foe, sued him for the money which he was, after his fashion, dilatory about repaying.[84] In a later case with Ireland over debt, Daniel simply closed the door on an order served him to appear in court:

> When the said Witcherley seeing this Depont he imediately hastened into his house And this Depont following him into the hall of his house where the said Witcherley then was, he the said Witcherley asked this Depont how his Matr [master] did, but he . . . perceiveing this Dept to be takeing the Writt of Execucon . . . out of his Pockett . . . in Order to serve him therewith . . . Witcherley imediately hastened out of the roome into another roome and imediately sent his servt to this Dept who Informed this Dept that his Master had wthdrawne himselfe apprehending that he . . . came hither to serve him . . . with a Writt of Execucon but that he was resolved he would not be served with the said Writt til he came to London [27 April 1686].[85]

Near the same time, he was forced to cancel what appears to have been a long standing order with Shrewsbury cloth merchant Arthur Dunn (or Donne) to deliver whatever "clothes and stuffes" Bethia and her family wanted.[86] For possibly the same reason of financial pressure throughout the 80's, Daniel was reneging on payment of lewnes, or taxes, to the parish Church of Wem.[87] These debts even from the early years of the decade brought Daniel to face a most unpleasant and disappointing necessity: he would have to sell the Manor.

[178]

Sir George Jeffreys, Lord Chief Justice and later Lord Chancellor of England, was interested in the estate for it was "near his own country and amongst his old acquaintance."[88] He had grown up in Shrewsbury and attended Shrewsbury School, perhaps contemporary with William Wycherley, who was four years older. This was the Jeffreys whose severity as Lord Chief Justice earned him the bitter reputation as the hanging judge of the Bloody Assizes in the summer of 1685 when he executed nearly 200 persons for treason in the rebellion of James, Duke of Monmouth, against his father King James II;[89] Monmouth was himself captured and executed on 15 July. Jeffreys approached Daniel in the fall of 1684 through his agents to negotiate a purchase and they agreed on a price of 7600£. On 23 December a deed of sale was drawn up and signed by which Daniel "in consideration of the 7600£ thus paid and of a further sum secured to be paid your orator did grant and convey the sd premises . . . to Sir George Jeoffreys"; the advowson to the church was 1000£ and the "other 6600£ should go toward the payment of the rest . . . and that 20 years value should be the rate of the rents."[90] To assure equity on the purchase, both parties agreed that agents designated by each should assay the true value of the properties, with the understanding that whatever the agents valued over or under the agreed-upon price would be paid by the affected party. Daniel's confidence in the great value of the Manor and the certainty of his receiving much more than the agreed price dissolved when the agents returned their verdict: Jeffreys was to pay only 54£ 10s 2d. Daniel instantly cried "unfair" and was about to seek vengeance at the law, when, "advised for quietness sake and to obtain his own peace," as he soberly expressed it, he accepted the judgment and "gave him a receipt of acquitance for the same on or about the 26th May 1686." Daniel was no longer the protagonist, the man of consequence; Jeffreys held all the options and controlled the flow of influence. So the Manor was sold, at a price usually declared to be 9000£,[91] a rounded figure of approximation, and Daniel could at last pay his debts and plan to settle into something like the quiet life of country retirement.

But no business of Daniel's ever ended easily or decisively, so when Jeffreys, who had taken the title Baron of Wem, died in April 1689, his son and heir became Baron and refused to honor the agreement that Daniel would receive all rents, herriots and so forth which fell due prior to 23 December 1684. Daniel presented a list of "the fines due from several copyholders . . . to be reced by Daniel Wycherley . . . for his own use as by a deed . . . made the 23rd December 1684," the total of which fines from forty-seven tenants was 1090£. The defendant answered, however, that ten tenants' fines, worth 230£, fell due after the Manor was sold. It seems that once again Daniel obscured his sound claim with such a show of acerbity that he lost a good part of what was due him. The petitioner, Jeffreys claimed, "has stuffed his bill with much scandalous and impertinent" argument, so that "itt was therefore pray'd yt the same may be purged."[92] On 8 July 1690 Daniel, who had so stuffed his bill, was ordered "to dismiss his bill with twenty pounds Costs,"[93] but he probably received his just rents.

The Wycherleys still had, of course, sufficient property in Shropshire. We have seen that when George took over the Rectory of Wem, Daniel kept Trench farm. One deponent reported that "he heard Daniel say that he had not any of the tythes of the sd Rectory of Wem but only some tythes arising out of some part of the said farm called Trenchfarm that he held in his own occupation which Complt George had given him." Another verified this view: "George had given his father the tythes of such part of the Trenchfarm as was in his own occupation" since Daniel had many years before given George the whole Rectory of Wem.[94] The farm was certainly a profitable one as one tenant testified who was "tenant for seven years" for 60£ per annum, during which time "Daniel let land to other tenants for 110£" but he kept only 80£ of the rent and George was to receive the rest.[95] Adam Wycherley, a relative, also observed the value of the land: Daniel got a great deal of corn from Trench farm, more than anyone else in the country did yearly.[96] There were other properties as well in Daniel's possession, for in the Church Wardens' books, he is regularly charged for four separate pieces of land in the Aston quarter of the parish:

Trench farm	1£	13s	4d
Trevers farm	-	13s	-
Bakers farm	-	1s	-
Trevers land	-	-	10d
and in Wem quarter: the white house	-	-	8d[97]

There is always another lewne listed at about 1s 3d without a place-name given which is probably the Wycherley residence. The book lists these properties from the beginning of its entries in 1683 till Daniel's death in 1697 and after. We have seen previously his erratic payment of the church taxes but one can assume his continuous ownership of these properties and therefore assume as well a reasonably profitable income from tenants occupying them—for instance the 1694 lewne is listed "Daniel Wycherley or tenant—7d" for each of two properties. But needs continued to constrict him and the debts never really disappeared. In the fall of 1696 a tripartive indenture was made between him, Robert and Richard Corbett and Thomas Grant, and Daniel's heir, William (the complete details of which we will see later in reference to him) for the settling of Daniel's debt "of One Thousand pounds owing to Thomas Lyster" of Shrewsbury, as well as a debt of William's for 1000£, through the efforts of the three men, the second party. This indenture was sealed on 10 September; on the 12th an indenture between Daniel and Lyster was made for the farm "lyeing and being in Tilley and Trench . . ." at one peppercorn rent, a token payment commonly used, and then on the next day, the same property was mortgaged to Lyster "for the Sume of One Hundred Pounds of Lawfull money . . . in witness whereof I have hereunto putt my hand this thirtieth

Day of September Ano Dom: 1696."[98] The signature of old Daniel was rather unsteady.

Dealing in land and money, shrewd and aggressive, often quarrelsome, he was to the end of his life much the same Daniel Wycherley Esq. we saw busying himself about the interests of the Marquis of Winchester, which were after all his own interests. He was at unpredictable moments at his best and at his worst. Showing a quick emotional response to persons both known and unknown, he was very generous with his time and ability, and money if possible: when he was seventy-five years old, he trooped off to London to look up in the Prerogative Office a will concerning his kinsman Thomas Wycherley and came back ready to depose in his defence.[99] But just as suddenly he would turn vindictive, and pursue a debtor past his grave to quibble over 200£ (see Appendix II). He had little sense of measure or proportion but a vehement sense of right, justice, and law, which was quite unrelated to the quality or relation of the person involved. Gough mentioned that Daniel never contended "with persons unable to deal with him, butt with great . . . persons," but Gough is seldom reliable.[100] At the last he overshot his ambitions, or misjudged the barriers he had to overleap by underestimating the people he dealt with, who were frequently his match in shrewdness, and by miscalculating what he could do with money. As he looked back over his life, amidst the successes, there were painful memories, dead children, dead grandchildren, dead daughter-in-law, dead friends. His wife would outlive him, and his son William would as well, and two grandsons, William and Daniel, sons of John; but none of the other children outlasted him, a fate one is inclined to view as prophetic. The Wycherley line Daniel had so proudly carried forward with title of gentry and arms, he would at last fail to continue into posterity. His noted son would insure the memory of the name in years to come, but no children would continue it.

"Mr. Wycherley made a handsome appearance, being of

large stature and comely countenance, his hair white with age. He had a clear understanding and good courage. His behaviour was genteel and plausible. He would speak courteously to the man he designed to ruin."[101] Old Daniel was eighty-one years old when he died on 5 May 1697. He was buried two days later near the altar of the church of All Saints, Clive, under a stone inscribed: "Here Lyeth The Body of Daniel Wycherley, Esq. Who Deceased the Fifth Day of May Anno Dom. 1697 In the 81st Yeare Of His Age."[102] To this day he is the only Wycherley buried at Clive whose grave is memorialized by a plaque, now in the churchyard wall.

Chapter V
Footnotes

1. Connely, p. 26. See Chapter 1, n. 1, indicating that Daniel reportedly built Clive Hall, though there is no further information on that notion.
2. Gough, p. 86.
3. Information on Knight case drawn from following: C10, 64/88; C6, 46/230; C9, 35/32; C10, 490/197; C5, 512/57; C10, 158/186; C22, 986/7; C24, 910/94; C22, 388/59; and cf. C8, 312/168 on Daniel's being seized in fee simple of Manor of Frobury, with others, 1657.
4. See C8, 140/120; C8, 144/96; C24, 891, part II, 106.
5. Gough, p. 86.
6. Cf. Chapter I, n. 45, and also C10, 489/157.
7. C24, 968/57.
8. The property consisted of "certain . . . Messuage or tenements or mansion house scituate and being in Augustine Fryers near Breadstreet in the Parish of St. Peter the Poor London"; back in 1669, one William Cutler sold the lease on 27 March to William Kiffin, a merchant of the city. Then

three or four months later . . . [it] was entered upon by one Daniel Wycherley of the Inner Temple London gent. pretending a title to part of the sd premisses and brought an action of ejectment for the part in Court . . . that is to say, for such messuage and a piece of ground east to west 18 feet of assize, and north to south 18 feet 6 inches with the rooms over the same . . . and also a piece of ground 3' by 5'.

Daniel's claim to this rather specialized bit of property was in a deed "bearing date 26 March 1669," which he had not gotten around to execute for several months. "The Sherriff of London gave Daniel Wycherley possession of the premises and [Kiffin] was outed," that is, Daniel "did stopp up the back door and back passage . . . and also the way into the

Orchard and garden." So Kiffin leased from Daniel for a yearly rent of 6£ 13s 4d and paid regularly until 1676 when he stopped and Daniel moved to evict him. Daniel's answers to Kiffin's complaint on 30 June 1685 traced the property through the Marquis of Winchester to his acquisition; depositions were taken in 1686 and Kiffin struggled on, but to no avail. No evidence indicates how long Daniel held this property but again it was probably for some time after Kiffin gave in. Information drawn from following: C5, 510/60; C24, 1095/87, and affidavits: C41/24, no. 166, no. 227, no. 232; 26, no. 12; note that 25 was declared Unfit for Production, that is, it was too damaged to be read. The last dated affidavit was 20 April 1686. These cases presented detailed measurements of property, which may be of value to an historian of London. I have not traced rate books for this property.

9. *The Statutes of the Realm*, V, Charles I—Charles II, 1625–1680 (London, 1819), 466, 527, 572, 582, 619, 624, 648, 768, 821, 869, 917.

10. *Calendar of Treasury Books*, IV, 1672–75, ed. Wm. A. Shaw (London, 1909), 790, 697. On p. 694 is the royal mandate on the commissioners' functions.

11. "Biographical Data on William Wycherley and his Father," *N&Q*, ccxvi (January 1971), 35.

12. Connely, p. 54. Gough, p. 86, indicated incorrectly that Daniel became Lord of the Manor of Wem, and was "afterwards put into the commission of the peace for this country."

13. Gough, p. 86.

14. He is specifically listed in 1677, 78, and 79, in *Statutes*, V, 821, 869, 917.

15. Garbet, p. 69.

16. C10, 183/81; C9, 43/105.

17. C10, 90/147, Daniel's complaint.

18. C10, 158/184; see also Jebb's reply to the above-mentioned case.

19. Court Rolls for the Manor of Wem, 167/12, 1666–69, and 167/13, 1670–1740; Salop Record Office. Roughly translated, the Latin means that the manor court, Daniel Wycherley lord of the Manor, was held on 7 August in the reign of Charles II by the grace of God King of England, Scotland, France and Ireland and defender of the faith, with Richard Jebb seneshal, or steward.

20. C10, 169/116.

21. C10, 170/116.

22. C10, 121/2.

23. This list is taken from E126, vol. 12, f. 126 verso, Easter, 27 Charles II; the list appears in many other cases and is reprinted by Gough, p. 70, with places of dwelling. The widow Harwood's name was probably Isabel.

24. These charges are taken from E126, vol. 12, f. 126v as above, but are listed in several places; though there are others, these are the chief complaints. Daniel confessed to the court and jury harassment.

25. These fines are taken from E126, f. 341, Michaelmas, 23 November, 28 Charles II, and are as follows:

1) the sixe Customes hereafter following vizt That the burroughholdrs within the said Mannor of Wem may aliene their burroughhold estates without Surrender

2) And that as to the Custome within the said Mannor that an Herriott is payable to ye Lord upon Alienacion or Surrender of the whole Copyhold estate only & not upon alienacion or Surrender of part of the same for which two Customes there hath beene a verdict at the Barr of this Court for the said ptts as aforesaid And as to the

3) Custome laid in the said Complts bill that if any person take to his wife any woman Inheritrix Customary holder of any Customary lands of the said Mannor & had or have issue by her & the same wife decease ye husband surviveing shall hold all his wifes customary

4) lands dureing his natural life And as to that Custome that at the death of every Customary tennt which was seized of any Estate in fee simple or fee tayle Generall in the said Customary lands the wife of such Tennt surviveing her husband should have & enjoy all such Customary lands as her husband dyed soe seized of dureing her wid-

5) owhood & noe longer And also that Custome in the said bill that all Customary tennt that are seized in fee simple fee tayle generall or speciall of any Customary lands within the said Mannor may lawfully cutt downe give sell all the timber trees & other trees growing & being upon their customary lands att their will & pleasure without the contradiccion or molesta-cion of the Lord of the said

6) Mannor or of any other And alsoe that Custome laid in the said bill that every Customary tennt & burroughholder ought to appeare at the Court Leetes or Law dayes or in default of appearance at one of the said Courts the maker of such default is to be essoyned with one penny if it bee proferred And at the next Leete or Law daye if such tennant soe essoyned make default in appeareing then to be amerced sixpence & noe more.

26. E126, vol. 13, f. 336, 9 February, Hilary, 33–34 Charles II. The chief documents of the case are as follows in chronological order: C10, 171/148; C10, 169/117; *Exchequer Decrees Calendar*, E126, Vol 12, f. 117; E126, f. 126; E126, f. 185; E126, f. 194; E126, f. 222; E126, f. 295; E126, f. 326; E126, f. 341; E126, Vol. 13, f. 2; C6, 66/74; C6, 79/120; C6, 564/74; E126, Vol. 13, f. 21 (containing three orders, 4, 11, 13 February 1678); E126, f. 38; *Register of Affidavits*, C41/42, Easter, #179; #298; Hilary #190; /23, Easter, #65; *Chancery Affidavits*, C31/41, Easter, #65; C24, 1049/99; E126, Vol. 13, f. 213; f. 216; (two entries, 17 and 25 May) f. 216; f. 225; E126, f. 336; C41/24, Easter, #47; C10, 206/95; C41/24, Michas, #324; #750; Hilary, #288; E126, Vol. 14, f. 112; f. 125; f. 153. See also for survey of case *Exchequer, Decrees Calendar*, Vol. III, E126, 16 Charles II, Easter—29 Charles II, Trinity, with names, dates and brief listing of case. See also Summers, I, 8, for

Wycherley v. Tyler in *Historical Manuscripts Commission Reports, House of Lords MSS,* 1690; Eleventh Report . . . , Appendix I-II (London, 1887) pp. 214 ff. and Thirteenth Report, Appendix Part V, *House of Lords MSS,* 1690-91 (London, 1892), p. 288n.

27. Summers, I, 8, thought the Tyler case was separate.

28. C6, 289/62.

29. *Historical Manuscripts Commission Report,* Eleventh Report, pp. 214-15.

30. E126, vol. 14, f. 112, f. 125, f. 153, dated respectively, 6 December, 13 February and 20 February 1684.

31. *Historical Manuscripts Commission Report,* Eleventh Report, p. 215.

32. C10, 206/95.

33. Garbet, p. 79.

34. *Ibid.,* p. 84. I have no information about Mr. Smith, unless he is the trustee of George's trust discussed below.

35. C41/24, Michas, #750.

36. C41/24, Hilary, #288.

37. C6, 253/88, Daniel's statement; C24, 1095/88, Richard Wycherley's dep.

38. C6, 253/88, Daniel's statement; all information about George's schooling and following are from Daniel unless otherwise indicated, and almost all statements are verified by other depositions and testimony.

39. C22, 856/8, testimony of Mary Cotton: "Bethia wife of Daniel about 1672 borrowed . . . 40£ which Bethia received herself . . . such sums were to be sent to George at Oxford."

40. *Shropshire Parish Registers,* Vol. IX, Wem Register. Note that he is here listed as brother to George.

41. *Ibid.*

42. C6, 253/88.

43. John Walker, *An Attempt toward Recovering an Account of the Numbers and Sufferings of the Clergy . . . who were Sequestered . . .* (London, 1714), p. 157; Walker says he was charged on "Sixteen Articles." A. G. Matthews, *Walker Revised, Being a Revision of John Walker's Sufferings of the Clergy During the Grand Rebellion, 1642-1660* (Oxford, 1948), p. 348: "Warned by note at parsonage, but had not appeared. Living worth 80£ per year. House and barns much decayed. Charges given by Walker not mentioned." Charges are in Bodleian, Rawlinson D MS 924. 202: "Hemingstone, Suffolk. Articles against Daniel Wicherley, rector, 1644." See also *Alumni Cantabrigiensis,* comp. J. A. Venn, (Cambridge, 1927), IV, 398.

44. *Calendar of State Papers,* ed. M. A. E. Green, Vol. 1670 (London, 1895), p. 296.

45. *Ibid.,* p. 387.

46. *Calendar of State Papers,* ed. Blackburne Daniell, Vol. 1672 (London, 1899), p. 554 and p. 618. For references, see *Index to Act Book of Archbishop of Canterbury, 1663-1859* (London, 1938), p. 464; and very probably E127, 7 Michas, #325m, a case "inter Daniel Wycherley Sacrae Theologie Professor et Edwin Rod, gent." in 1672, Hereford.

47. Some said that debt to Charleton was 400£: C22, 213/5, William Wenton's dep. For repayments to Charleton, see a very interesting suit, C5, 197/63.

48. C22, 213/5, Thomas Trevor's dep.; C24, 1095/88, Thomas Ryder's dep. The Rectory was a large house of nine hearths, for which the 1672 hearth-tax was 18s; *the Shropshire Hearth-Tax Roll of 1672*, Shropshire Archeological and Parish Register Society (1949), ed. W. Watkins-Pitchford, Also listed are houses for Mr. Dan Witcherly (1 hearth), Daniel Wicherley Esq. (12 hearths in Clive, the Manor house), and a Wm Witcherley (2 hearths in Bradford Hundred), not the playwright presumably.

49. C22, 213/5, John Isaw's dep.; and C24, 1095/88. His wife was perhaps Dorothy Witcomb, spinster, to whom he was indebted by bond 18 September 1674: C22, 213/5, Edward Bailey's dep.

50. C6, 253/88; the sum is repeated in many other suits and depositions.

51. Garbet, p. 84.

52. C6, 253/88.

53. Connely, p. 184; he gives no proof but cites Summers, I, 5, who says nothing; I have found no evidence on Henry's college career.

54. C6, 253/88.

55. *Shropshire Parish Register*, Vol. IX, Wem Register, 222. She was born on 28 November, and died in 1685. The infant mortality rate was higher in the 1680's in Wem, according to Peter Laslett, *The World We Have Lost* (New York, 1965), p. 125, rising from an average of 120 per thousand in the 70's to 139 in the 80's.

56. C22, 213/5, Thomas Jebb's dep.

57. C6, 253/88, George's statement.

58. *Ibid.*, Daniel's statement.

59. C22, 213/5, John Isaw's dep., who also mentions sundry small unpaid loans to George.

60. C6, 253/88.

61. C10, 222/97.

62. *Ibid.*, answers of Watkis, Lovekin and Pay.

63. C22, 213/5, John Isaw's dep.

64. *Ibid.*, Roger Hussey's dep.

65. C22, 856/8, various depositions; C22, 209/25, John Staine's dep.

66. C5, 197/63.

67. C22, 856/8, Christopher Mathew's dep.

68. *Ibid.*

69. For specific details of her purchase of meats for the family, see C22, 856/8, John Gittin's dep.: 29 April 1675, 10s 4d for veale; 8 May 3s 8d for veale; 13 May 4s 6d for mutton and veale; 29 May 7s mutton and veale, and so on. For details of her business activities, see depositions of Mary Cotton, Christopher Mathews, Mary Evans, Edwards Phillips, Robert Husband, who provide many details of sale price for amounts of grain, wheat, barley, hay, etc. Gough's remark, p. 85, "if shee wanted beauty had a large share of tongue," appears to be mere prejudice, though she obviously was not one to hide timorously in the kitchen all her life.

[187]

70. C41, 24, Michas, 1683, #741: John told George that they "left the whole managemt of ye Trust to" Daniel.

71. C41, 27, Easter, 1687, #750.

72. C41, 27, Trinity, 1687, #490.

73. C22, 213/5, John Isaw's dep. and John Wright's dep., both of whom were arrested. Teague was in Wem prison for at least three years; Prichard said he "is now and for some years past . . . a prissonr for debt": C41, 27, Easter, 1687, #750.

74. C6, 253/88.

75. C41, 27, Easter, 1687, #733.

76. C33, 266, p. 177v. 13 January.

77. C41, 27, Michas, 1687, #961.

78. In addition to previously cited documents, see: C41, 24, Trinity, 1682, #44; Easter, 1683, #160; Michas, 1683, #834; C33, 258, 1684, p. 53; p. 524; p. 596; C33, 266, 1685, p. 16; p. 114; p. 560; p. 831; C41, 26, Trinity, 1686, #1037; Hilary, 1686, #399; 27, Michas, 1687, #1467. C22, 732/62 is indexed as Witherley v. Carol; when I examined this I saw the name George but the document broke into dust and it was returned as unuseable: no date, no information what this may contain. Thomas Vernon, *Cases Argued before The High Court of Chancery*, I, 283n. reference to Wicherley v Wicherley, post 470; 470 reference to Whicherley v Whicherley, De Term Trin 1687, a citation to the case; vol. II, 176n to same, I, 283.

79. C41, 24, Michas, 1683, #741.

80. *Fleet Prison Committment Book*, Pris I, la, p. 232, 26 September 1688, with the following list of debts: 100£, 100£, 10£, 500£, 200£, 40£ (for a total of 950£); and on p. 239, as follows: 13£, 10s 1d, 2£, 200£, 100£, 100£, 100£, 100£ (for a total of 615£ 10s 1d). His widow is mentioned but not by name and nothing is said about her.

81. Connely, pp. 214–17; see his account to Grahme's wealth, p. 217.

82. Garbet, p. 156, places his burial at the Fleet; *The Shropshire Parish Register*, Vol. IX, Wem Register, 329, indicates Wem, which is more probable.

83. If we take the Wycherleys as members of the Gentleman class, we find the average annual income per family to be 280£, according to "Gregory King's Scheme of the Income & Expenses of the Several Families of England Calculated for the Year 1688," in Peter Laslett, p. 32. If we take them as Esquire, the next step up in the group of lesser nobility, the annual average is 450£, which is closer to the Wycherley's income of 500£, at the minimum. Their level of living was, in other words, quite high.

84. C6, 565/169.

85. C41, 26, Trinity, #104. Cf. also C41, 26, nos. 103, 1920, 2045; Michas, 137, 616.

86. C6, 66/82, with itemized list of cloth and respective prices. The "ready money" Daniel normally had no longer existed and Dunn was told to deliver only on specific order, but Dunn of course ingenuously sent several "parcels of goods for the use of the complt and his wife and daughter" (at this time Elizabeth only, Frances having married and in

1678 passed away) but at the same time he was receiving no payment; consequently he demanded to be paid and "seized some goods" from Daniel's house in Clive. His outstanding bill for goods purchased from 30 August 1678 to November 1680 was only 9£ 5s 8d. See also C6, 564/28.

87. Parish of Wem, Church Wardens' books, 1683–1734. The Church Warden Randle Griffis wrote in his Book: "I crave allowance for Mr. Witchurleys lewnes for the years '82 and '83. 3£ 9s 8d." Daniel paid the amount in small bits, but then in 1686 the Church Warden again wrote: "I crave allowance for Mr Wycherley's lewnes due for the old White House 10d," and in 1689, ". . . for Daniel Wycherley Esqs several lewnes which I cannot get being 1£ 3s 4d."

These books are handwritten documents, unpublished, which were shown to me by the generosity of the Parish Vicar, Mr. John Ranford (14 Tilley Road, Wem). They are kept in an old wooden chest in the loft or balcony of the church. The present volume was only recently discovered; the following volume, 1735–c.70, is yet lost, and the next following volume is extant. My thanks to Mr. Ranford are gratefully expressed for his great kindness and assistance in opening his home and church to me. These books contain much of historical interest about the ongoing business of a parish; for instance among disbursements for Aston quarter, 1683, are:

for timber iron wire and other materials			
about the chymes	1£	8s	9d
for making the chymes	1£	10s	-
to carpenter for them	-	10s	6d
for leade to add to chyme waite and rope	-	6s	-

Each quarter was assessed for the repair of the bells and tower which the fire had destroyed. The disbursements are thoroughly detailed.

88. C10, 239/92.

89. H-Montgomery Hyde, *Judge Jeffreys* (London, 1948), pp. 19, 223.

90. C10, 239/92.

91. Garbet, p. 84, See *King's Bench Deeds and Wills*, Hilary 36–37 Charles II & I James II, Deeds, 39: "Wycherley, Daniel and Geo. Duc Jeffreys Ch. Justice." Note that Hyde says, p. 195n, that Jeffreys probably did not visit the property, but C10, 239/92, George Chambre's answer suggests otherwise: ". . . being neighbor to the estate and an acquaintance of his lordship this deft did as his friend assist him in and about the sd estate."

92. C33, 274, 11 December 1689, p. 492.

93. *Ibid.*, p. 582.

94. C22, 209/25, Thomas Spendlove's dep. and John Staine's dep.

95. *Ibid.*, first dep.

96. C22, 213/5.

97. Parish of Wem, Church Wardens' books, 1683–1734. Lewnes are variable from year to year but are roughly at the indicated rate; Trench farm for example varied from 1£ to 17s.

98. Spurrel Papers, Trench Farm, Wem, 172/1 and /2, Salop Record Office. One debt Daniel died without paying was to The Corporation of

Shrewsbury for non-payment of tithes, and William had to pay it in 1700; Summers, I, 8.

99. Exchequer Deponents, E 134, 5 William & Mary, Easter, 1692, #29.
100. Gough, p. 87.
101. Garbet, p. 84.
102. Summers, I, 10.

Chapter VI

The Final Years

In the years after his release from prison, life quieted for William Wycherley but it did not slow down to a genteel retired pace for a number of years. There were, of course, friendships to continue or renew or develop, the delights of conversation at Will's Coffee House with Dryden and Dennis and a host of others, the solace of composing and planning to publish his poems, but the practical realities of his family and obligations in Shropshire and in Ireland had to be dealt with before he could rest.

In Ireland, the suit of Henry Earl of Drogheda against William, alone now without his wife, continued on after 1685. The Robartes family, who were of course still very much interested in the process of the suit since they were to receive much of the Moore property according to the deed of 1677, added to their strength of numbers Aramintha's husband, Ezekiel, Bishop of Londonderry. To their suit, entered 3 June 1686, Henry replied eleven days later with a bill against them and Wycherley (who answered 28 April 1687).[1] In desperation at "soe many vexatious Suits, as they have brought these 8 yeares past" by which he had become "greatly impoverished," Henry petitioned King James II to "Settle . . . the Estate to yor Petr and his issue Male according to the sd Deed of 1669 and that the sd deed of 1677 be demur'd and that the sd persons claimeing under the same may be Barr'd."[2] In this petition Henry traced the treaty of marriage of 1669 of his brother and Letitia-Isabella, their new deed of 1677 that transferred the estate to her heirs, gave his version of the torturing of Charles, claimed to have had to pay 11,000£ toward Charles' debts, and on the basis of his helplessness before the law, begged the King to come to his aid—through what Wycherley would have called "custom." At Windsor, 19 September 1687, the King "was graciously inclined to give the Honble Petitionr all just Reliefe in this matter," and recommended the Earl of Tyrconnel prepare a bill for the next Irish Parliament.[3] A word on this parliament: historian David Ogg stated that, "a revolutionary parliament, consisting mainly of Roman Catholics, sat in the summer months of 1689, but all its acts were annulled; otherwise, there was no meeting of the regularly constituted parliament between 1666 and 1692; nor, in William's reign, was there any session after 1698."[4] This being the case it is certainly problematic what strength the King's petition had, or Henry's, or Tyrconnel's. Probably Henry's was a suggestion hopefully submitted, and at any rate his last recourse. Ordinarily, a plea at the King's behest would receive ready support by the parliament, but this time the case merely crept onward. The *Chancery Entry Books* record "Henrici Moore Con Drogheda Regno Hiberno v. Francis Roberts Ar deft" on 13 February 1688 for a stay in proceedings until Roberts could answer the bill, and on 3 March it was argued the defendants were entitled to the premises in question for "there have beene sevll tryalls had hereupon & sevll speciall verdicts found by sevll Inquiries in Ireland."[5] In short, the defendants continued to win their suit against Henry, and they were allowed to proceed to argue the special verdicts.

By 13 July Wycherley was listed as a defendant again and a delay was sought by the defendants until next Michaelmas term, apparently because "ye deft Wycherley [was] in towne," probably London.[6] Olympia claimed that Wycherley had a copy if not the original of the 1677 deed, which was, of course, his key to his late wife's property; the Robartes family had taken the property allowed them by the deed, Olympia herself "being intituled to the fee simple & Indenture of the town of Stallings in Co. Meath & the

Rectoriall tythes thereof with appurtenances which were part of the said late Earl Charles his estate." Wycherley and his wife "had some right," she said, "to the Capitall Mansion House and Demisne of Mellifont," which they had claimed, and "she hath heard the said Mr. Wicherley claim some part of the Lands settled upon the Lady Leticia Isabella and her heirs," but she was not certain which they were, but had heard "some parte of the Estate is made by the said Lady . . . to the said Mr. Wicherley,"[7] a repetition of her prior statement. In his letter from prison to George Legge, Baron of Dartmouth, Wycherley mentioned "an estate in Dublin" of which his wife had "levied fines to my use." This may or may not have been the "jointure . . . of four thousand pounds on the St. Mary Abbey Estate," mentioned elsewhere as property Letitia-Isabella willed to him.[8] According to the legality of the deed Wycherley seemed proper heir to his wife's property, though sentiment, family attachment and custom were strong resentment against him, for he had married hastily above his station to a Countess and gained thereby the hatred of Henry, the newly succeeding Earl and newly deprived brother, and the condescension of the Earl of Radnor's family.

The case ended for Wycherley at about the turn of the century. Gildon reported it happened not long after Daniel Wycherley's death in 1697; "the Relations of the Lady *Drogheda*, who possess'd her Estate, thought fit to pay him Fifteen hundred Pounds for his Right to the said Estate."[9] A picayune vindication, fifteen years too late. It is worth observing that, though Wycherley was freed of its encumbrances, Henry's legal history went on in mad career into the future; in 1709 he was sued by Arthur Viscount Loftus of Ely "the principall summe of 4000£ together with the Int. then due and the accruing Int. thereof at the rate of 7£ 10s p. Cent pann."[10] Somehow he had managed to gather up a dowry of 3000£ for his daughter, Lady Elizabeth, when she married Robert Rochfort Esq. in 1704,[11] but until the end of his life on 9 July 1714,[12] he was struggling in constant litigation.

[193]

Wycherley had received prior to the turn of the century his inheritance at the death of his father—again, not nearly the amount he anticipated and felt his due as eldest son, but a considerable assistance nonetheless. His father arranged an Indenture, sealed on 10 September 1696, between himself, his eldest son, and a third party consisting of Richard Corbett, Robert Corbett and Thomas Grant who were to act as trustees for the indenture. In brief, the indenture stipulated that the trustees pay off Daniel's debt of 1000£ to Thomas Lyster and William's debts of 1000£. Daniel was to have "for and during the terme of his naturall Life" use of the properties, and

> after his decease then as Touching and concerning All and Singular the Messuages tenemts Lands heredamts & premisses aforesd (Excepting onely the Messuages Lands and premisses in Clive aforesd) To the use and behoofe of the sd William Wicherley . . . And from and after the determination of the sd Estate of William Wicherley To the use of them the sd Robert Corbett Richard Corbett and Thomas Grant & their heires during the Naturall Life of the sd William Wicherley To the Intent onely to Enable them to make Entries for preserving the contingent Remainders hereafter menconed And in Trust nevertheless that they permitt and suffer the sd William Wycherley to have & Receive All the Rents & proffitts of the sd premisses during his life.[13]

He could settle all the houses and lands, except those of Clive, upon a wife he might possibly marry and on his possible male heirs, or next in line upon his late brother John's children William or Daniel, as long as the trustees provided payments of the debts of Daniel and of William, and dowries for possible daughters of William. But nowhere in the indenture was William allowed to sell any of the properties: this was the rub for which everyone then and thereafter has harbored ill feelings for Daniel.[14] He effectively restricted his son's financial flexibility and set a fixed annual income as if he were still in his minority. Even the payment of his debts was limited to what "he now oweth or hereafter shal during his father's life contract & not

amounting to above One thousand pounds in the whole."
The properties listed were large in number; apart from

> that Capitall Messuage or Mansion House & tenement
> scituate and being in Clive . . . wherein the sd Daniel
> Wicherley doth now dwell And all the Barnes Stables
> Outhouses yards gardens Orchards Lands Meadowes Woods
> Woodgrounds pastures Leasowes feedings Moores Marshes &
> Comons thereunto belonging And All those ffoure tenemts
> scituate and being in Clive which were Antiently the tenemts
> & hereditamts of Daniel Wicherley Gent Late ffathr of the
> said Daniel Wicherley with All barnes . . . ,

which was the main domicile of the Wycherley family in
Clive, there were twenty other properties listed, even though
Daniel was no longer Manor Lord. In short, William
received ownership of a large amount of real estate which he
could only watch as it turned him a steady income of perhaps
a few hundred pounds annually. And he received enough to
pay off his debts, at least those on hand up to that time. Later
there would be others.

From the evidence of the Church Wardens' books for the
Parish of Wem, we see that, beginning exactly in 1697 at
Daniel's death, William paid his lewnes on the listed
properties regularly and faithfully. One property is listed
from the Wem quarter, of which Richard Jebb was warden,
and the other three including Trench Farm from the Aston
quarter.[15] Each year the one and the three properties were
listed and paid; for unknown reasons in 1698 there were only
one and two listed. On the surface then, it would appear that
he was not suffering serious financial want during these
years nor did he have any excess income to help him over
periods of emergency. With his brothers George, John,
possibly Henry, and sisters Frances and Elizabeth all dead,
and his father gone in May 1697, he had only the care of his
mother in that house in Clive, until her death on 10 May
1700.[16]

From the late 80's well into the 90's when he planned to
publish his poetry, he turned his attention regularly to the

[195]

welcome distraction and relaxation of composing poems, just as he had done with the early celebration of Charles II's restoration, the random love lyrics, and during the composition of his plays and later in his most difficult phase. Although the subject matter of his poetic canon is varied, certain groups emerge which range from the purely conventional to significant and in some cases quite original poems. There is, of course, the group of straight love poems, such as *"To* Love," *"A* Song, *against Reason in* Love," *"A* Song, *against Delays in Love,"* *"A* Song, *against* Variety *in* Love," and *"For* Variety *in* Love,"[17] Then there are those on specific love topics such as to a mistress, probably half real and half fictional ones, or *"To* Celia," the conventional recipient of a love lyric, *"A* Song *Proving* Love *more Pleasure, as more Pain. To a too easie Mistress,"* *"A* Song, *To a Mistress, who call'd her Lover Ungrateful . . . ,"* *"To a pretty* Young Woman, *who opening Oisters . . . ,"* *"The* Poor Poet's *Answer to his* Mercenary Mistress."[18] A large number of poems treat subjects other than love, such as drinking; with *"Sober Thoughts on* Drunkenness," which is also dedicated to a mistress, as is *"A* Song. *To a Mistress, who call'd her Lover* Beast *for Drinking,"* and several drinking songs,[19] and topics like *"Upon* Gold; *Preferring* Steel *to it,"* *"Upon a* Lady's *Fine* Back-Side, it being *Her Best Side."* There are poems to specific persons, either prominent ones such as Charles II, Buckingham, Boyle, and *"On His* Grace *the Duke of* Marlborough,"[20] or to such as "To W. O. *my* Jocky-Friend," *"An* Epistle, *to a Brave* Young Man, *making a* Campaign *in* Flanders," *"A* Song: *To a* City-Friend (*a* Rich Banker)."[21]

The poems to specific persons are revealing both biographically and thematically and most of these can be dated, with the exception of the one to his jockey friend or his *"Little* Drawer . . . *in* Lombardstreet" whom he could have known at any time.[22] It is interesting to compare this poem to the jockey who offered the poet a wife, with another poem *"To his* Friend, *who presented him with a Horse"*;[23]

Wycherley seemed to prefer the horse and may well have enjoyed horse races. A rather vague complaint about a Mr. Wycherley's greyhounds makes one wonder whether he was a dog fancier at home in Shropshire.[24] In the early or mid 1680's he wrote, "To that Incomparable Poet, Mr. *Waller, in his Old Age,"* to Edmund Waller, who died October 1687; Waller's fame for small lyrics was immeasurably greater then than now. It is a gentle poem, based on a Phoebus image of sun-fire-wit and rising-setting-dying.[25] To the playwright who wrote *The Rivals Queens* and collaborated with Dryden on *Oedipus,* he wrote, *"To* Nath. Lee *in* Bethlem (*who was at once* Poet *and* Actor),*"* sometime between the time Nathaniel was imprisoned in that asylum in 1684 and his death in 1692; the poem tells us that Wycherley knew Lee and yet denies us more information because it turns on the paradox of the fortunate misfortune:

> In Chains unfelt, more happy then you are,
> Since by them, free from Thought, Pain, Care, or Fear;
> More free, more happy, as your Sense is less,
> Since 'twas your Sense was your Unhappiness.

Wycherley's wit may seem nearly crude to us who are chary of mentioning insanity and prefer to lock away from sight those whose stability we choose to question:

> Whilst you grow Wiser now, for Want of Sense;
> Whose Fustian Nonsense now, gives none Offence,
> But rather by that, and your late crack'd Brain,
> You best, your Gaping Audience, entertain.[26]

A more interesting poem is one addressed to Sir John Cutler, satirizing his greed, *"The* Praise *of* Avarice." Cutler's daughter Elizabeth had married in the late 1680's Charles Bodville Roberts (1660–1723), grandson to the first Earl of Radnor and nephew to Letitia-Isabella, Wycherley's wife; but Sir John did not grant a dowry. When he died in 1693 worth several thousand pounds,[27] though he was a close friend of the Fanshawes,[28] Wycherley saw him as a subject worth satirizing, as Pope did later,[29] and the threat to his own and the Countess' estate by young Bodville Roberts worth defending. The poem is one of Wycherley's better ones, direct, emphatic and rhythmically smoother than his usual irregular efforts; it has something of the quality of Rochester's poetry as it plays on words like "thrift" and "want" in order to wring new senses from them.

> How falsly we that prudent Thrift despise,
> By which Man gains what he himself denies!
> Since he receives from voluntary Want
> More than his craving Appetites could grant . . .
> Then that blest Thrift, which aids us to controul
> The working Passions of the restless Soul,
> And keeps us guiltless, should be deem'd our Praise,
> Not load us with Reproach, and foul Disgrace.[30]

The poem suggests that for Wycherley the ironic mode was more agreeable than the panegyric, which is the mode of his *"On His* Grace *the Duke of* Marlborough":

> My Art and Hand too weak to touch your Praise!
> Yet I've a common Right, as *England's* Son,
> To thank you for the wound'rous Things you've done.[31]

This poem is not a direct appeal, as is the one to Lord Boyle or the more subtly couched praise to James Duke of York, but rather celebrates the recognizable themes of generosity and courage as opposed to tyranny and the "Monsters" of disorder.

These poems give us some biographical sense of Wycherley's interests and values, as some, such as *"To a* Bridegroom, *after having married an ill Wife to screen him from his Debts,"*[32] seem almost autobiographical. A last group of poems on abstract subjects, usually satiric in tone, reveal more about the ideas which consistently fascinated him and which were commonly treated in the plays. Working from a theme out of Gracian, Wycherley in *"Upon the most useful* Knowledge, Craft *or* Cunning," takes craft as worldly wisdom—"Profit before Praise, is Cunning's aim"— and not as true wit or its equivalent plain-dealing.

Then Cunning shou'd for the best Science go,
Which, without Learning, does best Knowledge show;
Does Wit, Pow'r, Art, by Nature best out-do;
Strange Science; since all Wisdom, Courage, Wit,
Must to it universally submit.

This cunning is like Freeman's plain-dealing which works
well, or like Horner's craft which works remarkably well;
but finally,

Tis Bastard-Sense, and like all Bastards so,
Does in the World but more successful grow,
Than the True, which does True Wits most undo.[33]

There is mature reflection in these lines, a wisdom of
experience (though not the wisdom of craft as Wycherley
here and Rochester often meant it) echoing back to the song
in *Love in a Wood* and to his life which was neither
successful, cunning nor "wise."

Another poem, *"In Vindication of Simplicity, and* Good
Nature" equates the two without irony:

. . . by good Nature more than good Sense, Man
Does much more his Humanity maintain,
Obtains his Mind's, and Conscience's best Peace. . . .

Worse nature is imposing one's will on another which shows
"most his Malice, but as more his wit," the term here once
more used pejoratively:

Good-Nature is,
. . . the best Sign of Human Prudence, . . .
The sole Proof of God's Image, on Mankind; . . .
The best Distinction, of Humanity,
From Brutishness, . . .
To make frail Man above all Self-Love Grow,
And of a Man, become a God below.[34]

Wycherley's general moral stance is here stated as un-
ironically and unequivocally as possible; an ethic orthodox
and traditional in its outlook and terminology, and
essentially that which the plays appear to reflect.

Pope remarked once, when trying to suggest the wasteland

[199]

of Wycherley's memory after his fever, that Wycherley would
write a poem on avarice and then a year later another against
liberality, obviously forgetting the first one.[35] In fact,
however, Wycherley's poems often deal with similar topics
in opposing manners, one ironic and the other straightforward. For instance, just as his *"against Variety in Love"*
noted above is followed by *"For Variety in Love,"* his *"A
Song, in praise of Solitude"* is followed by *"In Praise of
Industry,"* which is followed by *"Against Industry,"* each of
which approaches its topic differently so there is no
redundancy or confusion of point of view. The first begins
with a nod to the *beatus vir* tradition,

> Most Happy he himself may boast
> Whose Happiness depends on none;[36]

and concludes with a line again from Gracian: the more self-
sufficient one becomes, the more "to himself a God on Earth
alone," a notion which opposes the plain-dealer's involvement in society, and which Wycherley may be exploring
rather than advocating. *"In Praise of Industry and Action . . . in Business or Love,"* repeats the craft-and-
cunning theme,

> In Love, as Bus'ness, Industry (we see)
> Will, more than Idle Wit, prevailing be.[37]

As a reply to a mistress' request that her lover be quiet, the
ironic tone shapes the dramatic context of the poem and the
view of business, which as in the plays is a frequent
metaphor for sexuality, or mercantile pursuits, or giddy,
purposeless motion. The poem *"Against Industry"* is
addressed to a "Laborious Poetaster, *who preferr'd* Industry
to Wit."

> . . . for a Man to be stil'd Labourer,
> In Wit, as Law, but his discredit were;
> He's the Best Wit, as the Best Gentleman,
> Who, for his Wit, or Money, takes least Pain;
> For Wit, to gain Esteem, like Beauty too,
> Must seem, as Artful Negligence, to show;

> Must, for its Fame on Nature, more rely,
> Than either upon Art, or Industry.[38]

The disdain not only for the labor of poor poet's wit but for the business of moneyed mercantilism is typical of Wycherley's attitudes since his first play; but he seemed to like to explore further the ramifications of business, as in *"Upon the Idleness of Business."*

> Your Man of Bus'ness, is your idlest Ass.
> Doing most, what he least can bring to pass;
> To satisfie vain Aims, at Wealth, Praise, Pow'r, . . .
> His Aim at Rest, becomes his Restlessness;
> Since his Desires, with his Success, augment.[39]

Business is here depicted as a "Monster," a creature of unreason which makes man a beast, since as man imposes drudgeries on beasts he similarly through business imposes them on himself; so he is

> . . . the Beast-Man, . . .
> more a Beast, as against Nature so,
> . . . and his Reason, he
> . . . most a Drudge will be.

This intelligent and strongly felt satire leads quickly to the next development of the beast image in *"Upon the Impertinence of* Knowledge, *the Unreasonableness of* Reason, *and the Brutality of* Humanity; *proving the Animal Life the most Reasonable Life, since the most Natural, and most Innocent."* It at once recalls to mind not only Swift, later on, but the best English statement of theriophily, the expressed preference for animals to humans, by Rochester in "Satyr against Mankind" in the late 1670's. Professor Vieth observes that Rochester "attained his full growth as a poet"[40] in early 1674 at the same time Wycherley was reaching the heights of his achievement with *The Country-Wife*; not improbably he saw Rochester's poem and built his own from it, but he assuredly did not merely imitate it. The poem, whose name seems more an argument than a title, examines the implications of the nature of man and the nature of beast,

[201]

and like Rochester, places more reliance upon sense and nature than upon reason:

> Why shou'd Man's vain Pretence to Reason be,
> From Beast, his just Distinction? . . .
> Who, for his Knowledge, and Humanity,
> Lives, deals with his own Kind, more Brutally. . .
> Since Reason serves us, but to justifie,
> By Reas'ning more its Fallibility, . . .
> Man's Reason does his Want of Sense betray
> Who, by his Reason, wou'd his Nature sway.[41]

Rochester's approach is more brisk but the sentiments are similar:

> I'd be a dog, a monkey, or a bear,
> Or anything but that vain animal
> Who is so proud of being rational. . . .
> . . . before certain instinct, will prefer
> Reason, which fifty times for one does err; . . .
> Reason . . . leaving light of nature, sense, behind, . . .
> 'Tis evident beasts are, in their degree,
> As wise at least, and better far than he.[42]

In Wycherley's version *sense* and *nature* are undermined by reason, for "Reason's none, which against Nature goes"; thus reason "does things more unreas'nably," and urges "unbridled Sensuality." Conversely, beasts' reason is sense, or rather their sense is without reason; they are led by nature, "more just and more sensible than man," and their desires are not "constant sensuality," which in man demands "no End of Drudgery," his way of saying servicing of women, complying "with others Appetites . . . For forc'd Delight." The sexual revulsion of this poem recalls some of the ideas in the divorce poem to Lord Boyle as well as those in *"To a* Bridegroom,"

> Constrain'd to Drudg'ry, each dull Husband beats
> The Hemp of Wedlock in the Wedding Sheets;
> And the gross Work of Love, in Form and Fear, repeats.
> By Wedlock then thou art remov'd, not freed
> From that *Fleet*-Prison thou so much didst dread.

It would seem that such sexual disgust became current in

Wycherley's verse as an argument for divorce, rather than from imitation of a convention of contemporary poetry. The inescapable biographical implications emphasize again not only the bitterness that overwhelmed him in his marriage, but also the antipathy toward his wife and, at this time at least, toward women.[43] In the poem on reason's misuses, Wycherley does not provide a solution to this condition of man, except to expose reason's traps and to promote the natural norms of sense which should lead to "Happiness," "Content," and "Ease," frequent ideals in the later verse.

One critic takes several of Wycherley's poems on solitude as typical of his thought, while at the same time pointing out that he can "scarcely be called an exponent of the philosophy of retirement," and might be better cited for "his frequent attacks on business, zeal, ambition and avarice," which is exactly the case.[44] We might best typify his fundamental theme by observing the lines from "The *Various Mix'd* Life, against the *Constant Publick* or *Private* Life,"

> We from our selves alone, and not from Fate,
> Derive our happy, or unhappy State;
> Since by a publick Life, or private one,
> The Busie, or the Idle, are undone, . . .
> 'Tis not as either can more Pleasure give,
> But as in both, we more contented live.[45]

Though there is indeed much of a negative attitude in these best poems of Wycherley, it would not be fair to think of them as wholly exploratory, questioning without ever affirming. Professor Vieth writes of the Restoration age, "It questions, though it does not doubt; it wishes to believe, but is not sure it can. Analytic rather than synthetic, it nevertheless opens up possibilities for syntheses such as those of Swift and Pope."[46] To a great extent this characterization is accurate, but synthesis and positive suggestions are indeed offered in these poems, just as they had already been in the last plays.

This survey of select poems by no means reveals the whole of Wycherley's canon but indicates some of the prevailing themes which captivated his mind. As Lansdowne wrote, his poems are rough-set diamonds—one reads them not for Walleresque polish but for the statements made. Though these last discussed poems are much better examples of his versification, and make much less plausible the question of memory failure, one does wish he had placed less emphasis on the "careless" aspect of wit and a little more on "business" or "labour." As we have seen before in his use of materials from courtesy and morality books, he based his thoughts and dramatic materials solidly on contemporary life of the street and coffee-house and intellectual discussion, and then dealt with them in his own distinctive manner, going beyond convention, not so often in the early poems as in these satiric and abstract works, and most plainly in the plays, toward the new Augustan direction soon to appear with Swift and Pope.

Sometime about the mid-1690's, Wycherley began to plan seriously for the publication of the poems he had been busily composing. In late 1696, his plans had reached the stage where he felt he could issue the following advertisement:

> Mr. Wycherley's Miscellany Poems, Satyrs, Epistles, &c. Printed in Folio by way of Subscription, for the Benefit of the Author; for which Proposals having been already made, have received Encouragement from the Nobility and Gentry.[47]

Wycherley had asked Samuel Briscoe, a bookseller in Covent Garden, to print the proposals for the project, and he did so, sending out two thousand of them. Gathering subscriptions was reasonably successful for there was among those of "first Ranke & Quality" genuine interest in Wycherley's work and Briscoe took in fifty pounds toward the project. But arguments between printer and author arose about the amount, shades of Barnaby all over again: whose accounting of monies received and expended was correct? Briscoe claimed he had received 32£ in subscriptions, so Wycherley demanded an accounting of receipts and expenses. Briscoe replied that Wycherley owed him 30£ to defray costs of printing the proposals, but later it was 53£ 8s when Briscoe claimed bankruptcy and called upon a friend, Marmaduke

Browne, a Ludgate Hill stationer, for assistance. Briscoe finally agreed to return the manuscript but said that since he was in debt for 100£ it was proper for Browne to sue Wycherley for the 53£ 8s owed to Briscoe. Wycherley was thus arrested for "a great Summe of money," at the suit of Browne. We do not know how long he was imprisoned or how he was released, though he had received inheritance money at the death of his father in 1697 and a settlement of the Ireland suit in 1700.

Needless to say, the delays thus effected were very embarrassing to Wycherley who realized that he "hath sufered very much in Character amongst those persons of quality who subscribed theire names and paid their money" for the edition of his poems. Dryden mentioned to Walsh in May 1699,

> Mr. Wycherley's Poems will not come out until Michaelmas Terme: if his versification prove as well as his wit I shall believe it extraordinary.

He did not seem especially alarmed by the delay of three years since the advertisement; he still was ready to subscribe to it:

> However, Congreve and Southern and I shall not faile to appear before it, and if you will come in he will have reason to acknowledge it for a favour.

After Michaelmas had gone by there was still no edition, but at last the *Miscellany Poems* did appear in print in 1704. For the frontispiece to the folio volume there appeared an excellent mezzotint portrait engraved by I. Smith from the painting of Sir Peter Lely when Wycherley was twenty-eight. It was here under this engraving that Wycherley had written, "Quantum Mutatus ab illo." One wonders with what emotion Wycherley placed the words there; he mocked his face in a poem, *"The* Author *to the* Book-seller, *who desir'd his* Picture *before his Book, in Front of his* Follies; *pleading the Custom for it,"*

> Poet's Wares, like others, great or small
> Must have their Sign, to put 'em off to Sale, . . .

The worse it is, have but the better Sign, . . .
For as good Wine wants no good Bush, or Sign,
Were not my Wit flat, you'd ne'r ask for mine:
So where there is but scanty Furniture,
Bare Walls to cover, Pictures we procure.[48]

He as resolutely refused to be serious about his face as about his volume, which, he noted, could be included in its entirety in the "Errata."[49] Nevertheless it was with unabashed pleasure that he wrote to Lord Halifax on 12 May 1704,

My Lord
Since Presents of this kind, are seldom made, without Apollogys, for makeing them; yesterday Dr. Garth told me that your LordP did me the honour, to subscribe to this Book, wch I never knew before for the Knave ye Bookseller, who shoud have printed, this scurvy miscellany, broke for the credit of ye Book, before he printed it; and never told me what he had recd, or from whom, so robs me, of the Subscriptions which I suppose he thought his due, for not being accessary to my shame in publishing so scurvy a Book; But (My Ld) least this shoud seem as epistle Dedicatory I conclude it, assureing your Lordsp if I had the confidence, to have prefix'd any illustrious name, before it, your Lordsps might have been in danger, tho', I seldom use my Friends so scurvily as that comes to neither, . . .

W. Wycherley.[50]

Only days later he sent a copy of his poems to John Caryl in response to an invitation to visit Caryl:

As to ye Scurvy present I make you, I wish, there were any thing in it, coud entertain you, perhaps in the Country where ye Gazetts are wellcome . . . my damnd Book may be admitted at least as less impertinent.[51]

And there seemed to lurk under all the clowning about "my Nonsense . . . , My Fictions, flimflam Poetry," a real doubt about his abilities as poet, a fear for the prudence of submitting himself to the exposure of print after a quarter century of public silence. He dedicated his book "unfeignedly . . . To thee, Great Aid to Fancy, Vanity," half anticipating from "damn'd . . . Readers . . . Criticks! or Anti-Wits!" the "Severity of your Malice," because he was, in defiance of them, "no Poet, since a Lover of Truth, and no Wit, since the Plain-Dealer."[52]

Dryden did not live to see the publication of the *Miscellany,* and one wonders whether his anticipated pleasure would have been satisfied. Some certainly praised Wycherley's efforts, but some as certainly did not. Gildon explained:

> As the Conduct of some of his Acquaintance of *Will's* Coffee-House, in regard of these Poems, was, what was by no means agreeable to Mr. *Wycherley,* so it caus'd a Coldness between them, especially on our Author's side, who cou'd not but resent a Behaviour he thought the Effect of either Ignorance or Envy.
>
> This made Way to his Reception of some Men into his Favour and Intimacy, by their deference to this Book, who wou'd never have been admitted to that Favour without so particular, and taking a Bribe.[53]

Gildon did not, of course, name names, and his sneering reference to the latter group is suspect because of his sharp animosity against Alexander Pope, who came into Wycherley's circle about this time. But Gildon mentioned that the sale of the book was "not the success . . . as might have been expected from so celebrated a Name."[54]

Whoever these acquaintances were who disparaged his work, the generality of men who knew Wycherley continued to accept him as a celebrity and welcomed him into the circle of wits at Wills. Wycherley was a great talker, a marvelous talker. In the years before their falling out, Charles II, "a nice Discerner of Men, and himself a Man of Wit, often chose him for a Companion at his leisure Hours, as *Augustus* did *Horace.*"[55] Although it had seemed that his reputation declined and that he was forgotten during the years of his marriage and his term in prison, it actually stayed as steady as it was during his playwrighting days. Clearly he was more engaging at this dramatic game before a lively audience when his maxims and aphoristic habit could be best exercised, than at writing discursive thoughts in verse. It is perhaps because Wycherley was so sought after and so

[207]

responsive to the enchantments of conversation that so little has been recorded of his activities. There was almost no political involvement in his life at any time, with the exception of his messages to Buckingham in disfavor and to James in exile, nor any at this time when he might be expected to take more vocal part in public affairs. Thus many exchanges of letters do not mention him. Sir George Etherege's letters do not. Rochester and Savile's correspondence does not; Dryden does a few times relative to his poems and illness; but one searches in vain the diaries and correspondence of public men and women for references to him.[56] Strange as this disaffection from the public aspects of life was, it had one main effect besides the absence of mention by most important persons of the day, and that was his freedom from the fickle cycles of fame. He maintained a very constant esteem and respect among his contemporaries, probably comparable to that of Dryden who was, till his death in 1700, the dean of wits at Will's Coffee House.

Mr. Will Urwin opened the coffee house after his own name sometime before 1660 at 1 Bow Street, Covent Garden, a place readily accessible to all the town. From the first, its character was distinctive. "So to Will's with Mr. Pinkney," Samuel Pepys wrote in his diary in 1660.

> In Covent Garden to-night, going to fetch home my wife, I stopped at the great Coffee-House there, . . . where Dryden the poet (I knew at Cambridge) and all the wits of the town, and Harris the player. . . . And had I had time then, or could at other times, it will be good coming thither, for there, I perceive, is very witty and pleasant discourse.[57]

Pope asserted, "It was Dryden who made Will's Coffee House the great resort for the wits of his time. After his death, Addison transferred it to Button's, who had been a servant of his."[58] Dryden could be frequently found there; when, for instance, a young man named Francis Lockier at the age of seventeen came to London to find Dryden, he "thrust [himself] into Will's to have the pleasure of seeing the most celebrated wits of that time."[59] He heard that day in 1685

Dryden holding forth on his preference for *Macflecknoe* among his own works. Many others attended the rites of wit at Will's, a place one visitor characterized as holding "the first Rank," as

> being consecrated to the Honour of Apollo, by the first rate Wits that flourish'd in King *Charles* II's Reign, such as the late Earl of *Rochester*, the Marquis of *Normanby*, the Earl of *Dorset*, Sir *Charles Sidley*, the Earl of *Roscommon*; Sir *George Etherege*, Mr. *Dryden*, Mr. *Wycherley*, and some few others.

And if one were to divide the company into wits and would-be wits, among the first there would be:

> Men of distinguish'd Merit and Abilities, such as Mr. *Wycherley*, Dr. *Garth*, Mr. *Congreve*, the Honorable Mr. *Boyle*, Colonel *Stanhope*, Mr. *Vanbruk*, Mr. *Cheek*, Mr. *Walsh*, Mr. *Burnaby*, Mr. *Rowe* and some others.[60]

Among these "others" would be the actor Thomas Betterton, George Granville, Lord Lansdowne, Sir William Trumbull, George Savile, Marquis of Halifax, Thomas Shadwell perhaps, Thomas Southerne, the playwright, who borrowed from Wycherley's *The Plain-Dealer* for his own plays,[61] Sir Henry Sheer, and Henry Cromwell;[62] and perhaps also several residents of Bow Street, Grinling Gibbons, Sir Peter Lely and Sir Godfrey Kneller. All these were known to Wycherley on a constant and close basis. And Wycherley's place among them was recognized high. "He was esteem'd by the *Rochester's*, the *Buckingham's* the *Howards*, the *Drydens*, the *Ethereges*, and the *Dennises*; and lived in a Friendly and Intimate Correspondence with them, being mutually esteem'd of them, and esteeming them."[63]

Wycherley was on good terms with William Congreve, who knew Wycherley's plays very thoroughly; his own plays ring with verbal echoes and quotations, from "plain-dealing is a jewel," in *The Old Bachelor*, to "Dreames and *Dutch* Almanacks are to be understood by contraries," in *Love for Love*, and one may easily see *The Double-Dealer* as a continuation of the plain-dealer theme as well as other

Wycherley themes, though Congreve was a free-handed borrower from all sorts of sources. To Jacob Tonson, Congreve wrote in 1693, "If you see Mr. Wycherley pray tell him with my service that I wrote to him in Shrewsbury"; and Moyle asked Congreve to convey "my humble Service to Mr. Wycherley."[64] Perhaps it was through Congreve that an aspiring young playwright, Miss Catherine Trotter, at the precocious age of sixteen, asked of Wycherley and received a prologue to her play *Agnes de Castro* in 1696. She no doubt thought Wycherley's name would benefit the reception of her maiden drama, though as Gerald Weales reminds us, possibly the new edition of *The Country-Wife* brought the playwright renewed prominence and prestige. Wycherley's sometime friend Samuel Briscoe printed Trotter's play with the prologue, which was designed to be spoken by a woman. It is a rough piece of verse, indicative of Wycherley's writing something he scarcely cared about, a little bawdy in places, a little clever in places, but uninteresting in all others:

> *Ladies, and Gallants, you we hope to find*
> *To her, who brings you now together, kind;*
> *That you will to your pleasing her consent,*
> *Not out of your own Nicety prevent,*
> *But to spight her, your own divertisement.*[65]

When Wycherley was away from London, tending to his affairs in Shropshire, he corresponded regularly with friends like John Dennis, passing along little of substance but great quantities of verbal ingenuity and banter. Wycherley had to endure listening about Dennis' latest "passion" or about his illness coming or going, and sometimes he had to fend off, or make a show of fending off, Dennis' praise of his plays. Dennis wrote:

I thought that your Works were the only things that could make me full amends for the loss of your Company. By them you have been able to give me Joy even in the midst of my Pain. For, the *Country Wife*, and the *Plain Dealer* are stores of Delight, which you have laid up by a Noble Charity, to supply the Poor in Spirit thro all Posterity.[66]

The reply was amused and mildly punning;

> When you talk of the Store of Delights you find in my *Plain-Dealer*, you cease to be one; and when you commend my *Country-Wife*, you were never more a Courtier; and I doubt not but that you will like your next Neighbour's Country Wife better than you do mine, . . . but enjoy my Wife and welcome in my Absence; I shall take it as civilly as a City Cuckold.

Dennis did, however, cite significant virtues in Wycherley—his letters were not wholly fluff—his force of mind, his generosity, and "while the force of your Fancy and Judgment makes all the World admire you, you remain your self unmovd by it; . . . it plainly appears that you have beyond all this a Greatness of Soul, from whence you look down on your own Merit,"[67] the same greatness of soul we saw as the traditional virtue which became Restoration Generosity. Dennis so carefully defined and enumerated the virtues that he appears to be writing not to Wycherley but to another about him; he is certainly not being fulsome for the sake of compliment. From what Dennis called "the Clear Air on your Mountain at *Cleve*," Wycherley was doubtless pleased and he valued Dennis' friendship. While he was in Clive, he could, through Dennis, keep up communication with his friends in London, not because he disliked Clive so much, though writers such as Connely insist he hated it,[68] but because he loved both. His letters reflect no true distress at being in Clive, and he was there frequently; some of his complaints were merely conventional for he could scarcely tell his coffee-house associates he did not miss them:

> I would not have my Rivals in your friendship, the *C——s*, the *D——s*, the *W——s*, and the rest of your Tavern Friends enjoy your conversation while I cannot; Tho I confess, 'tis to their interest to make you dumb with Wine, that they may be heard in your company. . . .
>
> Pray let me have more of your Letters, tho they should rally me with Compliments undeserv'd . . . for like a Countrey Esquire I am in love with a Town Wit's Conversation, tho it be at a Distance that I am forced to have it. . . .[69]

In return, when he was back in London in December of 1694, where he had "been very busie this last Week about Law Affairs," perhaps about the Ireland suit, he chided Dennis who was then absent, as he himself would be the following April when he was "forced to take a little Turn out of Town":[70]

> I've given your Service to your Friends at the *Rose*, who since your absence own they ought not to go for the Witty Club, nor is *Wills* the Wits Coffee-House any more, since you left it . . . ; therefore expect not a Witty Letter from any of them, no more than from me, since they, nor I have conversed with you these three Weeks.

and supplied the gossip and compliment:

> Your friends of the Coffee-House and the *Rose*, whether Drunk or Sober, Good Fellows or Good Wits, show at least their Sense, by valuing you and yours, and send you all their Service . . . For News, *W*— lives Soberly, *Ch*—goes to bed Early; *D'Urfy* sings now like a Poet, that is, without being ask'd: And all the Poets or Wits-at-Wills since your departure, speak well of the Absent.[71]

There were apparently at Wills, clubs within the Club— those who would on cue act dramatically dour, and those who would similarly pantomime good humor. This Grave Club and Witty Club maintained their *il penseroso-l'allegro* posture with a kind of self-conscious dramatizing and submerged hilarity. Walter Moyle wrote to Congreve, "I believe not a Man of the Grave Club durst assist at this ridiculous Scene, for fear of laughing outright."[72] Probably Wycherley was of the Witty Club, if he bothered to take part in this game at all, though if cynicism were grave enough, he could have moved in both groups.

The year 1704 saw the appearance of the much delayed *Miscellany Poems*. It also witnessed a perhaps more significant event, the meeting of the sixty-three-year-old playwright with teenage Alexander Pope. "About this time there came to Town," wrote Gildon, as if narrating a folk tale of mythic moment, "and to *Will's*, one *Pope*"—in

Gildon's eyes the ogre of the tale—"a little diminutive Creature, who had got a sort of Knack in smooth Vercification, and with it was for setting up for a Wit and Poet . . . I remember I was once to wait on Mr. *Wycherley*, and found in his Chamber this little *Aesopic* sort of an Animal in his own cropt Hair, and Dress agreeable to the Forest he came from."[73] Wycherley's response to Pope was, in Gildon's recollection, even more droll: "*Wycherley* afterwards told me he was Poetically inclin'd, and writ tolerably smooth Verses," but the drollery was Gildon's interpolation.

Pope had come to London to look for Wycherley, as he had come as a boy of twelve to peer in the door of Will's for a glimpse of Dryden—"Virgilium tantum vidi"[74]—and as Lockier had come twenty years before to see the poet. Wycherley was still a man eminently worth meeting in the literary circles of London. Pope was an emerging poet and needed the association and support of cultural leaders, so his earliest friends were exactly selected to correspond to that need: William Walsh, Wycherley's long-time friend, of whom Pope wrote in the "Epistle to Arbuthnot," "knowing *Walsh*, would tell me I could write"; Lord Lansdowne, George Granville, to whom he dedicated *Windsor Forest*; Thomas Betterton the great actor, and of course Wycherley. Maynard Mack has observed that Pope's friends were from the beginning the alienated, men out of place.[75] And there is a perceptive appropriateness in Dennis' naming Wycherley, "the Humble Hermit at *Cleve*,"[76] for he was both a Jacobite and like Pope a Catholic (at the end of his life); his reputation was neither general nor popular but primarily among the great, within the collegiate isolation of the wits of Will's.

The two, standing at the end and at the beginning of something like epochs, must have been a strange looking pair from any point of view: Wycherley a tall man, still imposing in stature without the handsomeness of youth, and Pope already crippled at seventeen, never to be taller than

[213]

four feet six inches, though as Sir Joshua Reynolds recalled, he had large fine eyes and a long handsome nose.[77] Wycherley, who had been well schooled in classical learning and in the erratic ways of fame, had had his success as playwright. Pope, equally well educated but as yet untested by the excoriation of the dunces, was only beginning his great career as poet. Wycherley referred gently to his "little tender crazy carcase," but others like Gildon would seize on his deformity and insult him and mock his verse. Pope was accused of every self-aggrandizing literary impropriety; for instance, it was spread about that Pope wrote the epistle in praise of his own *Pastorals* under Wycherley's name, and that he stole lines from the old man and called them *An Essay on Criticism*.[78] It is true that Pope's revisions of Wycherley's poems and his tamperings with Wycherley's and his own letters for publication opened him to such attacks, but the passions of Grub Street far outran the offense. For all these vicissitudes, the relationship between Pope and Wycherley lasted, though not always smoothly of course, until the dramatist died— "I went to see him on his death-bed," Pope said. "We were pretty well together to the last," he went on; "sometimes we were out a little and sometimes in. He never did any unjust thing to me in his whole life."[79] To Swift in 1729 Pope commented, "My first friendship at sixteen I contracted with a man of seventy, and I found him not grave enough or consistent enough for me, tho we lived well till his death."[80] Pope's own consistency is somewhat fluid; when Spence remarked to him, "surely 'twas a very difficult thing for you to keep well with him," he answered, "The most difficult thing in the world."[81] This "out" and "in" becomes somewhat clearer as we trace the progress of their association.

The early correspondence of Pope and Wycherley is full of, to us, unnatural and implausible compliment— especially after one has read *The Plain-Dealer*—but such rhetorical flourish Sherburn assures us was "essential to letters written in the tradition of Voiture."[82] Pope's first printed letter was clumsily composed of sixteen-year-old similitudes which were unnatural even for him:

> For Critics, as they are Birds of Prey, have ever a natural inclination to Carrion: And though such poor Writers as I, are but Beggars, however no Beggar is so poor but he can keep a Cur, and no Author is so beggarly but he can keep a Critic. . . .[83]

Wycherley's reply was so predictably in his style as to border on self-parody:

> So Scribblers to the Publick, like Bankers to the Publick, are profuse in their voluntary Loans to it, whilst they forget to pay their more private and particular, as more just Debts, to their best and nearest Friends. However, I hope, you have as much good Nature as good Sense (since they generally are Companions) will have Patience with a Debtor. . . .[84]

Throughout the correspondence we find, of course, moments of serious exchange, such as when Pope cried Hold!: "I must blame you for treating me with so much Compliment, which is at best but the Smoak of Friendship." Wycherley tried to turn this to some advantage, "But since you say you do not write to me to gain my *Praise*, but my *Affection*, pray how is it possible to have one without the other? We must admire before we love."[85] In reply Pope offered a rather pat argument that old and young friends get on better than two old or two young because the interest of each is in the former case not threatened, a false notion which his enemies would soon bring to his attention.

Within the first year of their acquaintance, Wycherley had a chance to read Pope's *Pastorals* and was very impressed with them; they were the stimulus for much of the praise he forced upon the young poet. While assuring Pope that the poems were "safe in my Custody . . . from any one's Theft,"[86] Wycherley in fact sent them to Walsh to read, and he too was astonished at their excellence:

> The Author seems to have a particular Genius for that kind of Poetry, and a Judgment that much exceeds the years you told me he was of. . . . 'Tis no flattery at all to say, that *Virgil* had

[215]

written nothing so good at his Age. I shall take it as a favour if you will bring me acquainted with him; and if he will give himself the trouble any morning to call at my House, I shall be very glad to read the Verses over with him, and give him my opinion of the particulars more largely than I can well do in this Letter.[87]

Walsh's words here and his promise of further discussion seem to be of a considerably more practical advantage to Pope than what Wycherley offered, but then, Dryden had singled out Walsh as "the best critic of our nation."[88] Wycherley for his part had some ulterior motives, it seems.

It was not long before he took the first presumptive advantage of Pope's youthful abilities and handed him copies of his poems to be retouched. In February 1706, he wrote from London,

> I have receiv'd your kind Letter, with my Paper to Mr. *Dryden* corrected. I own you have made more of it by making it less. . . . Well; you have prun'd my fading Lawrels of some superfluous, sapless, and dead Branches, to make the remainder live the longer. . . .
>
> Now, Sir, to make you another Excuse for my boldness in inviting you to Town, I design'd to leave with you some more of my Papers, (since these return so much better out of your Hands than they went from mine) for I intended . . . to spend a Month, or six Weeks this Summer, near you in the Country, for you may be assured there is nothing I desire so much, as an Improvement of your Friendship—[89]

Pope's father knew such an arrangement would come to grief for his son,[90] and Wycherley should have known as much, but once again his practical wisdom was sadly lacking and he ran eagerly to Pope for help, seeing only his own advantage in publishing better poems. And when Pope did not make instant, serious protestations, Wycherley seized the opportunity to "Submitt all I writ, to the infallibility of your Wit, Judgment, and Sensure who are my Pope," Wycherley's usual pun, and sent on to Pope his *Miscellany Poems*, "that Damnd Miscellany of Madrigals of mine to pick out (if possible) some that may be so alterd that they may yet apeare in print again I hope with better Success than they hether to have done."[91] Pope was suddenly sobered into realizing exactly what complex arrangement he had become party to; his reply of 10 April was direct:

> By yours of the last Month, you desire me to select, if possible, some Things from the first Volume of your Miscellanies, which may be alter'd so as to appear again. I doubted your meaning in this; whether it was to pick out the best of those Verses, (As that on the *Idleness of Business;* on *Ignorance*; on *Laziness*, &c.) to make the Method and Numbers exact, and avoid Repetitions? For tho' (upon reading 'em on this occasion) I believe they might receive such an Alteration with Advantage; yet they would not be chang'd so much, but any one would know 'em for the same at first sight. Or if you mean to improve the worst Pieces, which are such to render them very good, would require a great addition, and almost the entire new writing of them? Or, lastly, if you mean the middle sort, as the Songs and Love-Verses? For these will need only to be shortened, to omit repetition . . . .

He sent along his revisions of the poems to Waller and to Marlborough, and some others, explaining that he had cut from some, added to others, and some "I have entirely new expressed, and turned more into Poetry." Consequently, Pope urged Wycherley to send along only new poems, and to let the published ones be. But this too became a problem when Pope found he had to compare new with old to see the extent of repetition; he was, in short, much put upon and constrained to do a great deal of work. The more he was put upon and the more work he expended on the project, the more annoyed he became. When he sent back a packet of corrected poems in November 1707, he emphasized that the carrier, a Mr. Englefyld,

> is ignorant of the Contents, and I hope your prudence will let him remain so . . . Since if you should reveal any thing of this nature [that Pope revised his poems], it would be no wonder Reports should be rais'd, and there are those (I fear) who would be ready to improve them to my disadvantage. I am sorry you told the great Man, whom you met in the *Court of Requests*, that your Papers were in my hands: No Man alive shall ever know any such thing from me; and I give you this warning besides, that tho' your self should say I had any way assisted you, I am notwithstanding resolv'd to deny it.[92]

Pope must have early considered himself a candidate for greatness to be so angry with Wycherley's casualness; but significantly, he continued this letter with a detailed examination of the structure of the poem on Dullness rather than throwing over the whole matter and rejecting Wycherley's project entirely. Was it respect that kept Pope at it? An exact motive is difficult to ascertain.

Even the exasperation Pope showed when he found "much more repeated than I till now imagin'd" in the former volume of poems, did not stop his activity; even when Wycherley encumbered matters yet further by asking Pope not to deface or blot the copy but to tick off in the margin questionable lines, Pope responded,

> Do not be so unjust, as to imagine from hence that I would decline any part of this Task: On the contrary you know, I have been at the pains of transcribing some Pieces, at once to comply with your desire of not defacing the Copy, yet to lose no Time in proceeding upon the Correction. I will go on the same way if you please; tho' truly it is (as I have often told you) my sincere Opinion, that the greater Part would make a much better Figure, as *Single Maxims* and *Reflections* in Prose, after the manner of your favourite *Rochefoucaut*, than in Verse. And this, when nothing more is done but marking the Repetitions in the Margin, will be an easy Task for your self to do, notwithstanding the bad Memory you complain of.[93]

In this last recorded letter written between the two men, Pope's patience was obviously wearing very thin and the civility of both was strained about as far as it would reach. Some years later, Pope told Spence, "I was extremely plagued up and down for almost two years with them. However, it went off pretty well at last."[94] In fact, the correspondence indicates that the revisions were going on from 1706 till this last letter of 2 May 1710, so Pope probably was referring to the major burden of the task, not the relatively minor tinkering he did at first. Pope cannot be blamed for his annoyance at Wycherley; admittedly his egocentric jealousy for his reputation is not admirable, but through the course of years, Pope was generally fair to Wycherley. Wycherley's behavior to Pope was often petty over the poems. He began to use his reputed bad memory as an excuse: "(You say,) you find numerous repetitions of the same thoughts, and Subjects, all which, I must confess my want of memory has prevented me from imagining."[95] One can see that his continuing a weak poetic career in the hope of regaining that old dramatic genius was hopeless and unfortunate and a little degrading to the dignity of the old man.

The fact that they continued their friendship through this period of strained emotions indicates something of the respect each was able to maintain for the other apart from the irritations of human frailty. Pope had always referred to Wycherley with respectful praise in his letters to Cromwell and others even when he could have safely derided the old man behind his back:

> next the pleasure of Serving my friends is that I take in hearing from them & in this particular as beyond all others I [am] beyond all acknowledgments Obligd to Our friend Mr W[ycherley] who as if it were not enough to have excelld all *Men* in Wit is resolvd to excell them in *Good Nature* & Humanity too. I know I need no Apology to You for speaking of Mr. W[ycherley] whose Example as I am proud of following in all things, so in Nothing More than in professing my self Like him.[96]

But the uncertainty of the relationship and a touch of defensiveness crept into Pope's letters to Cromwell when he lamented the silence of Wycherley; since the old man left London, he wrote,

> I have not heard a word from him; tho just before, and once since I writ to him, & tho I know myself guilty of no Offence but of doing sincerely, just what he bid me. . . .But the greatest injury he does me, is keeping me in Ignorance of his Welfare, which I am always very sollicitious for.[97]

He continued to mention Wycherley in his letters, one time reporting one of his asides about going to Shropshire "to

[219]

Rob the Country," again questioning when Wycherley would be in London, another time suggesting he had "once hop'd to have possesst in" Wycherley[98] a friend, a hope now apparently vain. His feelings emerged more and more strongly as time passed, and he wrote to Cromwell on 28 October 1710:

> I hope it will be no offence to give my most hearty Service to Mr. Wycherley, tho' I perceive by his last Letter to me, I am not to trouble him with my Letters, since he there told me he was going instantly out of Town, & till his Return was my Servant, &c.

On the basis of the last letter of Wycherley extant, Pope would have no reason for such suspicion; he appears to intensify possible differences, to invite jealousy for causes one cannot clearly find in the letters, though there may have been other ways of his discovering Wycherley's feelings. He nevertheless conveyed his regard and esteem for Wycherley, perhaps in an attempt to break their supposed impasse:

> I guess by yours he is yet with you; and beg you to do, what you may with all Truth and honour, that is assure him, I have ever born all the respect & kindness imaginable to him, & all that is His. I protest by all that is holy, I do not in the least Know to this hour what it is that has Estrang'd him from me; but this I know, that he may for the future be more Safely. . . my friend, since no Invitation he can make shall ever more make me so free with him. I cou'd not have thought any man had been so very cautious and suspicious, as not to credit his own Experience of a Friend. . . . There is but one way I know of Conversing safely with all men, that is, not by concealing what we say or do, but by saying or doing nothing that deserves to be concealed, & I can truly boast this Comfort, in my affairs with Mr. W. I beg you Sir to pardon my speaking well of myself in this One thing, since I doubt not but Mr. W. speaks ill enough of me in some others. But I pardon his Jealousy, which is become his Nature, & shall never be his Enemy whatsoever he says of me.[99]

The silence between them that seemed to have ensued after the last printed letter was broken in a fashion in Cromwell's letter to Pope on 26 October 1711:

[220]

> Mr. *Wycherley* visited me at the *Bath* in my sickness . . . ; hearing from me how welcome his letters wou'd be, he presently writ to you. . . . whenever we met he talk'd of you. He praises your [*Essay on Criticism*], and even outvies me in kind expressions of you. . . . I arrived on *Saturday* last much wearied [and] Mr. *Wycherley* came to town on *Sunday* last, and kindly surpriz'd me with a visit on *Monday* morning. We din'd and drank together; and I saying, *To our Loves*, he reply'd, *'Tis* Mr. Pope's *health*.

Pope was relieved that the friendship was restored:

> I am highly pleas'd with the knowledge you gave me of Mr. W[ycherley]'s present Temper which seems so favorable to me: I shall ever have such a Fund of Affection for him as to be agreable to myself when I am so to him, & cannot but be Gay when he's in good humor.[100]

Wycherley wrote regularly to Pope then and they associated very closely during these years. "I visited him for a whole winter, almost every evening and morning," Pope told Spence.

They had in fact planned more meetings than they accomplished. Wycherley was traveling about a good deal and when he was stationary, ill health was often the cause. Shortly after they met, Pope moved from London to Windsor Forest, whence he often thereafter invited Wycherley to visit him, and Wycherley in return as often found reason not to. It became something of a game between them; as late as 1710, Wycherley remarked: "I know not, but I may See You very suddenly at Binfield, after all my broken promisses."[101] In March 1706, a little over a year since they met, Wycherley went to Shropshire, his main business there being the overseeing of his properties ("I have receiv'd some Monny" from his tenants). He reported his painful journey by coach to Pope who could well sympathize since he travelled in such jostling manner at the peril of his dwarfish limbs and life; if, he wrote, you should be

> inquisitive, how I bore my long Journy, att this time of the Year, you must know, it went harder with me in the Coach, than out of it.[102]

He planned to go to Bath, about 100 miles directly south of Shrewsbury, and then to "spend two Months (God Willing) with You att Binfield." By November 1707, he was back in London, where he awaited "My Mans return from Shropshire,"[103] and was soon recalled home to handle business there; he wrote on 9 January,

> I have receivd your most extream kind and entertaining Letter, written upon New Years Day, and I must confess was the best New Years Gift, I receivd this Yeare, tho' some of my Tennants brought me that Day some Monny; . . . my Journy (as you apprehend) was very Tedious to me, by reason of the season . . . But necessity . . . made me, the old Gelding, Jogg down into Shropshire, haveing two Farmes of some Concidderable Rents thrown upp into my hands which might have been unlet . . . for this whole Yeare following, had I not come down nor had I stayd above, woud my Tennants, have come down with the Ready.

Apparently Wycherley stayed in Shrewsbury during this trip to handle business at the county center, since he said his being out of Shrewsbury four days accounted for the delay in answering Pope's letter.[104]

After returning to London, Wycherley remained there silently into the following year, causing Pope to worry over his health, which did in fact take a sharp turn for the worse in the spring of 1709 through an accidental fall.

> I have had a very odd Accident befall me; upon Friday was fortnight, or rather Saturday morning, the last of April, when I went to, and came from the Painters Tavern, with one Mr. Balam, who, being something drunker than I, (because he thought himself sober,) wou'd needs lead me down the Stairs; which I refused, and therefore, went down very well, but at the Steps, going into the Street, he turn'd short upon me, to help me again from falling, and so procur'd my Fall; for Balam turning back upon the Ass, not the Ass upon Balam; he fell upon me, and threw me backward, with his Elbow, in my Stomach, and the Hilt of his Sword, in my Eye, bruis'd me so sorely, I was forced to keep my Bed, for two Days; with a great pain in my side, which by the help of Surgeons, is but lately gone; so that I have been almost a fortnight in pain.[105]

For a man of seventy this was a serious injury which he slowly began to realize when his indefatigable intentions to go to Shropshire were delayed week after week. In mid June he repeated his intentions to go to the country in a week's time, but admitted being "troubled with an akeing side."[106] Over the following months, Pope heard nothing from him, and shared with Cromwell his apprehension for Wycherley's health, indeed his life. Not until the spring of 1710 did Wycherley write again, and by April, a year after his injury, he was in Shropshire, hastening to finish "my Business at *Shrewsbury* in a Fortnights time,"[107] so he could hurry back to Pope and plan toward printing some of his poems, a venture that did not occur during his lifetime.

Wycherley's sometimes precarious physical condition certainly did not hamper seriously his energetic travels. To some extent, these were necessitated by obligations to oversee his properties in Shropshire and deal with that insistent perennial problem of debt. He had already in 1699 mortgaged some property in Clive to stave off debt, and in 1713 he was again obliged to arrange a quick loan. With the assistance of his nephew William, John's son, he demised a piece of property in Wem called Pools to one John Cartwright as security for 200£.[108] Nevertheless with typical abandonment of caution, he ignored expense and travelled frequently to Bath where he visited Cromwell in 1711. Since Bath had overtaken Tunbridge as the fashionable watering spa, especially after the arrival there of Beau Nash early in the eighteenth century, he no doubt loved to visit there for the pleasure of conversing with friends as well as for the salubrious waters. The population of Bath was in process of leaping from a village-size of 1,000 in 1660 to over 6,000 near midcentury,[109] and though the Roman baths were not rediscovered till much later, the city was building and expanding its status as the premier resort of inland England. When Pope himself went to Bath to escape the irascible dunces who both despised and feared him, he wrote on 25 September 1714 to John Caryll:

Upon the whole, I walk about here as innocently, and as little dreaded, as the old lion in satire. Mr. Wycherley, who now goes tame about this town. I named you to him, and [he] speaks such things of you (to give him his due) as may be heard by your friend with satisfaction.[110]

This meeting may have been one of the very few times in the last three or four years that Pope and Wycherley were actually together. Pope had mentioned that he "visited him for a whole winter," probably in 1710 or 1711,[111] but the letters indicate little personal contact after that. And this meeting assures us that their reconciliation was more genuine than an epistolary cordiality.

If we look ahead for a moment beyond Wycherley's death to the disposition of his papers, we find that Pope's relationship with him continued, in a manner of speaking, well after Wycherley was gone. Wycherley's papers fell into the hands of his cousin Thomas Shrimpton who, as we shall see, controlled much of Wycherley's estate after his death. Shrimpton disposed of the papers to his acquaintance, the noted Shakespearean editor and scholar Lewis Theobald who "purchased them at a considerable Expence,[112] but who was apparently Shrimpton's only choice as editor of the works. The task was reportedly a taxing one, so that "*a great Delay in its Publication, is owing to several unavoidable Embarrassments which have befallen*" the editor, none of which are presently known, and the volume eventually appeared in 1728, *The Posthumous Works of William Wycherley Esq. in Prose and Verse.* The "Reader" was informed that since "*what is here offered, being but one Moity of Mr. Wycherley's Manuscripts, the Remainder . . . according to the Reception of these, will in a short time follow.*" In fact, Theobald did not have a chance to present a second volume, for Pope intervened.

Pope's response to the volume was intense and varied, partly an already dedicated hostility to Theobald whom he later skewered as "pidling *Tibald*" for his *Shakespeare Restored* (1726) and whom he had selected for the chief dunce of the first *Dunciad* (1728), and partly because Theobald was encroaching on Pope's self-declared territory in printing his revisions of Wycherley's poems. Thus, Pope hastened to print *The Posthumous Works of William Wycherley, Esq.* . . . Vol. II the next year, a volume consisting of the poems not in the *Miscellany Poems* of 1704, the collection of three hundred and eight maxims Wycherley had borrowed, written or distilled from some of his over-wrought poems, and the edited correspondence between him and Pope. Just as Theobald's *Shakespeare Restored* was a reply to Pope's edition of Shakespeare, so, as Professor V. A. Dearing has observed, Pope challenged with his own *Wycherley Restored*.[113]

In the introductory "To the Reader," supposedly composed by the publisher, Pope explained the procedure of the volume, for he wished to point out those poems which "were touch'd upon, with the Author's own Consent and Concurrence, by his Friend; and which may have been finger'd after his Death, by others, without any Warrant, but their own Arrogance, or Motive but their own Lucre."[114] The volume began with an index to Volume I, annotating the poems printed there which were spurious, in whole or part, or had been altered from Wycherley's original or from Pope's own revision by Theobald, who had "Revised and Corrected . . . every Sheet" in his volume. For example, concerning "To Celia, who, flying from him into a Grove," lines 13–33 are *"not* Mr. Wycherley's"; "For Solitude and Retirement Against the Publick, Active Life, . . . *very much disagrees with Mr.* Wycherley's *Original"*; as also "On His Grace the Duke of Marlborough . . . *Disagrees with the Original Manuscript . . . and seems to have been added to."*[115] In the index to his volume, Pope placed asterisks beside the seventeen poems he had revised, noting also those printed in error by Theobald. We have discussed several of these above without specific consideration of the lines Pope may have altered or added, but as Wycherley's own at least in intention—poems such as *"Various Mix'd* Life," "To that

Incomparable Poet, Mr. *Waller*," "An Epistle to *Mr.* Dryden," and "*The* Praise *of* Avarice." Pope's inclusion of his correspondence with Wycherley therefore acted as a proof of his hand in the poems, for instance his detailed analysis of the structure of "on *Dulness.*"[116] Pope's versions of the poems are generally shorter than the originals and than Theobald's versions, for the obvious reason that he cut heavily, as Wycherley had urged; "slash, cut, and lopp of the Excressness and dead parts of my wither'd Bays, that the little remainder may live the longer."[117] Professor Dearing judiciously observed, "Pope's version is uniformly the more carefully articulated, and it is normally the more euphonious. The syntax of Pope's version is clearer, effective parallelism is more pronounced, and harsh collocations of sounds and forced emphases are fewer."[118]

To this volume of *Posthumous Works* an "Introduction" by Wycherley was fixed, written apparently as late as 1714, if we judge on the basis of a quote from Pope's *Rape of the Lock* (Canto IV, 1. 125; 1714) in the line, ". . . for Men with full Pockets, plump Cheeks, and *round unthinking Faces* . . ."; though the essay was probably planned earlier when Wycherley was hoping to print, with Pope's assistance, the remainder of his poems—the *Miscellany Poems* of 1704 concluded with a tentative "Volume I." Pope had, for some time, urged Wycherley to restraint on the projected second volume. He even considered this introduction *"most certainly written by some other hand, tho' some of the Thoughts are* Mr. Wycherley's":

> Worn as I am with Age, and harrass'd by Fortune, I find many of my Vices still faithfully troublesome, and amongst the rest that impertinent Itch of Scribbling, which has betray'd so many Authors to Ridicule, and almost undone our Notions of Reason and common Sense: Tho' at the same Time, I must own, the Lust of Writing, like a Man's other Lewdness, should forsake us in our State of Impotence: But we grow most vicious when we have least Power left to be so; as Beggars become more importunate, the more strenuously we deny them.[119]

The sentiments, images and comparisons are in Wycherley's manner, though the essay is generally less heavily repetitious or conscious of comparison than much of his prose.

While this edition of Wycherley's works by Pope may be viewed as a service to the memory of the playwright, Pope's characterization of Wycherley has served to fix a peculiar image, for the delay in producing these poems was caused, Pope said, by

> The known Inability of Mr. *Wycherley* in *Versification*, added to the Decay of his *Memory*; the *Impossibility* which his Friend at last found of rendring them perfect *Pieces of Poetry*, even tho' he should have entirely new-written them; the Conviction by several instances, that [the more he revised them, the less they would] pass for Mr. *Wycherley's*; and lastly his sincere Opinion that they would make a worse Figure as Verses unequal and undigested, without Ornament Method or Musick, than as single *Maxims*.

Finally he noted Wycherley's "Temper, Sense of his own Deficiencies, and Deference to the Judgment of a Friend" and his own "Sincerity, Candor and Zeal for the Reputation of a Friend."[120] How far was Pope self-serving, how far showing Wycherley truly or fairly? Like much of their relationship, there is about this posthumous edition an ambiguity and irreducible complexity, beyond which it is difficult to perceive, though there is clearly some truth in all that Pope wrote of his old friend.

Wycherley visted Bath the next summer, 1715, and at Michaelmas term came back to London to Mrs. Watkins' large and noisy rooming house in Covent Garden where he had lodged for some time. She would watch him stagger across the street and remark to her daughter that he would never live through the coming winter.[121] As he rested in his rooms there, his health gradually declining toward death, he was visited by a relation of his mother's family, one Captain Thomas Shrimpton, a man of thoroughly predatory instincts whose motive for visiting the old man was to grasp

[227]

the only material thing he had left, besides his debts, his right to settle a jointure of his properties upon a wife. Preposterous as the motive may seem, as we consider Wycherley, seventy-five years old, in declining control of his faculties, plainly dying, it was nevertheless the one which drove Shrimpton and the one which accompanied Wycherley in his last months, a period more degrading and pitiable than one would have thought possible, even bearing in mind the truth of his prologue to *The Plain-Dealer*:

> And where else, but on Stages, do we see
> Truth pleasing; or rewarded Honesty?

Shrimpton's assault on the weakened old man was both swift and covert. Pope, who visited him on his death bed and from whom Wycherley borrowed 20£,[122] did not have any sense of what was going on; and when he wrote in January following to a mutual friend Edward Blount, with "some circumstances of the last Act of that eminent Comick Poet, and our Friend, Wycherley,"[123] he had only part of the story right. Shrimpton first undermined what remained of Wycherley's health and perspicacity by killing him with the kindness of late night pub life:

> Shrimpton . . . did use to call upon him very frequently in a morning and keep him out all day & bring him home again to his Lodgings at 2 3 or 4 of the Clock in the morning & it was a very Early hour if he brought him home at 12 o' th' Clock at night & when he soe brought him home the sd Wm Wicherley was allways or usually soe intoxicated with Wine . . . that he could neither speak nor help him self.

Then, reminding Wycherley of what he quite well knew, his debts, he began to suggest to him that if he would marry, he could convey his property to his wife and thus settle his debts. He was not yet so dead as to misconstrue Shrimpton's intentions, and he would shout out "his aversions to marry & saying they should get him a Consult of Physitians for it was that he wanted & not a wife." In order to salvage some of his debts, he sent an agent, who happened to be Shrimpton, to Shropshire in his stead to collect the rents due, and with a letter of attorney signed by the lawyer and scholar Lewis Theobald and one Marmaduke Kilburne, Shrimpton went off to do Wycherley's business.

Doctors meanwhile who were called in to examine the old man were convinced that he was in no condition to marry and needed a wife only for a nurse; five doctors declared him in early December to be dying. Thus when Shrimpton returned to London, he discovered his victim to be nearly beyond the scope of his plan, and he was compelled to work even faster.

Though he had actually received at least sixty pounds from Wycherley's tenants, he "told . . . Wycherley that he was a miserable man for noe money could be got for him & . . . pressed him to marry the sd Mrs Jackson, . . . telling the sd Wm Wicherley that without money noe Dr would come neer to him & sayed the sd Gentlewomans money would furnish him with what he wanted & swearing that the sd Wm Wicherley if he did not marry . . . might lye & starve. . . ." To this Wycherley replied that he would rather "run his Head into the fire as Marry." At this time, William, the son of John Wycherley, came to see his dying uncle since he was first inheritor of the property according to Daniel's indenture of 1696 and was gravely concerned that old William's marriage would bilk him of that inheritance. While it has been traditionally believed that old William deliberately cheated his nephew, as Pope remarked, "the Nephew he left to comfort himself as well as he could, with the miserable Remains of a mortgaged Estate,"[124] such does not seem to have been the case; he did, in effect, destroy the nephew's hopes and the two did quarrel, but the destruction was wrought by Shrimpton's accomplishment of old Wycherley's marriage.

Shrimpton's efforts by 19 December were redoubled; he raged at the old man, "By God he should marry & he would force him to marry for he was money out of Pocket & he should be a Looser if he did not marry telling him that he could not now Live long." Then Shrimpton had Wycherley moved to a quieter rooming house run by Mrs. Armstrong,

[229]

and was there visited by Elizabeth Jackson, Shrimpton's protégé, mistress and the intended bride. Already a deed of marriage and the jointure had been presented Wycherley by the lawyers Theobald and others, but he dozed through the attempted presentation, asking vaguely what papers these were, knowing he had sent for none. Shrimpton then got a special licence declaring Wycherley to be "perfectly in his right sences & desirous of ye sd Marriage," and returned to his rooms with that and the other necessary papers, demanding Wycherley sign them. Though he would fly "into a Passion" and complain "he was in great Pain," Wycherley could not resist the constant pressure, and while knowing what the lawyers and Shrimpton were scheming, he found himself unable to drive them away. "Soe I will doe it & not give these Gentlemen the trouble to come again & did thereupon voluntarily sign the sd affidt & swear to the Truth of it."

The next morning, 20 December, his nurse, Elizabeth Davis, was ordered to dress him in clean clothes, but he disliked "to have clean Linnen on & soe averse that" she was compelled to put the clean shirt over his old one. Later that day he received the sacrament of the sick, "according to the Church of Rome as a Dying Man & been anointed with Oyl," by Dr. Harris of St. Paul's, Covent Garden.[125] Pope could not resist the observation that, in the usual order of things, one received Extreme Unction after marriage, not before. Later that day, Dr. Harris was recalled to marry the couple.

> While the said Ceremoneys were performing the sd Wm Wicherley did not stand or kneel but sat in his great Chair & seemed . . . to be much dejected hanging down his Head & . . . not to mind what was then doing & tho the Parson bid him hold up his Head & speak after him this Dept did not hear that he sayed one Word but . . . heard the Complt Elizabeth speak very distinctly. . . .

After the ceremony Shrimpton told Wycherley to open his hand where Shrimpton had placed two guineas to pay the minister. So it was accomplished except for the consummation. With Shrimpton apparently observing with greedy concern, the couple went to bed that evening but in no way satisfied Shrimpton, for Wycherley took "noe manner of notice of her," and only after sufficient harrassment by Shrimpton, "his mother & Grand mother & of . . . Elizabeths mother" he relented and the marriage was validated on the books. What is more probable is that Shrimpton and Elizabeth were quickly in bed together, a circumstance Wycherley may have been aware of, for when his former landlady Mrs. Watkins came and "wished him Joy," he snorted "in a great Passion & . . . with great Heat a ffart of Joy."

Pope stopped to see Wycherley "twice" after the marriage and jointure, and he seemed to Pope "less peevish in his Sickness than he used to be in his Health; neither much afraid of dying, nor (which in him had been more likely) much ashamed of Marrying." Wycherley was beyond shame, beyond concern for what the world might think of his actions. His wife treated him poorly when she did deign to do him any service, and he seems not to have cared. He did, however, shortly before he died, call her into his room and ask her to grant him one request.

> Upon her Assurances of consenting to it, he told her, *My Dear, it is only this; that you will never marry an old Man again.* I cannot help remarking [Pope continued], that Sickness which often destroys both Wit and Wisdom, yet seldom has power to remove that Talent which we call *Humour*: Mr. *Wycherley* shew'd his, even in this last Compliment.

Pope seemed to think this was humor on his part, and perhaps there was a glint of irony in his eye.

Among his final acts was of course the drawing and signing of his will, eleven days after his marriage, dated 31 December 1715, the day of his death. After commending his soul to God in hopes of a joyful resurrection according to customary form, the will's particular items began with his desire that all his debts be properly settled, along with the charges of his funeral, and thereafter all "my Estate ready Money Plate Jewels Goods" would go "unto my dear & well beloved wife Eliz. Wycherley And of this my last Will & Testamt I do hereby make and appt my loveing kinsman Thos Shrimpton . . . sole Exe[cutor]."[126] Captain Shrimpton had his way to the last detail: young William had lost the inheritance, and he had gained it both as executor to the property and as imminent husband of Elizabeth, for after three months, the two had the sanction of the Church placed upon their liaison and his plan was neatly completed. Within a few years, the Church Wardens' books for the parish of Wem record Shrimpton as owner of those properties which had passed from Daniel to William,[127] and the Shrimptons had the last laugh on Daniel's elaborate plan to cling to all his Wycherley property.

As repellent to one's sensibilities as Wycherley's final humiliation is, there is about it a certain inevitability, as if it were a necessary last insult dealt by the man of business and cunning to the man of no business acumen, the man helplessly out of place in that arena of city life. The virtues he and others celebrated of generosity did not have a real chance against the designs of the Shrimptons, or Brownes or even the Barnabys. He could draw the character of greed in his plays, he could ridicule the cits' passion for money, but after the plays were done, after the stage was darkened, he had to live in this world and pay his way; for unlike his and most comic heroes, he did not marry into an easy fortune for a comfortable and carefree life. So it was nearly of necessity in the nature of things in his world that he would be visited by a Shrimpton, and that he would be visited by a fine poet, Pope, who would not understand what the relative was engineering. To all appearances Wycherley died a fool and dupe. Only his fierce anger to Shrimpton and his final peace before Pope tell us that he retained his strong sense of himself and bore a firm inner assurance even while ignominious circumstances made him seem the least stock cuckold.

On the evening of 31 December 1715 William Wycherley

died. In his will he had declared himself a member of the parish of St. Paul's, Covent Garden; there he was buried on 5 January 1716.[128]

Chapter VI
Footnotes

1. *Chancery Bill Books*, 1685–87, p. 237, and p. 244. Ireland PRO.

2. D21, 912, National Library of Ireland.

3. *Ibid.* State Papers, SP 44/71, p. 377. "Upon the Petition of Henry Earle of Drogheda representing that his Brother the late Earle of Drogheda did by the contrivance of his Wife and her Relations settle from him a great parte of the Estate entailed on the family and charged . . . with severall debts and payments, and praying since he can have no other relief but in Parliament that his Majty will order the examination & the preparing a Bill. . . ."

4. *England in the Reigns of James II and William III* (Oxford, 1955), p. 8.

5. *Chancery Entry Books*, C33/270, Hilary, 1687/8, p. 340, and p. 333. "Ar" stands for Armiger, Gentleman. Ireland PRO.

6. *Ibid.*, Trinity, 1688, p. 596.

7. C8, 435/23.

8. Anne Moore, Countess of Drogheda, History of the Moore Family (Belfast, 1902), p. 79. In spite of her erroneous notion that Wycherley's debt from this litigation cast him in prison, one is inclined to believe this fact of the St. Mary Abbey property.

9. Gildon, p. 13.

10. *Chancery Order Books*, Vol. 10, 1709, 29; see also p. 74 and p. 339 for more on same; and see Vol. 9, 390. Ireland PRO.

11. Indenture, 20 January 1704, M6992—4. Ireland PRO. See also document #2, on a payment to Henry of a small debt, 3 June 1699; and document #3, on land demised 16 August 1699 to Henry's son on his marriage to the daughter of Lord Loftus of Ely. For other cases involving Henry not mentioned previously, see: *Repertory to Decrees of Chancery*, 1685–1732, III, 57, Trinity, 1685, which actually involves his mother, Alice; p. 169, Michas, 1685, a decree that Henry repay 200£ of a loan of 668£ borrowed to pay off Charles' debts; *Chancery Entry Books*, C33/272 Michas, 1688, p. 106, and 9 June 1691, both references to suit of Henry vs. Francis Roberts; *Repertory to Decrees of Chancery*, III, 48, Michas, 1693, a decree that Henry repay monies received from lands and tithes, which were settled for payment of debts of Charles; and *Chancery Bill Books*, November 1692–November 1696, p. 22, a case with Elnathan Lumm, in 1692; p. 139, a case with Hercules Davys and Lettice his wife, in 1694; and p. 157, Henry a deft.

12. Anne Moore, p. 79.

13. Indenture of Daniel Wycherley, 10 September 1696, 1452/1, Salop

Record Office. Connely, pp. 253–55, printed an abbreviated form and omitted "And all that Messuage or Tenemt scituate and being in Clive aforesd now in the holding of One Benjamin Rogers"; misstated the prior ownership of the property in Houlson or Howson to be James Wycherley when it was "lately purchased of the sd Richard Wicherley"; omitted what I believe is relative, "And all that peice of ground in Wem aforesd which is designed for the erecting another new house upon but the same is not yet built"; as well as the following last entries: "And all those sevrall other parcells of Land besides and sd Trench Farme which are now occupied with the said ffour last mentioned tenents: And all other the Lands & Meadowes & Pastures which now or formerly belonged to the said Trench Farme. . . ."

14. Sherburn, III, 363: Swift remarked to Pope about a friend: "he is befathered worse than poor Wycherley." Connely, p. 255.

15. Church Wardens' books, 1683–1734, for 1697 to 1716.

16. W. G. D. Fletcher, *Shropshire Parish Registers*, Register of Clive (Shropshire Parish Register Society, 1909), p. 133: "May 10, Bathia [sic] Whychley . . . bur."

17. Summers, III, 37–57.

18. *Ibid.*, pp. 178, 100, 89, 169, 183.

19. *Ibid.*, pp. 84, 96; and 83, 119, 130, 186.

20. *Ibid.*, p. 221; IV, 10, 231.

21. *Ibid.*, III, 87, 210, 165.

22. *Ibid.*, p. 215.

23. *Ibid.*, IV, 247.

24. *Orders of the Shropshire Quarter Sessions*, Vol. I, 1638–1708, ed. R. Lloyd Kenyon, Salop Record Office: 113, January 1686, "Mr. Wicherley is fined 1s. and paid to the sheriff for keeping a greyhound, and not to keep one any longer without a qualification." It is just as probable that this is Daniel rather than William, or any of a number of other members of the family. This volume has reference also to Richard, p. 26, and Thomas Wycherley, p. 148.

25. Summers, IV, 151.

26. *Ibid.*, III, 233.

27. *Ibid.*, I, 56.

28. *The Memoirs of Ann Lady Fanshawe* (London, 1907), p. 120.

29. *The Poems of Alexander Pope*, ed. John Butt, III, ii, *Epistles to Several Persons*, ed. F. W. Bateson (London, 1951), 116, "Epistle to Bathurst," 11. 321–26.

30. Summers, IV, 234.

31. *Ibid.*, p. 231.

32. *Ibid.*, p. 192; see further discussion below, n. 43.

33. *Ibid.*, III, 28–31.

34. *Ibid.*, pp. 33–35.

35. *Spence, Anecdotes*, #89.

36. Summers, IV, 13–14.

37. *Ibid.*, pp. 14–15.

38. *Ibid.*, pp. 17–18.

39. *Ibid.*, III, 103 f.

40. David M. Vieth, ed., *The Complete Poems of John Wilmot, Earl of Rochester* (New Haven, 1968), p. xxxviii.

41. Summers, III, 149.

42. Vieth, pp. 94–95, 98.

43. The poem was probably written in the late 1680's, after marriage and the Fleet. The most striking parallel to this poem is, again, Milton's divorce tracts, where he wrote: "O perverseness . . . that to grind in the mill of an undelighted and servile copulation must be the only forced work of a Christian marriage, ofttimes with such as yoke-fellow, from whom both love and peace, both nature and religion, mourns to be separated." *John Milton, Complete Poems and Major Prose*, ed. Merritt Y. Hughes (New York, 1957), p. 712.

44. Maren-Sophie Røstvig, *The Happy Man* (Oslo, 1962), I, 277–80. She finds "Song, *in praise of* Solitude" "close to seeming cynically insincere"; perhaps this is because, as I believe, Wycherley was not promoting this severe self-sufficiency since it was too remote from society.

45. Summers, IV, 149–50.

46. Vieth, xxxiv. I believe his emphasis on ambiguity may be overstated in the following interesting observation: "The Restoration temper is most sensitively reflected in the pyrrhonistic scepticism of Etherege's comedies, the almost mystical ambiguity of Wycherley in *The Country-Wife* and *The Plain-Dealer.*"

47. Howard P. Vincent, "William Wycherley's *Miscellany Poems*," *PQ,* XVI (April 1937), 145. This article is the source of information on litigation prior to actual publication of the *Miscellany Poems.* For Dryden's letter, see Charles E. Ward, ed., *The Letters of John Dryden* (Durham, N.C., 1942), p. 54.

48. Summers, III, 23–24.

49. *Ibid.,* p. 279.

50. *Ibid.,* II, 242.

51. *Ibid.*

52. *Ibid.,* III, 18: "The Dedication to the Greatest Friend of the Muses Vanity"; and 4, 5, 13: "The Preface."

53. Charles Gildon, p. 15. Note that Gildon, p. 17, included Pope by name as "such a Wretch" who had made his way "into his Conversation and Intimacy."

54. *Ibid.,* p. 14.

55. Lansdowne, "A Letter with a Character of Mr. Wycherly," in *The Genuine Works in Verse and Prose. . . ,* p. 435.

56. Frederick Bracher, ed., *Letters of Sir George Etherege* (Los Angeles, 1974); John Harold Wilson, ed., *The Rochester–Savile Letters, 1671–1680* (Columbus, Ohio, 1941).

57. Robert J. Allen, *The Clubs of Augustan London* (Hamden, Conn., 1967; originally Cambridge, Mass., 1933), pp. 27–28. Pepys' second statement is dated 3 February 1664.

58. *Spence, Anecdotes,* #68.

59. *Ibid.,* #644.

60. Abel Boyer, *Letters of Wit, Politicks, and Morality* (London, 1701), p. 216. Rochester died in 1680; Mulgrave became Marquis of Normanby in

1694; Roscommon is Wentworth Dillon, author of "An Esssay on Translated Verse," 1684, who died 1685; Samuel Garth was author of *The Dispensary*, 1699, very well edited in *Poems on Affairs of State, Augustan Satirical Verse, 1660–1714*, VI, 1697–1704, ed. Frank H. Ellis (New Haven, 1970), with a reference to Wycherley, p. 102:

In Sense and Numbers if you wou'd excel,
Read *Wycherley*, consider *Dryden* well.
In one, what vigorous Turns of Fancy shine,
In th'other, *Syrens* warble in each Line.

The Key to the poem, 1709, identified Wycherley, "A Poet famous for solid Wit and Sense." Mr. Boyle is Robert, a religious and scientific writer who died 1691; Vanbruk is Sir John Vanbrugh, architect and author of *The Provoked Wife*; in a letter to Pope, Wycherley referred fondly to "drunken poetical Tom Cheek," Sherburn, II, 208, and Summers, II, 313; Nicholas Rowe wrote tragedies.

61. John Wendell Dodds, *Thomas Southerne, Dramatist* (New Haven, 1933), p. 95.

62. Betterton died 28 April 1710; Wycherley wrote to Pope; "the Gout, being gotten up into his Head, and (as the Physicians say) will certainly carry him of suddenly," Sherburn, I, 85. Henry Cromwell too was friendly with Wycherley and Pope: "Soft Cromwell salutes you," Wycherley wrote Pope, Summers, II, 208; Sherburn, I, 36.

63. Gildon, p. 17

64. John C. Hodges, ed., *William Congreve, Letters and Documents* (New York, 1964), p. 91 and pp. 191–92.

65. Gerald Weales, "A Wycherley Prologue," *The Library Chronicle*, Friends of the Library, University of Pennsylvania, XXXII (Spring, 1966), 101–04.

66. *Letters Upon Several Occasions*: Written by and between Mr. Dryden, Mr. Wycherley, Mr. [Moyle]. Mr. Congreve, and Mr. Dennis. Published by Mr. Dennis (London, 1696), p. 22, written 20 November 1694. The reply following was written 1 December.

67. *Ibid.*, pp. 10–11, written 19 January 1694.

68. Connely, p. 108.

69. *Letters Upon Several Occasions*, pp. 15–16, written from Clive, 4 February 1694. The blank names are probably Cromwell, Dryden, and Walsh, according to Summers, II, 310.

70. *Ibid.*, p. 27, and p. 31. The journey out of London may have been to Ireland or Shropshire.

71. *Ibid.*, pp. 26–27. The blank names are probably Walsh, and according to Summers, II, 310, Cheek and Balam.

72. Quoted from Allen, p. 31.

73. Gildon, pp. 15–16.

74. *Spence, Anecdotes*, #57; and Sherburn, I, 2.

75. *The Garden and The City* (Toronto, 1969), p. 62.

76. *Letters Upon Several Occasions*, p. 7.

77. Taken from Marjorie Nicolson and G. S. Rousseau, *This Long Disease, My Life* (Princeton, N. J., 1968), p. 8.

78. J. V. Guerinot, *Pamphlet Attacks on Alexander Pope*, 1711–1744 (New York, 1969), p. 207; pp. 245–46.

79. *Spence, Anecdotes*, #96.

80. Sherburn, III, 80.

81. *Spence, Anecdotes*, #91.

82. Sherburn, I, 1, headnotes.

83. *Ibid.*, p. 2.

84. *Ibid.*, p. 3.

85. *Ibid.*, p. 6.

86. *Ibid.*, p. 7.

87. *Ibid.*, p. 7.

88. Watson, II, 261.

89. Sherburn, I, 13.

90. *Spence, Anecdotes*, #82.

91. Sherburn, I, 14–15.

92. *Ibid.*, p. 31.

93. *Ibid.*, pp. 86–87.

94. *Spence, Anecdotes*, #83.

95. Sherburn, I, 84–85.

96. *Ibid.*, p. 38 (editorial brackets).

97. *Ibid.*, p. 96.

98. *Ibid.*, pp. 97–98.

99. *Ibid.*, pp. 101–02.

100. *Ibid.*, p. 135, with reference to Cromwell's letters, p. 134.

101. *Ibid.*, p. 85.

102. *Ibid.*, p. 14.

103. *Ibid.*, p. 35; the letter is dated 6 December, but he had received Pope's letter in November in London. Cf. pp. 29–30.

104. *Ibid.*, pp. 38–39; in this letter he advises Pope to care for his weak eyes: "your Eyes I suppose know when they have read enough, tho you do not; therefore pray look to your Eyes, because they usd to look so kindly on me." Though he puns on sight, he sincerely pleads with Pope to have care.

105. *Ibid.*, p. 58, letter of 17 May.

106. *Ibid.*, p. 65.

107. *Ibid.*, p. 82.

108. H. P. Vincent, "The Death of William Wycherley," *Harvard Studies and Notes in Philology and Literature*, 15 (1933), 223.

109. C. W. Chalklin, *The Provincial Towns of Georgian England* (London, 1974), p. 24.

110. Sherburn, I, 256.

111. *Spence, Anecdotes*, #87.

112. *The Posthumous Works of William Wycherley Esq. in Prose and Verse* (London, 1728), p. iii.

113. Vinton A. Dearing, "Pope, Theobald, and Wycherley's *Posthumous Works*," *PMLA*, LXVIII (1953), 224.

114. *Ibid.*, p. 225.

115. *Ibid.*, pp. 226–27.

116. Sherburn, I, 31–32.

117. *Ibid.*, p. 80.

118. Dearing, p. 234.

119. Summers, IV, 105. Pope's doubts about authenticity of the essay from Dearing, p. 226.

120. Dearing, pp. 225–26.

121. H. P. Vincent, "The Death of William Wycherley," p. 223. All information on the death of Wycherley will be taken from this article, unless otherwise specifically noted. His n.4 on p. 220 lists C24/1364; the source I found was C24, 1367/90. His mention on p. 222 of *David*, as son of John Wycherley, should be *Daniel*.

122. *Spence, Anecdotes*, #95.

123. Sherburn, I, 328–29. All following references to Pope are from this letter, dated 21 January, unless otherwise indicated. Pope concluded this incident with the comment, "I cannot help remarking, that Sickness which often destroys both Wit and Wisdom, yet seldom has power to remove that Talent which we call *Humour*." This observation is used by Dr. Cox Macro in his handwritten annotations on Wycherley's life placed in the margins of Anthony a Wood, *Athenae Oxoniensis* (London, 1721), II, 975, to be found in the Bodleian. Macro (1683–1767), an antiquarian collector and correspondent of various notables, used the standard biographical materials, e.g., Middle Temple, prison for 700£, and so forth with the usual errors. His correspondence in the British Museum, Add. MS., 32556–7 contained no reference to Wycherley.

124. *Ibid.*; see also *Spence, Anecdotes*, #92: "Wycherley's nephew . . . would not consent to his selling any part of it [the estate] which he wanted much to do to pay his debts about a thousand pounds. He had therefore long resolved to marry in order to make a settlement from the estate, to pay off his debt with his wife's fortune, and to plague his damned nephew (as he himself used to express it)." Ms. Jackson's fortune was apparently 1000£. Pope's view here suggests that Wycherley's expressed intentions and his actions were not in agreement.

125. See *Spence, Anecdotes*, #94: "Wycherley died a Romanist, and has owned that religion in my hearing." Connely, pp. 207–08, believed he converted to Catholicism in 1678 (citing Alexandre Beljame) to coincide with the accession of Catholic James II. It certainly seems likely that Wycherley returned to Rome well before his death, but there is no new evidence to fix that date.

126. Copy of the Will of William Wycherley, Esq. 1452/4, Salop Record Office.

127. Church Wardens' books, Parish of Wem:

Wem 1716   Esquire Wycherley or Tent,

and thereafter William Wycherley, until 1720 when the listing changed to

Wem (no listing)

Aston Captain Shrimpton for Trench Farm. . . .

I selected at random 1734 and Shrimpton was still listed as owner.

128. Vincent, p. 236, reprints the marriage entry from *The Registers of St. Paul's Church, Covent Garden*, ed. Wm. H. Hunt (Harleian Society, London, 1907).

Appendix I

The Fire of Wem

The fire of Wem has figured significantly enough in the history of Daniel and his family and in the welfare of many of the tenants of the Manor of Wem to warrant inclusion. The fire began on Saturday evening, 3 March 1676, when a young girl named Jane Churm accidentally ignited the thatch in her cottage, and then due to the "very dry season" and a "violent tempestuous wind," as Garbet tells us,[1] the fire spread through much of the town. The village was so badly ravaged that King Charles issued a Royal Proclamation Elemosynary, 31 May, sanctioning the collection of alms for the victims:

> between seven and eight of the clock in the evening there happened a most dreadful fire in the Towne of Wem in the said County of Salop which burned the church steeple five bells the markett house and sevenscore dwelling houses besides treble the number of outhouses and buildings to the value of fourteen thousand seven hundred threescore pounds and tenn shillings and in household goodes to the value of eight thousand nine hundred sixteen pounds thirteen shillings and a penny—as appeared to our said Justices by a certificate under the hands of diverse persons of quality naybours to the said place as also by the oathes of Andrew Holdbrooke and John Bradman carpenters and Richard Cureton mason and bricklayer, who carefully viewed the several houses, by reason whereof the said poor sufferers are brought unto soe miserable condicion even to their utter ruine and undoeing unless assisted by the charitable benevolence of well deposed Christians. . . .[2]

Thereupon, four justices of the peace, Sir Vincent Corbett, Edward Kynaston, Charles Maynwaring, and Thomas Hill, were named agents or treasurers for the collection and a considerable number of collectors were duly appointed to go about collecting "within the Kingdom of England Dominion of Wales Towne of Barwick upon Tweed." Some went to London and Westminster and the suburbs; a London fishmonger was deputed to cover the South counties of "Kent, Surrey, Suffolk, Hampshire and Essex,"[3] and the collectors brought in surprisingly large amounts of alms, 50£ by John Shenton in London, a London fishmonger Williams 500£, Thomas Astley 72£, Thomas Jebb 100£, Samuel Roycroft several hundred pounds, and so on. It was a well organized and efficient method of gathering charity, remarkably widespread in its national scope, and very effective in the amount of money collected, though the totals were not certain, either then or now, for some collectors made off with their money and a few died and their collections were misplaced. The manner in which this event impinges upon the story of the Wycherley family is at least partly apparent already—the losses of the fire placed many tenants who were suing Daniel under severe hardships, ruining them entirely; George we have observed refusing to open his door to the homeless. Daniel, of course, also suffered losses in the fire, estimated by Thomas Hill to be "for private and pticular losses . . . four hundred pounds or thereabouts,"[4] but his reaction to the alms gathering, prompted quite likely by a sense of pique at not being appointed a treasurer, is complicated and confusing.

He insisted first that he and those of the fire victims he was representing ought to have had a proportionable share of the alms but the three treasurers, Corbett being dead by this time (February 1682), neglected to do so and refused to distribute money to the "sufferers" or to him. He added, however, in apparent contradiction, that he had asked for no money himself except for rebuilding the "Almshouse in the towne of Wem (consumed by fire)" and other charitable uses for benefit of the poor. Then, the heart of the complaint: "the Treasurers have converted great sumes to their own use or gave it to their close friends and slighting others."[5] Thomas Hill pointed out that Daniel had "never required or demanded such share but to the contrary hath often given out in speeches . . . that he desired no such share," and never "gave in any amount of his losses in apportion of such share"; Hill denied "there ever were to his knowledge any Almshouses belonging to the lord of the Manor consumed by the fire," and as a result, concluded, "noe jot of the sd money was distributed to the Complt."[6] Daniel pursued his investigation and demanded proof of all treasurers and collectors[7] of amounts received and disbursed, to whom, when, for what. In 1687 Samuel Roycroft was still replying to Daniel's complaints and queries, even though Daniel was no longer Lord of the Manor of Wem.[8] The suits are marked by a candor of response by the defendants, a readiness to admit Daniel's losses—"the chancell Market house and some other shops," Shenton said, similar to Daniel's claim, "Church Steeple Bells Market house and a great number of dwelling house"—or surprise or shock at being assailed: Shenton "doth admire that the Complt should so injuriously prosecute him since Complt often told [him] that he took more pains with the sufferers than they could ever requite,"[9] and Thomas Jebb observed that such a request was "a thing below a man of his estate and temper to doe."[10] Though the townspeople accepted the high position Daniel held and respected his character at a certain begrudging distance, his crabbed persistence after justice was as patently illusory to them as it is to us now.

Appendix I
Footnotes

1. Garbet, p. 223.
2. Duplicate of a Proclamation Elemosynary for the Inhabitants of Wem, 484/240, Salop Record Office. The above is taken from a typescript transcription of about one-third of the whole.
3. C6, 66/58, Hill's answer.
4. C6, 66/59.
5. C6, 564/72.
6. C6, 66/59.
7. Daniel seemed to believe that the King's letter-patents granted him, because he was commissioner, authority to receive alms as if he were a treasurer, but he did not insist on this attempt at usurpation of authority.
8. C6, 293/103.
9. C6, 293/111.
10. C6, 66/81.

Appendix II

Law Cases on Daniel Wycherley

The following stories suggest the paradoxical nature of Daniel's personality in his dealings with various persons. The first especially reveals the complexity of the man; for though Daniel had so thoroughly demonstrated to everyone his proclivity for the unpopular and unfriendly that it is easy to credit Henry Felton's assertion that Daniel's friends absented themselves from his company, such is not an entirely accurate portrait. In 1669, a widow Margaret Skremsher was beset by her daughter-in-law, Elizabeth, also a widow, with several suits demanding the inheritance of John Skremsher, Margaret's husband, which Margaret naturally claimed as her own, that being the intent of his will which had been proved and executed. Elizabeth exhibited her bills in Chancery in 1667 and '68 and followed them with a bill of ejectment against her mother-in-law and about twenty tenants who had leased land from John. Margaret was in desperate straits and could get no legal assistance from lawyers in her town in Staffordshire, for they had reportedly been instructed by Elizabeth to ignore her. So she travelled the fourteen miles or so to Clive to Daniel Wycherley whom she knew only by reputation and to him "much lamented her condition . . . that she and her children should be totally ruined in case she could not get some assistance and advice from some able lawyers and such persons as would not discover or betray her cause to her adversaries."[1] Daniel, "perceiving the great hazzard the said Margaret was in of loosing what her husband had left for her and the maintainence and education of her children," accepted the challenge, hastened to London, filed a cross bill both to defeat Elizabeth's bills and lease in ejectment, and to confirm the prior lease the late John had made to the tenants, and "much to his trouble" won the case and restored Margaret to her estate "to her great satisfaction and content." She had chosen her counsel well. But the story does not end there, and the image of Daniel as generous champion of the oppressed does not survive entirely intact.

As payment for his efforts, he said he would choose the common recompense of "a fatt bucke and a fatt doe of each season out of her parke every year . . . as long as he and she did live." In a few years, after Margaret married Joseph Venables, the payments began to lapse, "sometimes pretending [the deer] were lean . . . sometimes pretending they were all dead . . . to deprive your orator of what was so justly promised and due to him."

Margaret replied to Daniel's suit that she could not recall any such agreement about a buck or doe, but had sent him some venison from time to time "which she did merely out of kindness and respect but not as his due or upon any agreement." The complications escalated when Margaret loaned Daniel 200£ (2 August 1675) which she had been reserving for her daughter Katherine's dowry, but when she and Venables sought the repayment, Daniel answered that he had borrowed not from them but from the daughter, even though Venables was acting as her guardian during her minority and loaned the 200£ in her stead.[2] Daniel and his son George had given bond on penalty of 400£ for the loan, and when Daniel urged Venables to exhibit a bill against him in order to gain legal certitude whose the 200£ actually was, Daniel fought the bill, executing the same kind of dupe he had on Felton and others. As with so many other cases, this one began to take on aspects of infinity. In Hilary term 1678, Katherine replied to the bill of complaints filed by Daniel and George, citing 50£ received from them of the amount due. In Easter 1681 Daniel was ordered to pay 174£, and on 11 May Daniel was nowhere to be found with that 174£ for he "about two months sithence went into ye Kingdome of Ireland & . . . hee is not since retorned."[3] In 1686 a bill was submitted to the Right Honorable George Lord Jeffreys Baron of Wem by William Bradshaw, who had married Katherine Skremsher, and was bringing Daniel to the bar about the well-worn 200£.[4]

Among various suits and arguments Daniel became party to, which are too many to enumerate or describe,[5] one of the last was "a great suite," Gough called it, "with the Towne and schooles of Shrewsbury, about the maintenance for the Minister of Clive Chappell," the church at Clive being part of Wem parish. The salary of the Clive ministers had been neglected some years when Daniel brought the issue to suit and managed to double the annual salary to 10£; but this was not satisfying so he pressed a new suit and won an increase to 31£. Lord Newport, "who allways opposed Wicherley," Gough observed, caused a rehearing and had the verdict overturned, but Daniel was too ill to continue the battle.[6] In 1690 Daniel was charged to pay costs of 20£ and 40£ and later of 66£, which he paid in Michas 1690.[7] Twenty-six residents of Clive and

[243]

its neighboring village Sansaw swore a statement in Daniel's defence on 6 October 1691, pointing out that his father had provided ministers for Clive chapel, such as Mr. Sugar, and subsequently several others were nominated and approved, "and by the care of and friendship of Daniell Wytcherley Esq now of Clive . . . most of the sd Ministers since Mr. Sugars death [1674] were paid with the sd Mr Wytcherleys owne money and sd Maior of Salop and other persons refuseing to pay them as they formerly did and ought to have done."[8] But Daniel had to pay the costs just the same.

Appendix II
Footnotes

1. C10, 196/69; subsequent quotations are taken from various sections of same case.
2. C10, 195/53.
3. C41, 23, Easter, # 220, and # 226, for Humphrey Perry's affidavit on Daniel in Ireland.
4. C8, 397/8.
5. These miscellaneous suits are as follows: C9, 72/69, property suit with John Vaughn and others, 1676; because of the poor condition of C9, 414/161 on the same case, PRO officers would not produce it for examination; C10, 495/203, property suit with Thomas Bishop and John Meeson, 1678; C6, 564/80, property suit with Rowland Gouldesborough, 1679, with some interesting details on Daniel's fierce approach to tenants, and C10, 196/76 on same case; C9, 488/89, property suit with William Stanton and others, 1683, in very poor condition, mostly illegible; C41/27, Trinity, #676, affidavit on suit with Charleton, 1687; C10, 48/185, property suit over Steele Manor with Samuel Stanford, 1679, and C10, 136/83; C10, 495/217, property suit with John Watkis of London dyer, 1680, and C10, 214/110, with answer also by George, son of Richard Higginson, 1684; C41, 26, Trinity #103, #104, #1920, #2045 (misnumbered 1045); Michas, #137, #616; and *Chancery Entry Books*, C33/268, p. 220v., all on debt suit with Thomas Ireland; *Calendar of Treasury Books*, Vol. XIV, ed. William A. Shaw (London, 1934): 1699, April 25, p. 325; and *Calendar*, Vol. XV, p. 208, references to properties of Daniel.
6. Gough, pp. 86–87.
7. E127, 17 Trinity, #40; 18, Michas, #222; see also C41, 28, Trinity, #941, Michas, #1535; E127, 17, Hilary, #99; Easter, #169; 18, Trinity, #161; also indexed but not available: E127, 18 Hilary, #236; Order books from Michas 4 William and Mary to near end of Easter 5 William and Mary are not present. Possibly related to this case: E127, 17, Trinity, #95, #116, information therein too uncertain to declare referent.
8. *MSS Calendar of Deeds and Charters*, Vol. V, no. 5097, Shrewsbury Borough Library.